Rawdon Wyatt with Jacky Newbrook and Judith Wilson

NEW first certificate

Gold

teacher's book

Longman

Contents

Introduction

Student profile

The students with whom you will be using this course will have studied English for around 500–600 hours, and will now be planning to take the Cambridge First Certificate in English (FCE). They may already have taken the Cambridge Preliminary English Test (PET) or one or more Certificates in English Language Skills (CELS) at Preliminary or Vantage level. They may also be intending to take the Cambridge Certificate in Advanced English (CAE) after another year of study.

The FCE corresponds to the **Council of Europe Framework** level B2. According to the framework specifications, learners of English at this level can function as follows in the language and skills areas described below.

Grammar

Students at B2 level have a good degree of grammatical control, and do not usually make mistakes which lead to misunderstanding. However, errors are still common, and they may have difficulty in using structures naturally. They will need to revise and practise some familiar grammatical areas such as verb tenses, reported speech, passives, etc., and to work on eliminating errors they are still making with some structures (which are often the result of carelessness rather than lack of understanding). They will also need to look at structures which can cause confusion if incorrectly used (for example, verbs where the meaning changes according to whether they are followed by a gerund or an infinitive).

Vocabulary

Students have a good range of vocabulary for most general topic areas. They are able to use a variety of expressions in order to avoid repetition, and have the ability to paraphrase when they don't know a particular word. However, there are some gaps in their vocabulary and this may cause them to hesitate when they are speaking. They may feel that they lack vocabulary and want to increase the number of words they can recognise and use easily. They will need to expand their knowledge of word formation, phrasal verbs and idioms, and should be encouraged to make use of a good monolingual dictionary in order to develop their vocabulary.

Reading

Their skimming and scanning skills are fairly well developed, and they can understand reasonably complex authentic and semi-authentic materials such as newspaper and magazine articles and extracts from fiction or non-fiction. In many cases, they are able to deduce the meaning of a word from its context. They can understand texts written in a variety of styles, even if some colloquial English is used. They are also able to follow a line of argument, even if the content is not entirely predictable, and can use text features to help with this. They may still need help handling more complex tasks, such as identifying the structure and organisation of a text, identifying reference and inferring implied meaning.

Writing

B2 level students are able to express opinions, give reasons, and can write informal letters expressing thanks, congratulations, etc. They can also present arguments, although limitations in their vocabulary and grammar may cause the reader some problems. They can write simple reports and advise, evaluate and suggest. Their writing may lack organisation, coherence and cohesion, at times, and their register may not always be appropriate or consistent, but generally they are able to communicate their main message and have a satisfactory effect on the target reader.

Speaking

They can communicate in a variety of situations, including conversations on a wide range of topics related to personal life and experience, current events, interests, friends and family, etc. They are able to present and justify their own opinion. More confident students can give clear presentations on familiar topics and are able to answer predictable or factual questions, but may have problems with more abstract concepts. They can ask questions for, e.g., clarification, reasons, opinion, etc., and they are able to express agreement and disagreement. Most students at this level feel that they still need a lot of speaking practice to increase their confidence in their own communicative ability.

Listening

Students at this level feel reasonably confident dealing with authentic or semi-authentic listening passages. They can understand much of what is said in a film or a television or radio programme, although they may be unfamiliar with many idiomatic, colloquial and slang expressions, and may have problems understanding some regional accents. They can understand some nuances of meaning and opinion. They are able to take and pass on messages. However, in some situations they may rely on being able to actually see the speaker in order to understand what they are saying, using gestures, expressions, etc., to help them.

The Common European Framework and the *Gold* series

The table below gives a general overview of the Common European Framework levels and the Cambridge ESOL main suite and CELS exams, and where the **Going for Gold** and **Gold** series fit into this.

Common European Framework	Guided learning hours from beginner	Cambridge ESOL main suite exams	Cambridge ESOL Certificates in English Language Skills (CELS)	*Gold* series
A2	Approx. 180–200	KET (Key English Test)		
B1	Approx. 350–400	PET (Preliminary English Test)	CELS Preliminary	*Going for Gold*
B2	Approx. 500–600	FCE (First Certificate in English)	CELS Vantage	*Going for Gold* *NEW first certificate Gold*
C1	Approx. 700–800	CAE (Certificate in Advanced English)	CELS Higher	*Advanced Gold*
C2	Approx. 1,000–2,000	CPE (Certificate of Proficiency in English)		*NEW Proficiency Gold*

Preparing for the First Certificate in English exam

An FCE course should consolidate, refine and extend what students already know, provide them with techniques for continuing to learn, and train them in the specific techniques and strategies required for the FCE exam. During the course, students should try to work independently at times, developing their own study skills and strategies for improving their own language ability. They should be thinking about ways of recording vocabulary that suit their own learning style, doing further grammar work to build on what is done in the Coursebook, and identifying other ways of continuing to learn after the course.

Features of the *NEW first certificate Gold* course

Components of the course

The components of the course include: the **NEW first certificate Gold Coursebook**, plus class cassettes or audio CDs; the **NEW first certificate Gold exam maximiser** available with or without Answer key and tapescripts, plus cassettes, (also available with audio CDs in some countries); and this **teacher's book**.

Supplementary materials

A selection of supplementary materials is also available for extra practice and development of vocabulary, grammar, fluency and exam skills, including:
- *Longman Active Study Dictionary*
- *Longman Essential Activator*
- *Grammar and Vocabulary for FCE*
- *First Certificate Practice Tests Plus 1 and 2*
- *Test Your Vocabulary for FCE* (Penguin English)
- *Test Your Structure and Usage for FCE* (Penguin English)
- *First Certificate Games and Activities* (Penguin English)

NEW first certificate Gold Coursebook

Organisation of the Coursebook

The Coursebook offers progressive preparation for the FCE exam, as well as developing and extending students' competence in the language. Exam-style tasks are generally at exam level from the early stages of the book, with graded support being gradually withdrawn as the course progresses.

Each of the 14 units in the Coursebook provides an integrated package containing practice for all five Papers in the FCE exam, as well as grammar, vocabulary and fluency practice, all linked to a theme which often features in the FCE exam. Basic errors which are typical of FCE students are highlighted in **Watch Out!** boxes. A key feature of each unit is the **Exam focus** section, which presents the techniques and strategies required for a specific task in the FCE exam, and provides exam level practice.

At the back of the Coursebook you will find: a section containing visuals for the **Paper 5 Speaking tasks** in the units; **Communication activities**; a **Grammar reference**, a **Writing reference** and a **Vocabulary reference**. The **Communication activities** include role-plays, information gap activities, answers to quizzes in the units, etc. The **Grammar reference** is a mini-grammar covering all the grammar points dealt with in the units. The **Writing reference** provides model answers for all the types of writing tested at FCE, together with a list of Dos and Don'ts, and examples of useful language. There are also authentic student answers which students can evaluate using the general marking guidelines provided on the inside back cover of the Coursebook. These student answers show clearly what is expected in FCE answers in different bands. The **Vocabulary reference** contains an alphabetical listing of multi-word verbs found in the Coursebook reading and listening texts, together with definitions and examples. It also contains a list of nouns, adjectives, verbs and expressions followed by prepositions.

Recycling and revision

Each unit ends with a Review of the language presented in that unit, except for Units 5, 10 and 14. These are followed by Progress tests which review students' knowledge of the language presented in the preceding five units, and contain a complete Paper 3 test. Since these relate directly to what has been taught, they can be used by the teacher in class as reviews, or as tests of the students' command of the language presented in the units.

Grammar

Various different approaches are used for the presentation and practice of grammar points. Structures to be presented are often taken from authentic texts used previously in the unit, and then presented through diagnostic activities such as analysis of errors. There are also a number of controlled practice activities, both spoken and written, followed by freer practice activities where students can use the target structure for themselves in writing or speaking. Use of English tasks in exam format also recycle the grammar that has been presented. Each Grammar section is cross-referenced to the **Grammar reference** at the back of the book. Students should be encouraged to develop the habit of checking their answers for themselves, as this will foster independence and make it easier for them to continue learning after the course. **Watch Out!** boxes are designed to pick up on mistakes that are commonly made by students. These are often language points that have already been taught at lower levels, but which students continue to find difficult. The boxes also identify possible problem areas with new structures so that students are less likely to have difficulty with them when meeting the structure for the first time. The boxes are interactive, making it easier for students to remember the point.

Vocabulary

A variety of presentation and practice techniques is used in **NEW first certificate Gold**. When reading, students are encouraged in early units to work out the meanings of unknown words for themselves and to recognise clues such as word formation, synonyms or explanations in the text, etc. They should be trained to continue doing this for themselves as this will help them with the reading tasks in the exam.

Dictionary use and ways of recording and learning new words are also emphasised. Students are encouraged to use a monolingual dictionary such as the *Longman Active Study Dictionary*, which gives information about meaning, pronunciation, grammar and collocations. This will help them to expand their active vocabulary.

Particular attention is also paid to word formation, with a structured syllabus which builds students' understanding of how prefixes and suffixes are used, followed by regular practice.

The practice activities give students the chance to use the words they have focussed on in speech or written tasks.

Reading

Authentic texts from a range of sources (newspapers, magazines, etc.) are used to develop reading skills and techniques for the FCE. Students are encouraged to use the title and subtitle of the text, as well as any photographs or

illustrations to help them to predict its content. Guidance is provided to help them do the task and apply appropriate techniques and strategies.

Vocabulary and discussion tasks following the reading texts allow students to develop the topic further and enable them to use and remember key vocabulary from the text.

Listening

The listening texts are also from a range of sources, and the recordings present students with a variety of (mild) accents. In addition to exam-style tasks, there are also four songs, which provide further skills practice as well as the opportunity for students to listen for pleasure.

Students are always reminded to read through the task **before** they listen, to help them predict what they might hear, and tips and guidance are often provided to help them complete the task.

Vocabulary and discussion activities usually follow the Listening tasks, to allow students to respond to the content and extend their vocabulary.

Writing

Each unit ends with a writing task of the type found in the FCE exam, which consolidates the topic and language covered in the unit. Each Writing section is cross-referred to the **Writing reference** at the end of the book. This is an important component of the course, as it provides model answers for each of the text types in the course, with advice on what makes a good answer. Students can refer to these for guidance when they meet a new text type. Students are encouraged to follow this procedure for their written work:

- Think about what the task type requires.
- Read the task carefully and identify what needs to be included.
- Make a paragraph plan before they write.
- Check their work carefully when they have finished, using the Checklist in the **Writing reference**.

When marking students' written work, you could use this correction code, to encourage students to edit and evaluate their own work.

Correction code

Vf = verb form, e.g. *My father always play football on Saturdays.*
Vt = verb tense, e.g. *Last year I have visited France.*
Ww = wrong word, e.g. *We arrived to the meeting five minutes early.*
Uw = unnecessary word, e.g. *I phoned to Jim three times.*
Wo = word order, e.g. *I do usually my homework in the evening.*
Gr = grammar, e.g. *Why you not tell me you were Italian?*

Sp = spelling, e.g. *I like going out with my <u>freinds</u>.*
P = punctuation, e.g. *Do you like tea<u>!</u>*
? = meaning or handwriting not clear, e.g. *I <u>went</u> to London <u>next week</u>.*
^ = missing word, e.g. *I wrote an <u>e-mail my</u> friend yesterday.*

Speaking

There is an emphasis on communicative language and strategies in the course. The grammar, vocabulary and skills sections all provide opportunities for speaking practice, which can be dealt with as a whole class or through pair- and groupwork. These fluency activities are an important part of the course and should not be omitted. Students should be encouraged to respond to what others say, so that their conversation sounds natural.

Each unit also contains a section with specific speaking practice for Paper 5 of the exam. These sections present functional language for talking about photos and for discussions, as well as techniques such as how to keep talking. There are also recorded examples of students doing a Speaking task. These provide the opportunity to evaluate performance and identify problems as well as good models to follow. There is also a recording of a complete Listening test in Unit 11, to familiarise students with the format of the test.

NEW first certificate Gold exam maximiser

The other major component of the course is the ***NEW first certificate Gold exam maximiser***. Working through the exercises in the **exam maximiser** will help students to consolidate the language and skills presented in the Coursebook and provide them with further exam-specific practice and preparation.

General features

Each of the 14 units corresponds thematically to the units in the Coursebook. The sections within each unit are cross-referred to the related Coursebook section, and provide consolidation both of language and skills work.

The grammar and vocabulary sections contain exercises which recycle the material presented in the Coursebook. This language is then further practised by means of topic related exam-style Use of English (Paper 3) tasks. Additionally, students may be asked to correct typical errors or fill in the gaps in model answers to Speaking (Paper 5) tasks.

Sections containing exam style tasks for Reading (Paper 1), Writing (Paper 2) and Listening (Paper 4) provide information about the exam, plus strategies for tackling each task type, and give students a further opportunity to put these into practice.

There is also a complete **Practice test** at the end of the book. This can be used for timed practice in the run-up to the exam itself.

Using the exam maximiser

The **exam maximiser** can be used in class in tandem with the Coursebook as a means of providing immediate follow-up work on specific grammar or vocabulary work. It also offers a source of additional Reading and Listening tasks for use in class. Alternatively, students can do the exercises and skills practice for homework.

Another way of using the **exam maximiser** is for intensive exam preparation after completing the Coursebook. The with key version can also be used by students preparing for the exam on their own.

NEW first certificate Gold teacher's book

This ***teacher's book*** provides suggestions on how to use the material in the ***NEW first certificate Gold Coursebook*** to best advantage. Answers to all exercises in the Coursebook are found at the end of each section of notes.

To facilitate lesson planning, the general **Aims** of each unit section are explained at the start. **Exam information** boxes give further useful information about the exam where appropriate.

Teaching tips and ideas suggest ways of presenting and practising the material in the Coursebook, or provide suggestions for further activities where appropriate.

Photocopiable resources

The recording scripts for all the Listening tasks in the units are at the back of the book so that they can be photocopied easily if you want to use them with your students.

There is also a section of **photocopiable activities** which provide extra communicative practice in key skills areas. These are linked to the units and provide extra practice of an important area presented in the unit. Detailed teaching notes state the aims and rationale of each photocopiable activity, and provide a step-by-step procedure for using them in class.

You will also find a bank of 14 photocopiable **tests**, made up of 11 Unit tests and 3 Progress tests. The Unit tests consist of exercises which test the language covered in a single unit. They are easy to administer and should take no more than 20 minutes for students to complete. The Progress tests are to be used after your students have completed Units 5, 10 and 14. These revise and test the language covered in the previous units. They should take about 40–50 minutes to complete. Answer keys to all the tests are provided and students can check their own work if you prefer.

Students need practice in filling in the **Answer sheets** used in the exam, and sample OMR (optical mark reader) answer sheets are provided. These can be used with the Practice exam in the ***exam maximiser***.

UNIT

1 What's on?

Speaking 1 p.6

Aims:
- **to review language for talking about films**
- **to provide a lead-in to Listening 1**

1 You can talk about the photos as a class. Students try to identify the films and then decide what kind of films they are. They could also try to think of an example of each type of film, either from their own country or from abroad.

2 Students can do this in pairs. This works well as an interview, with one student asking the other the questions. They should try to answer each question in as much detail as possible, using complete sentences (e.g. *'What was it called?'* *'It was a science fiction film called* The Matrix.' *'Who was in it?'* *'The main character is played by Keanu Reeves, but the film also features …'* etc.)
For question 5, students could add some of their own adjectives, or think of synonyms for the adjectives in the question (e.g. *outstanding = superb*).
Make sure they don't fall into the *-ed/-ing* adjective trap (e.g. *It was a very ~~bored~~ film. I was very ~~boring~~.*).

3 This works well as a small group activity and should promote a lot of discussion. Set a time limit of no more than ten minutes and then ask one or two students to tell the rest of the class their ideas. Encourage the other students to develop the story by adding some of their own ideas.

ANSWERS

Ex. 1
1, 2
The Godfather – thriller
Moulin Rouge – musical
Shrek – animation, comedy

Listening 1: note completion p.7

Aim:
- **to introduce techniques for completing notes: predicting missing information, listening for specific words**

1 Students should work individually to skim through the notes to find out what the survey is about, then read through them again more carefully to try to predict what the missing words are. In many cases, it is only possible to predict the type of answer (e.g. questions 1 and 2), but for e.g. question 3, students could predict that the missing word might be *crime* or *gangster* if they are familiar with *The Godfather*. Encourage students to highlight key words in the text that would help them to identify the missing words. This helps them to focus on the subject.
They can then compare their possible answers with a partner.

2 Play the recording twice (as in the FCE exam). Tell your students that, for this task, the information they hear in the recording always follows the same order as the questions. Feedback answers.

Exam information ▶ Cbk p.5

Incorrect spelling is not penalised in the Listening paper unless a word is spelled out in the recording. Difficult or unusual words, such as place names, are usually spelled out.

▶ Tapescript p.99

3
1, 2 Set a time limit of no more than ten minutes for the groups to discuss the questions, before feeding back their results to the rest of the class.
3 Set this as a homework task if you don't have time during the lesson. Alternatively, do it as a whole class activity, with one student writing the email on the board with help from the rest of the class.

Teaching tips and ideas

As an alternative to Exercise 3.1, ask students to work in pairs or small groups, choose one of the genres from Speaking 1, Exercise 1 (e.g. action, science fiction, etc.) and compile a list of their top five or ten favourite films from that genre. They can then get together with another group and discuss their results.

With mixed-nationality classes, this provides good cross-cultural discussion, as they can talk about films from their own countries which the other students may not have heard about.

ANSWERS

Ex. 1
Most popular type of film
Best plots
Most popular settings
Most popular stars
Titles of the most popular films

Ex. 2
1 2000   2 50,000   3 drama   4 boy meets girl
5 combination   6 exotic   7 future   8 character
9 two words   10 person

See also: *NEW FCE Gold exam maximiser* p.13

Vocabulary 1: recording vocabulary p.8

Aim:

- **to review/introduce different ways of recording vocabulary**

1 Students discuss the statements in pairs. Encourage them to use language of agreement (*I agree, Absolutely,* etc.) and disagreement (*I disagree, I'm not so sure about that, I don't think so,* etc.). Students may be unfamiliar with some of the highlighted key words, e.g. *stunts, flashbacks* and *close-up shots*. They could refer to a dictionary, or you could pre-teach these words through gapped sample sentences on the board (e.g. *The film takes place in 2004, but there are lots of _____ to the 1980s.*).

stunt: a dangerous action in a film, usually done by a stuntman or stuntwoman.
flashback: a scene in a film, play or book that shows something that happened before that point in the story.
close-up shot: when the camera gets very near to the subject it is filming.

2, **3** Students often record vocabulary in a rather haphazard way. These tasks show them different methods of recording vocabulary in a way that makes it easier for them to refer back to when they need to use the words again. Encourage them to organise their vocabulary records by topic, and to include sample sentences whenever possible. Most monolingual dictionaries include sample sentences, together with other linguistic features (pronunciation, grammatical function, definition, other forms of the word, etc.). A recommended dictionary at this level is the *Longman Active Study Dictionary*. More advanced or confident students would also find the *Longman Dictionary of Contemporary English* useful.

4 The methods shown in Exercise 3 are generally regarded by most teachers as being the most effective, but students often have their own ideas. For example, some carry vocabulary cards which they can flick through.

5 Your students can work in pairs to look at the first two pages of the unit and decide which words would be useful. Help them to choose by telling them to imagine that they have been asked to write a composition (e.g. *What kind of films do you like the best, and do you have a favourite?*), and then decide which words would be useful in this composition.

Teaching tips and ideas

Introduce a vocabulary box into your classroom. When your students come across a new word in the lesson, they should write it on a slip of paper and put it in the vocabulary box. At the beginning of the next lesson, take out slips of paper at random from the box and give the class a definition of the words on those slips. The class then tries to remember what the words are. Alternatively, students can take it in turns to take out the slips and give their classmates the definitions. This is a quick, enjoyable and very useful way of helping students to recycle vocabulary on a regular basis.

ANSWERS

Ex. 2
People: director
Story: happy ending, flashbacks
Parts of cinema: front row
Film-making: special effects, stunts, close-up shots

Ex. 3
2 1 b)   2 d)   3 a)   4 c)

See also: *NEW FCE Gold exam maximiser* p.7

Grammar 1: revision of simple tenses p.8

Aims:

- **to review simple tenses: present, past, present perfect**
- **to focus on the use of adverbials with these tenses**

1 The mistakes in Exercise 1.1 are typical of those made by students at this level. In many cases, these mistakes are the result of minor carelessness rather than lack of grammatical knowledge. Minor tense mistakes, which usually won't cause confusion to the listener/reader, will lose students marks in the FCE if done persistently. Students should do Exercises 1.1 and 1.2 individually, and then check their answers with a partner.

Watch Out! *British and American English*
North Americans often use the past simple instead of the present perfect when an action has occurred (or not

occurred) in the recent past. American English is acceptable in the FCE exam, provided it is used consistently.

You might like to ask students if they are aware of other differences between British and American English. There are many differences in vocabulary (e.g. *film – movie, biscuit – cookie*, etc.) and several spelling differences (e.g. *colour – color, theatre – theater, catalogue – catalog*, etc.). Your students might also like to know that in some cases, the same word can have different meanings in British and American English (e.g. *subway, bill*, etc.).

2 The words in the box are often featured in Paper 3, Part 3 (Key word transformations) of the FCE. Students should complete the sentence pairs individually, then compare their answers with a partner.

> **Teaching tips and ideas**
>
> As a way of checking answers, you could ask your students to close their books and listen while you read the sentences out to them, leaving a gap for the missing words. They should try to remember what these are.

3 Students complete the extracts with the same partner, then work with another pair to compare answers. They can use **Grammar reference** page 203 to check if they are correct.

4

1, 2 Working individually, students make questions from the prompts and then ask the questions to a partner. Explain that in addition to adding extra words, your students will also have to change the forms of the verbs.

ANSWERS

Ex. 1
1 I *met*   2 ✓   3 I *belonged*   4 ✓
5 I *don't understand*   6 I've *seen*   7 ✓   8 ✓
9 I *went*   10 ✓

Ex. 2
present simple: twice every weekend
present perfect: all my life, already, so far, ever, yet, for a long time
past simple: ago, from 2001 to 2003, twice every weekend, when I was young, for a long time

Watch Out! *British and American English*
True. (see notes above for explanation)

Ex. 2
1 1 a) ago b) since   2 a) since b) when
   3 a) for b) ago   4 a) ever b) never
   5 a) for b) when   6 a) before b) ever

Ex. 3
1 1 has just become   2 promised   3 've always loved   4 've thought   5 said   6 (has) won   7 fell
2 1 has become   2 made   3 accepted   4 (has) also appeared   5 won

Ex. 4
1
1 How many times has Brad Pitt been married? (Once, to Jennifer Anniston)
2 Who directed (the film) *Titanic*? (James Cameron)
3 Which football team has won the World Cup five times? (Brazil)
4 In which country was *Lord of the Rings* filmed? (New Zealand)
5 Has Mel Gibson ever won an Oscar? (Yes, one for directing and one for producing the 1995 Best Picture, *Braveheart*)
6 Can you name any musicals which/that have won Oscars in the last ten years? (*Chicago* 2003, *Evita* 1996)
7 Which famous English footballer called/has called his child Romeo? (David Beckham)
8 Who usually presents the evening news programme on television in your country?

▶ Photocopiable activity 1A *Missing words noughts and crosses* p.161
See also: *NEW FCE Gold exam maximiser* p.8

Reading: multiple matching (Part 4) p.10

Aims:
- **to practise skimming, scanning, identifying parallel expressions**
- **to practise working out the meaning of words from context**

1 Before your students look at this section, write the words *Reality TV* on the board, and ask them if they know what the expression means. Tell them to read the description, and then ask them if they have any examples of Reality TV in their own countries. *Do they enjoy watching programmes like this? What do they think is the appeal of such programmes?* In many cases, many of these programmes are examples of an international franchise (e.g. *Big Brother* began in the Netherlands, and now has versions all over the world).

2 Ask your students to look at questions 1–4. Focus on question 1, and ask them to think of a physical problem that the speaker might have had (e.g. he/she might be disabled, might have a speech impediment, might be deaf or blind, etc.). Then do the same for questions 2–4 (e.g. *What kind of island might the speaker have lived on? What kind of singing competition did the singer win? What did the speaker build?*, etc.). This kind of brainstorming activity is a useful pre-reading task, as it not only focuses the students on the topic, but also helps them to think of some of the words or expressions they should be looking for in the text.

Students should then skim texts A–D and answer the questions, checking their answers with the others in the class.

Exam information ▶ Cbk p.4

In Part 4 of the FCE Reading paper, it is rare for the words in the sentences to be the same as those in the texts – students have to look out for synonyms or parallel expressions (e.g. the word *ill* in one of the sentences may match *sick* or *under the weather* in the text).

3 Students work individually. They should read through questions 1–12, highlighting key words (these are usually nouns, verbs and adjectives), and then match the questions with the relevant text. They then compare their answers in small groups.

Ask them which words/expressions in the text helped them to identify their answers (e.g. in number 1, *gave away* in the question matches *donated* in the text).

4 Students discuss the question in small groups. Alternatively, if your classroom has enough space, they could walk around the room asking other members of the class for their opinion. They can then tell the class about one of the people they talked to.

Exam information

Dictionaries, including monolingual versions, are **not** allowed in Cambridge ESOL exams. Some students rely heavily on a dictionary to find out what words mean, although often the meaning of a word can be guessed from the context in which it is being used. Encourage students to use this technique when they come across a new word or expression in a piece of written text.

5 You could do this as a quick game. Divide your class into small groups and ask them to decide on the correct option for each word/phrase. As soon as they have done all 11 words and phrases, they should check their answers with you. If all their answers are correct, they win. If they have made mistakes, tell them that not all of their answers are correct, but don't tell them which ones. They can then use a (monolingual) dictionary to check their answers.

ANSWERS

Ex. 2
1 C　2 A　3 C, D　4 B

Ex. 3
1 B (line 25: *Craig donated his £70,000 prize money*)
2 A (line 17: *The television company has agreed to pay him £16,000 compensation*)
3 C (line 35: *Denise Leigh has won joint first prize*)
4 D (line 55: *Will Young shot to success*)
5 B (line 24: *'I don't know why I won'*)
6 A (line 5: *later accused the producers of the show of misrepresenting him*)
7 A (line 15: *other students wouldn't talk to him*)
8 D (line 59: *I don't think it's me myself they're voting for*)
9 B (line 30: *had a five-album deal with a record company but he was dropped after his first single*)
10 D (line 70: *which puts a distance between you and other people*)
11 C (line 45: *Keeping them safe is definitely more worrying than anything that can happen to you on stage*)
12 A (line 12: *the other contestants were glad to see the back of me but it wasn't true*)

Ex. 5
1 a)　2 b)　3 b)　4 a)　5 a)　6 b)　7 b)　8 b)
9 a)　10 a)　11 b)

See also: *NEW FCE Gold exam maximiser* p.10

Grammar 2: present perfect simple and continuous p.12

Aim:
- **to review the difference between the simple and continuous aspects of the present perfect**

1 Ask your students to work in pairs and discuss the differences between a) and b) in each pair. When they have finished, ask different students to illustrate the sentences on the board using time lines.

Watch Out! *stative and dynamic verbs*
Stative verbs like *know* are not normally used in the continuous aspect, although there are a few exceptions. For example, we can say *I've been wanting to meet you for years* or *I've been hoping you would call* when we want to emphasise the length of time.

2, **3** Students work in pairs to decide on the best form of the verbs in Exercise 2, and compare their answers with another pair. They should then work with the other pair to decide which sentences in Exercise 3 should be changed.

4   This role-play practises the present perfect continuous in an authentic context. Encourage students to react and respond accordingly using colloquial expressions (e.g. *Really? That sounds interesting. Lucky you!, Good for you!*, etc.). Monitor and check for stress and intonation as well as for accurate use of the present perfect continuous. Activities like this work best if your students are able to stand up and move to a different part of the class rather than just sit at their desks.

ANSWERS

Ex. 1

1 a) He has appeared on one show at some unknown time in the past.
 b) He has appeared on several shows – these appearances have probably happened recently and are continuing up to the present.
2 a) They live on the island permanently.
 b) They are staying there temporarily.
3 a) You have probably finished sending the emails, but it is still morning.
 b) This emphasises the duration of the activity, but does not say whether it is finished or not.
4 a) She has finished reading the book.
 b) She probably hasn't finished reading the book yet.

Watch Out! *stative and dynamic verbs*
The first sentence is not possible (see teaching notes above for explanation).

Ex. 2

1 both possible   2 has got back   3 have never smoked   4 have been going   5 both possible
6 have been eating   7 both possible   8 have always wanted

Ex. 3

1 A: Have you *been getting*
2 B: she's *been working*
3 A: How long have you *been sharing*
4 B: I've *been trying*
5 B: He's *been saving up*
6 A: You've *been reading*

See also: *NEW FCE Gold exam maximiser* p.11

Use of English: key word transformations p.13

Aim:

• **to practise the tenses studied so far in an FCE-style task**

Exam information ▶ Cbk p.5

Paper 3, Part 3 tests a wide range of grammar and vocabulary. Each answer in this part of the exam carries two marks, so students can get marks even if their answers are not completely correct. Remind students that contractions (e.g. *I've, you'd*, etc.) count as two words.

In the exam, students write their answers on a separate answer sheet. They should only write the missing words, **not** the complete sentence. In the exam, they must use a **pencil** for Paper 3.

Before your students look at this section, tell them to close their books. Write the first sentence in the example (*I can't remember the plot at all*) and ask them if they can think of another way of saying this sentence so that the meaning is the same or similar. If they can't, write *forgotten* on the board, and ask them to do the same, using that word. Finally, write the second gapped sentence (*I _____ what the plot is about*) on the board and ask them to complete it using *forgotten* and between one and four other words. Your students should then complete sentences 1–9 individually, before comparing their answers with a partner. Note that in some cases, more than one answer may be possible (e.g. question 2) In cases where this is possible, students should only write **one** answer.

ANSWERS

1 who has won / who's won
2 I can't find / I'm unable to find
3 have nearly all died
4 've / have just been talking
5 've / have been working here for
6 's / has never been
7 haven't / have not seen him for
8 haven't / have not found (out)
9 's / has run out of

Vocabulary 2: word formation p.13

Aims:

• **to provide preparation for Paper 3, Part 5**
• **to focus on the formation of nouns, adverbs and adjectives**

1 , **2**   Students should do these exercises in pairs and use a dictionary to check their answers.

3   Your students should cover up Exercises 1 and 2 before doing this. They should be particularly careful of *prepare, donate* and *finance* (the final e is removed in the new form: *prepareation, donateion, financeially*) and *explain* (the *i* is removed in the noun: *explaination*).

Although it does not appear in this exercise, one of the most common student word form mistakes is *pronounce* (they often spell it *pron<u>ou</u>nciation* instead of *pron<u>u</u>nciation*), and you might like to point this out to your class.

4 This exercise practises some of the word forms in a personalised context. Your students should do this in pairs or small groups, and try to answer in as much detail as possible.

> **ANSWERS**
>
> **Ex. 1**
> 1 shock<u>ing</u> differ<u>ent</u> flatter<u>ed</u> = c) adjectives
> 2 compet<u>ition</u> perform<u>er</u> determin<u>ation</u> contest<u>ant</u> = a) nouns
> 3 regular<u>ly</u> general<u>ly</u> = b) adverbs
>
> **Ex. 2**
> 1 confusion 2 confuse 3 performer / performance 4 perform 5 origin 6 originate
> 7 originally 8 flattery 9 flatter 10 flatteringly
>
> **Ex. 3**
> 1 enjoyable 2 performance 3 disappointment
> 4 preparation 5 explanation 6 survival
> 7 donation 8 financially

▶ Photocopiable activity 1B *First to the top* p.162
See also: *NEW FCE Gold exam maximiser* p.12

Listening 2: extracts (Part 1) p.14

Aims:
- **to provide a graded introduction to Paper 4, Part 1**
- **to help students understand what they have to listen for**

> **Exam information**
>
> In Paper 4, Part 1, the questions a) identify the setting and b) indicate what students have to listen for, e.g. specific information, the main point or gist, location, relationship of the speakers, opinion/attitude, function. The questions are read on the recording and each extract is heard twice. Students should listen out for key words and expressions which will help them to identify the answer. They may sometimes be helped by the **way** it is said (e.g. if someone is very angry, upset, etc.). Distracters are a common feature in this paper, both within and across extracts.

Before your students look at their books, you could do the following:
Write the following words on the board:
A the station B the shops C the airport

Then ask your students where you are going before reading the following passage twice at normal speed:
We'll have to leave quite early. The trains are all on strike and it's a Saturday, so everyone will be driving to the city centre to do their shopping. The traffic will be terrible. We don't want to get there and discover it's already taken off, do we?
The answer is C – the airport. Ask them why (the phrasal verb *taken off* at the end refers to an aeroplane. *Trains* and *shopping* are distracters).

Allow your students a few moments to read through questions 1–6, and tell them to identify the key words/expressions in the questions (but **not** the answer options). Then play the recording. They should work individually to choose their answers, and then compare them with a partner. Ask them for their answers and why they chose them.

▶ Tapescript p.99

> **Teaching tips and ideas**
> Make copies of the tapescript, so that you can show students where the answers are and how distracters are used after they have done the exercise. This is quicker and more effective than rewinding the cassette/CD while you go through their answers with them.

> **ANSWERS**
> 1 A 2 C 3 A 4 B 5 C 6 A

See also: *NEW FCE Gold exam maximiser* p.13

Vocabulary 3: entertainment p.14

Aim:
- **to review/introduce some common words connected with entertainment**

1 You could do this activity as a simple game. Divide your class into two teams, and write the gapped words on the board. The teams take it in turns to guess a letter. For each letter they guess correctly, award them one point.

2 This could be done as a student interview activity, with students working in pairs to ask each other how they feel about the different things featured using useful colloquial expressions, which you could review before they do the activity (*I adore it. I hate it. I'm quite keen on it. I can't stand it. I'm mad about it.* etc.)

3 , 4 Your students could do this as a homework task. For Exercise 4, they should not describe the show, concert or play in too much detail, although they should provide a brief synopsis. They should say how they felt about it and whether they think others would enjoy it. (Note that when we describe a show or play, we usually use the present tense to describe what happens.)

> Tapescript p.100

3 The questions that students ask each other in this section all regularly appear in Part 1 of the FCE Speaking test. Encourage your students not to give a very short answer, but not to talk for too long. For example, to the question *Where are you from?* the answer *I come from St Laurent du Var, a town to the west of Nice in France. It's quite a lively place with a great beach* would be sufficient.

> **ANSWERS**
>
> **Ex. 1**
> 1 play/theatre
> 2 reviews
> 3 audience/applauded
> 4 opera/performance
> 5 concert/symphony/composer/sold out
> 6 conduct/orchestra/instruments/musicians
> 7 pop music/singers/groups
> 8 night clubs/discos

> **Teaching tips and ideas**
> If your classroom is big enough, ask your students to walk around the class asking different students their questions. At the beginning of a course, this is a useful way of breaking the ice and helping students get to know one another.

> **ANSWERS**
>
> **Ex. 1**
> 1 I *have* two brothers. One is older than me; he *is* twenty-one years old.
> 2 Just now I *am staying* in a hostel but I want *to* have my own apartment …
> 3 I like playing computer games and doing sport *very much*, especially *swimming*.
> 4 I have been studying English *for* five years … I *have* never been to England.
> 5 I want *to* travel abroad, and maybe I'll *get/be* married.
>
> **Ex. 2**
> 1 D 2 A 3 C 4 B

Exam focus

Paper 5 Speaking: introduction (Part 1) p.15

Aim:

- **to introduce and practise Part 1 of the FCE Speaking test**

> **Exam information ▶ Cbk p.5**
>
> Paper 5 is usually done about one or two weeks before Papers 1, 2 and 3. Students do the test in pairs (although very occasionally they do it in groups of three). They are expected to work together, responding and asking questions, making suggestions, etc., in certain parts of the test. They are marked on their grammar, vocabulary, pronunciation, fluency and interactive abilities.

Before your students look at this section, ask them what they know about the FCE Speaking test. (You could refer them to the Exam information section of the Coursebook.) Ask them to read through the **About the exam** section (including the DOs/DON'Ts box), then tell them to close their books and ask them how much they can remember.

Writing: informal letter (Part 1) p.16

Aim:

- **to practise writing an informal transactional letter based on written input**

1 Before your students look at this section, ask them if they regularly write to their family and friends. *What is their preferred method: handwritten letter? email? text messaging? Why do they write to their friends? What do they usually include in a letter?*
Individually, students should read through the writing task. Ask them to close their books. Can they remember the answers to questions 1–3?

1

1, 2 Students can work in pairs to identify the mistakes (all of which are very common at this level) and match the sentences with the topics. Play the recording once so that they can check their answers.

2 Students find this kind of activity very enjoyable, especially if they are able to identify and correct mistakes that are made. Play the recording once, and ask your students to work in small groups to discuss how they feel about each person on the recording. Ask for feedback from the class, and why they decided on their answers.

2 In pairs, students put the letter into the correct order and identify the mistakes.

One of the most common mistakes students make is to include unnecessary or irrelevant information, or miss out information altogether, as a result of not reading the task carefully enough. This will lose them marks. Encourage them to highlight key words and expressions in the task, and to refer to these when writing.

Planning a letter or other written task before writing it is vital as it helps students to avoid making such mistakes. A simple plan only takes a few minutes to write, but will help with cohesion and organisation of ideas, as well as helping students to focus on what is required for the task. Encourage students to make a plan before they write anything.

3 , **4**   Students can do this for homework. They should allow themselves about 45 minutes: ten minutes for planning, 30 minutes for writing, and five minutes for checking.

Exam information

Students are advised to write between 120 and 180 words for each Writing task in the FCE. This is the recommended number of words needed to answer the task satisfactorily. If they write fewer words, they may miss out some necessary information. If they write more, they may include unnecessary information, their work will contain more mistakes and, they may run out of time.

ANSWERS

Ex. 1
1 Jack
2 To invite him to go to the theatre with you
3 See Post-it note

Ex. 2
1 Sample answer
Dear Jack
Thanks for your letter. It was very good to hear from you again after all this time.

I've been working really long hours recently preparing for my exams but now I'm planning to take a break and go out to the theatre next Saturday to see 'King for a Night'. It's on at the Alhambra. The reviews are excellent – and it's the last night.

Would you like to come along? I *emailed* Sue and Milo yesterday to see if they can come, and they say they can, so it should be a good evening. They suggested *going* for something to eat together after the show – I know you like Italian food so we could all go to Gino's Pizzas. I*'ve never been* before but everyone says it's very good.

Give me a ring if you're free and would like to come, then I'll book the tickets.

Hope to see you on Saturday.

Best wishes
Pedro

(164 words)

See also: *NEW FCE Gold exam maximiser* p.14

UNIT 1 Review p.17

ANSWERS

Ex. 1
1
1 How long is it since you started learning English?
2 When did you last have a holiday?
3 How many years have you lived in this town?
4 How long have you had this book for?
5 When did you leave home this morning?
6 How many films have you seen this month?

Ex. 2
1
1 Role.   2 Screen.   3 Box office.   4 Setting.
5 Plot.   6 Flashback.

Ex.3
1 Have you been running?   2 Have you ever been
3 I've had   4 I have never seen   5 She has been doing   6 I have known   7 I didn't know

Ex. 4
1 since   2 for / during   3 since   4 After   5 for
6 just / recently   7 never   8 yet

Ex. 5
1 for   2 to   3 in   4 of   5 on/in   6 in

▶ Photocopiable Unit 1 test p.112

UNIT
2 Worth the risk?

Speaking 1: p.18

Aims:
- to introduce the theme of the unit
- to provide a lead-in to Listening p.19

1 Before your students open their books, ask them to think about any dangerous sports and activities they have heard about. Write these on the board (e.g. *parachuting, deep-sea diving, mountain climbing, bungee jumping, hang-gliding*). If they don't know the English words, ask them to try to explain what it involves, or draw a simple picture on the board. Ask if any of them have done any of these, or would consider doing them. Why or why not?
Add the words *free diving* to the list on the board, and ask them what they think this might be.
They should then look at Exercise 1 in their book and discuss questions 1–3. For question 3, they should try to think of as many words as possible (e.g. *brave, stupid, mad, reckless, a daredevil, strong, fit, energetic*, etc.).

2
1, 2 Students work individually to answer the questions and then compare them with a partner. They should do this orally rather than just looking at each other's paper. You could make this more communicative by putting your students into small groups of three or four.
Question 9 could prompt some interesting/entertaining discussion. Ask your students if they have ever acted on a dare. *What did they do? What was the outcome?*

3 In pairs or small groups, students should try to think of at least one example (for question 1) of a positive aspect of taking a risk, and a negative aspect of taking a risk, or give examples of when they took risks that had a positive outcome and/or a negative outcome. They can then feed this back to the rest of the class in a whole class discussion which can be extended to include question 2. One possible reason that some people might not approve of risk-takers is that often **other** people are put at risk as a result; for example, if a climber gets stuck halfway up a mountain, someone has to take a risk by rescuing them.

ANSWERS

Ex. 1
1 Free diving involves diving as deep as possible without using breathing apparatus.

Listening: true or false? (Part 4) p.19

Aim:
- to introduce one type of Part 4 task: true or false?

> ### Exam information ▶ Cbk p.5
>
> In FCE Paper 4, Part 4, there are three or four different task types, which all involve selecting from possible answers. In this section, students have to decide whether statements are true or false. As in Parts 1 and 3 of the Listening paper, they have to listen for synonyms and parallel phrases to help them choose their answer, and should also beware of distracters.

1 Introduce Exercise 1, and tell students to work in pairs to underline the key words. Remind them that key words are usually *nouns*, *verbs* or *adjectives*. Very often, key **words** are grouped together to form key **phrases**.

2, **3** Play the recording once, and give your students a few moments to compare their answers with one another before playing it again. Ask them how they knew whether the statements were true or false (e.g. for number 1, the answer is false because she says *being in the water was always a natural feeling for me*).

▶ Tapescript p.100

4 Students discuss the questions in pairs or small groups. This can then be extended to a whole class discussion.

> **Teaching tips and ideas**
>
> Students can carry out a class survey to find out who has done the most dangerous or exciting thing. They could grade each activity 1–5 (1 is very dangerous/exciting, 5 isn't really dangerous or exciting at all). This could prompt some lively discussion as students decide how dangerous something really is.

```
ANSWERS
Ex. 2
1 F   2 T   3 T   4 F   5 F   6 T   7 T
```

See also: *NEW FCE Gold exam maximiser* p.15

Vocabulary 1: adjectives of feeling p.19

Aim:

- to review *-ed/-ing* adjectives to describe feelings

1 Students work individually to complete the adjectives, then check their answers with a partner. They should be careful with number 8 – the answer is *encouraging*, not *encouraged*, as the speaker is describing how the instructor treated him, and not how the instructor felt.

2 With the same partner, students complete these sentences. To make it more challenging, ask them to cover up Exercise 1.

3

1, 2 This practises the target language in a personalised context. Some of the more interesting student questions for Exercise 3.2 could be extended into a whole class discussion.

Note that the questions students ask should use a Type 2 conditional structure. You should decide whether or not to correct your students if they don't use this, but avoid going into detail, as conditionals are covered later in the course.

```
ANSWERS
Ex. 1
1 excited   2 flattering   3 frightening
4 depressing   5 interested   6 confusing
7 frustrated   8 encouraging   9 annoyed
10 irritating
Ex. 2
1 confused   2 depressed   3 exciting   4 flattered
5 excited / frightened   6 frustrating / annoying
```

See also: *NEW FCE Gold exam maximiser* p.15

Reading 1: multiple-choice questions (Part 2) p.21

Aims:

- to provide a guided introduction to the Paper 1, Part 2 exam task
- to practise working out the meaning of words from context

Exam information ▶ Cbk p.4

To find the answers to multiple-choice questions, students usually have to look for synonyms of words in the question. Occasionally, the information they need is **implied** in the text rather than overtly stated. The questions follow the same order of the text, although often the final question checks the students' understanding of the text as a whole.

1 Predicting the content of a text from the title and any accompanying picture is a simple but useful reading preparation skill. In addition to answering questions 1–3, your students could also cover up the text and predict some of the words they might read, which you can write on the board.

2 Always encourage your students to skim (quickly read) a text for general meaning before they attempt to answer the questions. If they do this, they will be better prepared to answer the questions (i.e. they will be able to find the answers more quickly because they are more familiar with what the text is about). Skimming the text should take about two minutes.

3 Before your students answer the questions, tell them to highlight the key words in each question. They should then work individually to answer the questions, using the clues provided to help them. Allow them about 12–14 minutes before comparing their answers with a partner, and explaining why they chose them.

foot (paragraph 1, line 7): An imperial measurement of distance equal to approximately 30cm. *The valley is 400 **feet** deep = It is a **400-foot** deep valley*

4

1, 2 Students do Exercise 4.1 in pairs, and then check their answers in a dictionary. They can then find one or two other words that neither of them know, and work out the meaning from the context.

Exam information

There is often a question in Paper 1, Part 2 that requires students to identify what a pronoun refers to. Referencing skills are also invaluable for Paper 1, Part 3.

5 Referencing skills are very useful, as they help students to follow what a text is about. Usually, to find what a pronoun refers to, students have to look backwards through the text, sometimes across a whole paragraph. Occasionally, they may have to refer ahead as well (e.g. *Although **he** is my best friend, **John** can be really annoying. He* refers ahead to *John*). Referencing is also useful for developing students' writing style, which can often be let down by repetition.

6 This personalises the theme of this section. Students should do this in pairs or small groups.

ANSWERS

Ex. 2

1 His name is Robinson Diaz. He lives in the Andes Mountains, South America.

2 a) Robinson works as a cable racer, and uses the cable to take the school teacher to work. It means he can cross the valley much more quickly than he could on foot.
b) The cable is the teacher's transport to work.
c) The cable links the village with the rest of the world – everything they need is brought by cable.

Ex. 3

1 C (line 3: *the difficult task of taking the local teacher to her school.*)

2 A (line 13: *does a quick safety check and then, without hesitating, throws himself off the edge of the mountain.*)

3 D (line 26: *Diana had no idea when she took the teaching job that just getting to work ...would be so dangerous.*)

4 B (line 30: *'But soon I got used to it.'*)

5 A (line 34: *the wire cable is a lifeline.*)

6 D (line 47: *'What I'm really scared of is the snakes,' he says. 'This is nothing in comparison.'*)

Ex. 4

1 b)   2 a)   3 b)   4 a)   5 b)   6 b)   7 a)

Ex. 5

1 a)   2 a)   3 b)   4 b)

See also: *NEW FCE Gold exam maximiser p.16*

Grammar 1: making comparisons p.22

Aim:

• **to review language of comparison, using comparative/superlative adjective forms and intensifiers**

1

1, 2 At this level, students are usually familiar with language of comparison and contrast, but make frequent mistakes (especially with intensifiers). The mistakes in Exercise 1 are typical of those that students make on a regular basis. Ask your students to work individually to find and correct the mistakes, before comparing their answers with a partner.

2

1, 2 Students work with their partner to match Alex and Ben's sentences. When they have done this, they can read the dialogue aloud as a mini role-play, and then underline the intensifiers and complete the table.

3 In their same pairs, students cover up the table from Exercise 3 and do the key word transformations 1–6. When they have finished, they should refer back to the table to see if they have used the language correctly.

4 This activity, if done in small groups of three or four, could promote a lot of lively discussion, and makes an excellent communicative activity. Your students could choose some alternative categories to those listed (pop groups, teachers in their school, local restaurants, etc.) and add their own adjectives before comparing their examples.

ANSWERS

Ex. 1

1 not as busy *as*   2 Transport is *easier*
3 *more* people   4 less *strict* than
5 the *least* populated   6 *more* exciting than
7 *better* at sport than   8 would *rather travel*

Ex. 2

1 1 e)   2 d)   3 b)   4 c)   5 a)

2 far/much; slightly; just

Ex. 3

1 the most amazing   2 a lot braver than
3 a bit less   4 far easier playing / to play
5 of the largest cities   6 rather go sightseeing than lie

▶ Photocopiable activity 2A *Key words risk 1* p.163

See also: *NEW FCE Gold exam maximiser p.18*

Vocabulary 2: word formation (negative prefixes) p.23

Aim:
- **to review the use of negative prefixes with adjectives and verbs**

1   Working in pairs, students choose the correct alternative for each sentence. Explain that they should read each sentence carefully, noting key words which will help them to decide on the correct form (for example, number 5 uses *so hard* and *you need to look after yourself*, which suggests that word needed will be negative, not positive).

2   Students do this in the same pairs. Remind them that it may not be enough to just add a prefix. Sometimes, the tense of the word may also need to change (number 4) or a suffix may *also* need to be added (numbers 7 and 8).

3   Ask your students to do this individually on a sheet of paper, then hand the paper to you. Read out the sentences. The others in the class can then try to guess who wrote those sentences.

ANSWERS

Ex. 1
1 distrust   2 insufficient   3 lucky   4 impossible
5 unhealthy   6 misunderstand

Ex. 2
1 insecure   2 incredible   3 possible
4 misunderstood   5 capable   6 conscious
7 inexperienced   8 unfortunately

See also: *NEW FCE Gold exam maximiser* p.19

Use of English: word formation (Part 5) p.23

Aim:
- **to provide a guided introduction to Paper 3, Part 5 word formation task**

1   Ask your students to look at the title and to think of as many reasons as possible why people take risks (e.g. *They are exciting, challenging; if we succeed we feel good; they make life more interesting;, in some cases they can make you rich*, etc.). Ask them if they have taken any risks recently.

2   Students skim the text for general information.

3   Your students should work individually to answer questions 1–3 (at this stage, they should **not** try to complete the text), and then compare their answers in small groups.

Remind them to read the **whole sentence** carefully, and not just the words immediately preceding and following the gaps.

Exam information ▶ Cbk p.5

In Paper 3, Part 5, the word form must **always** be changed.

---

4   Your students can do this in their same groups, and then compare their answers with another group. They should try to explain to each other why they chose those words.

ANSWERS

Ex. 3
1, 2, 3
 1 noun – plural
 2 noun – singular
 3 verb – gerund
 4 noun – singular
 5 adjective – comparative
 6 adjective
 7 adjective – negative
 8 adjective
 9 noun – singular
10 adjective

Ex. 4
1 explanations   2 excitement   3 facing
4 survival   5 easier   6 basic   7 unhealthy
8 interesting   9 curiosity   10 sensible

Exam Focus

Paper 1 Reading: multiple matching (Part 4) p.24

Aim:
- **to introduce and practice a procedure for Paper 1, Part 4**

Exam information ▶ Cbk p.4

Some students are better at some parts of the Reading test than others, so they may prefer to do these first (in the exam, it doesn't matter which part they do first). They should never spend more than 18 minutes on each part; if they haven't finished one part after this time, they should move to the next part, and return to it if they have time at the end.

Many students think Part 4 is the most complicated part of the paper, as they have to refer between the statements, the choice of answers and the text, and also because the answers do not follow the order of the text. With the right skills, however, this can be a fairly straightforward task, so it is important to guide your students through the procedure, and to make them aware of why they are doing it this way.

Allow your students a few minutes to read through the **About the exam** and **Procedure** sections. Then ask them to close their books, and tell you as much as they can remember. Focus particularly on the procedure, asking them why each stage is important.

1 Before your students look at the questions, ask them to brainstorm as many outdoor activities as possible, and ask them why people enjoy doing these things. (They should try to answer in complete sentences, e.g. *Some people enjoy camping because it's cheap, it's healthy and it gets you back to nature.*)

2 Before your students do the task, tell them to look at the example 0. *Why is the answer to this C?* (The answer is at the end of the paragraph: *My main concern now is encouraging people to take greater care of … sites of natural beauty. Concern* is an important key word, which also appears in the multiple matching statement; *natural beauty* is a synonym here for *the environment*.)
They should then work individually through the task, following the recommended procedure. Remind them that the information in the text must be **exactly** the same as that in the multiple matching statements.
When they have finished, they should check their answers with a partner, explaining why they chose them, and then check their answers with you.

3 This personalises the theme of this section. Students discuss in small groups.

ANSWERS

Ex. 1
1 hiking climbing mountain biking
2 Photo A = Text B, Photo B = Text E,
  Photo C = Text A

Ex. 2
1 D 2/3 A/E 4 B 5 E 6 C 7 E 8/9 A/D
10 B 11 A 12 E 13/14 A/B 15 C

Grammar 2: articles p.26

Aim:
- **to focus on the correct use of definite and indefinite articles**

1 Students should work in pairs to identify and correct the mistakes. You can then tell them to work with another pair and categorise each word where the article has been used (e.g. the Atlantic Ocean = Seas and oceans. These are

---

preceded by a definite article. *Weather* is uncountable, so it cannot have an indefinite article.). They can then think of some other examples for each category (e.g. the Pacific, the Mediterranean, the South China Sea, etc.) and develop a bank of these that they can refer to in future. They should note, however, that some words cannot be categorised (e.g. *by accident, at home,* etc.), and should be learnt and recorded as individual expressions.

2 In their groups of four, students complete sentences 1–10, referring to the bank they have developed, and/or to the **Grammar reference** on page 192.

3
1 For this task, ask your students to cover up parts 1 and 2, and try to do it without referring back or looking at their notes. They can either do this in pairs or small groups.
2 Tell your students that when they write the email, they should pay particular attention to whether or not they are using articles correctly.

ANSWERS

Ex. 1
1 ✓   2 was terrible weather   3 *a* footballer
4 *the* front door   5 *the* River Thames
6 Mount Everest   7 at home   8 by accident
9 ✓ 10 in Nepal

Ex. 2
1 the   2 (-)/(-)   3 The/a   4 (-)   5 (-)
6 the   7 the   8 (-)   9 The 10 (-)

Ex. 3
1 *a* hollow plastic ball   2 *a* hill   3 *The* first zorb
4 ✓   5 *The* Dangerous Sports Club   6 New Zealand   7 *the* late 1990's   8 *the* world
9 a/the dry zorb   10 *a* harness   11 *the* ball
12 ✓   13 *the* bottom   14 ✓   15 *a* washing machine

▶ Photocopiable activity 2B *Get it right!* p.164

See also: *NEW FCE Gold exam maximiser p.20*

Speaking 2: comparing and contrasting (Part 2) p.27

Aims:
- **to practise the language of comparison and linking words**
- **to compare and contrast two photographs**

Exam information ▶ Cbk p.5

For this task, students are not expected to describe the photographs in great detail, but they should be able to explain what they can see and what is happening, and then move on to answer the examiner's question. It is a good idea to start with a general comment that focuses on the main link between the photos.

1   Ask your students to look at both photos for a moment and decide which sentence best summarises the link between them.
Then briefly ask them what is happening in each photo. *What can they see? How do the people feel in each picture? Where would **they** rather be?*

2

1   Students underline the comparative structures individually, then compare their answers with a partner.

2   As an alternative to students reading for the incorrect information, tell them to close their books and read out the sentences yourself. They should try to remember what they saw in the photos, and then correct any mistakes you make.

3

1   Students should be familiar with most of the linking words in this task, but *whereas* may cause a few problems. Encourage your students to check for any unfamiliar words in a dictionary.

2   Ask your students for their answers, then play the recording so they can see if they were right or wrong. Encourage your students to keep a record of these words and expressions and how they are used, as they are used a lot in many areas of English.

3   Stress and intonation are important features of pronunciation that are often overlooked. Incorrect stress on individual words, or incorrect stress and intonation on expressions, can alter the meaning. Remind students that a good dictionary will show them the stress on individual words.

4

1, 2 Students work in pairs to compare and contrast the pictures, and then answer question 2.

5   Monitor the student pairs while they do this activity. Help any students who have stalled by asking them 'prompt' questions (e.g. *How do the people feel? Do you think you would enjoy doing something like this?*)

ANSWERS
Ex. 1
a)
Exs. 2, 3
1
1   much *older than* = younger
2   *fewer* people = more
3   *more* brightly coloured *than* = ✓

---

4   *more* nervous *than* = ✓
5   The man is taking a *bigger* physical risk = the woman
6   The man is enjoying himself *more than* = the woman

Ex. 3
1
1 While   2 but   3 whereas   4 while
5 but on the other hand
3
1 first, other   2 inside, air   3 first, nervous, other, relaxed   4 woman, man   5 woman, expert, other, first time

---

Writing: formal letter (Part 1) p.28

Aim:
- **to focus on the process of writing a formal transactional letter**

Exam information ▶ Cbk p.4

Both parts of the FCE Writing test should take about 45 minutes each, but students should allow themselves time to read the questions, highlight key points, make a plan and check for content, etc., when they have finished. Generally, students take longer to do Part 1 than Part 2.

---

1   Ask your students to read the exam writing task, and to highlight key words/expressions. Encourage them to do this for any writing task, especially those where specific information must be included in their answer. They can then answer questions 1–4 with a partner.

2   Point out that the basic function of a paragraph is to divide the letter into 'subject areas', with the aim of making it easier to read. With an FCE letter, five paragraphs (including the introduction and closing remark) is an ideal average.

3   You could ask some students to read out their completed sentences and compare their ideas.

4, **5**   Point out that in this letter we know the name of the person to whom they are writing (*Mr Spiller*), so they should begin their letter *Dear Mr Spiller* and end it *Yours sincerely*.
This can be done for homework. Your students should try to do it in about 30–35 minutes, allowing 5–10 minutes afterwards to check for content, organisation, cohesion, clarity, etc.

ANSWERS

Ex. 1
1 True.   2 False.   3 False.   4 False.

Ex. 2
Paragraph 1: thanks for the letter and general remark
Paragraph 2: which month you want to travel
Paragraph 3: preferences for morning classes and afternoon activities
Paragraph 4: request for further information
Paragraph 5: closing remark

Ex. 4 Sample answer
Dear Mr Spiller,
Thank you very much for your letter informing me that I have won first prize in the competition. I am looking forward to going to Australia and attending the course.

I would like to do the course in August because I have to go back to university in September. In the morning, I would like to join the grammar and vocabulary class because I think there will lots of opportunities for speaking and listening in the evenings.

In the afternoon, I would like to try making a class website because I think this would be a very useful skill to have in the future. I would also be interested in doing a scuba diving course because Australia is famous for the Great Barrier Reef and one day I would love to go scuba diving there.

Could you tell me what type of accommodation is provided and what kind of clothes I should bring with me?

I look forward to hearing from you.

Yours sincerely,
Francesco Vacca
Francesco Vacca   (164 words)

See also: *NEW FCE Gold exam maximiser* p.22

UNIT 2 Review p.29

ANSWERS

Ex. 1 Sample answers
healthy, relaxing (cycling); challenging, enjoyable (football); dangerous, thrilling (free diving); difficult, frustrating (windsurfing); boring, tiring (walking)

Ex. 2.1
1 *as* dangerous as   2 *the* most dangerous   3 *a* lot
4 *as* strong   5 *than* I am   6 *would* rather

Ex. 3
1 C   2 D   3 B   4 A   5 B   6 D   7 D   8 B

Ex. 4
1 *The* next bus   2 *the* Andes Mountains
3 *The* best   4 ~~the~~ Nepal   5 in ~~the~~ diving
6 *an* activity   7 ~~the~~ football   8 taking ~~the~~ risks

Ex. 5
1 ability   2 unbroken   3 unexpected   4 unsafe
5 frightening   6 unsuccessful   7 impossible
8 healthy   9 confidence   10 unadventurous

▶ Photocopiable Unit 2 test p.114

3 Fact or fiction?

Reading: gapped text (Part 3) p.30

Aims:

- **to provide a guided introduction to the gapped text task**
- **to focus on pronoun links between parts of a text**

1

1 This prepares students for reading by getting them to think about what the story is about. Students can discuss their ideas with a partner.

2 This provides a good opportunity to review and practise both information and *Yes/No* questions and language of probability (*Where did he come from? Why is he there? Does he want to be there? How does he feel? he might, he could*, etc.).

2 Students skim the text (allow them about one minute for this) to check their ideas.

3 Check that your students understand what these types of story are (*thriller* – an exciting story about murder or crime). Ask them if they can think of any other types of story. Can they think of any specific examples of these sorts of story, either in English or in their own language?

4

1, 2, 3 Remind your students that in order to identify which sentences are missing from each part of the text, they will need to refer back to the sentence **before** the gap, and often **ahead** to the sentence after the gap. They need to match pronouns to main nouns and vice versa (the pronoun in the missing sentence will usually – but not always – refer back to the previous main noun). They will also need to look for synonyms and parallel expressions. When they have finished, they should compare their answers with a partner, and explain why they chose those answers.

5, **6** Play the recording once and let students check their answers. They can then work in groups to discuss what is at the end of the road and how the story will continue. As a possible follow on, they can continue writing the story for homework, or continue the dialogue between Julian and the girl, which provides another opportunity to review question forms.

7 Your students will probably recognise the class these words belong to, but won't know what they mean. Remind them that they may be able to deduce their meaning from the context. Focus on number 1. *Julian has suddenly arrived in an unfamiliar place and he doesn't know how he got there. How would you feel in the same situation? Think of a word in your own language to describe that feeling.* *Disoriented* is probably an English synonym, or equivalent, of that word. Ask your students if they can think of any other words which might have a similar meaning – for this example, *dazed* and *confused* would be examples.

> **Teaching tips and ideas**
>
> As a follow-up, ask students to think of a famous author, dead or alive, from their own country, and tell the others in the class about them and the book(s) they are/were famous for. This could be developed into a class project, or students could be encouraged to find out about authors from their classmates' countries on the internet.

ANSWERS

Ex. 3
b)

Ex. 4
1
landscape
2
1 H   2 G   3 F   4 B   5 E   6 A   7 C

Ex. 7
1 *disoriented* – confused, not able to understand what is happening or where you are
2 *unsteadily* – shaking when you try to stand or walk
3 *trails* – pathways in the grass where people have walked
4 *scattered* – spread over a wide area
5 *murmured* – said in a low voice

See also: *NEW FCE Gold exam maximiser* p.24

Vocabulary 1: using a dictionary p.32

Aim:

- **to focus on the importance of dictionaries as a learning resource**

Before your students look at this section, ask them about the benefits of a good dictionary. What information can a monolingual English dictionary give them?

As well as providing the definition of a word, dictionaries (in particular, monolingual dictionaries) also show how that word is pronounced, part of speech (noun, adverb, etc.), how it is used in context, other forms of the same word and so on.

A recommended dictionary at this level is the *Longman Active Study Dictionary*, which is available with a CD rom of useful vocabulary exercises.

1   Students can work in pairs to decide if questions 1–8 are true or false, based on the dictionary entries.

2   Your students could try to do this initially without referring to the dictionary extracts, and then refer to the extracts to check their answers.

3   **1, 2** Phrasal verbs are an important area of language and are a common feature of Paper 3. Your students should be encouraged to develop their own bank of useful phrasal verbs.

They should do this exercise individually, then compare their answers with a partner before checking in their dictionary.

ANSWERS

Ex. 1

1 T   2 F   3 F   4 T   5 T   6 F   7 F   8 T

Ex. 2

1 I *got / caught* a glimpse – *see* does not collocate
2 stared *at* – stare is intransitive (cannot have an object) but can be followed by a preposition plus noun or pronoun.
3 a quick *look* – a gaze must always be long, and you can't give a glimpse.
4 *gave* him a stare – *make* does not collocate
5 He was unaware of his *gaze* this is always singular.
6 ✓

Ex. 3

1 looking into
2 looking forward to going
3 look it up
4 looked up to
5 look out for
6 looks down on

See also: *NEW FCE Gold exam maximiser* p.23

Grammar 1: *like, as, as if/though* p.33

Aim:

- **to focus on the different functions of *like*, *as*, *as if* and *as though***

1   Students can answer 1–12 individually, then compare their answers with a partner and/or check how the words are used in the **Grammar reference** on page 205.

Teaching tips and ideas

Instead of your students looking at questions 1–12, tell them to close their books, and then read out the sentences, using either the correct or incorrect words, and let your students work in small teams to decide if your sentences are right or wrong.

---

2   Working with the same partner from Exercise 1, students think of the questions for each answer. When they have finished this, they could think of some **other** answers that would require a question with *as* or *like*, and then hand these to another pair to make questions.

3

1, 2 This exercise practises the target language in context. Students should do this individually, then compare their answers with the rest of the class.

4

1, 2 This activity focuses on grammatical accuracy and language of description. As well as listening to their partner describing their picture, students could ask them questions to get more information or to clarify something (e.g. *What do you mean when you say she looks like a cat? Has she got a tail? Is she eating a mouse?* etc.)

ANSWERS

Ex. 1

1 like   2 What's   3 seems   4 as   5 as   6 like   7 as though*   8 as if*   9 as*   10 as   11 like
* Note: *like* is often used colloquial speech, but is not considered good English.

Ex. 2 Sample answers

1 What are your mother and father / parents like?
2 Are you like / Do you look like your brother / father? Has your brother / father got the same colour hair as you?
3 Do you feel like going to a disco? / Would you like to do something fun, like going to a disco?
4 What's your home town like?
5 Do you like working as a pool attendant? What's it like?

Ex. 3
1 as   2 like   3 as   4 like   5 as if / as though
6 as   7 like   8 as if / as though

See also: *NEW FCE Gold exam maximiser* p.25

Listening 1: multiple matching (Part 3) p.34

Aim:
• **to provide a guided introduction to Paper 4, Part 3**

Exam information ▶ Cbk p.5

In Part 3, students hear a series of short monologues or dialogues, and have to match what is said with words or short sentences that sum up, or highlight a main point of, what the speaker says. Each extract is based on the same theme (e.g. shopping, cinema, food, books, etc.).

1   Students can discuss questions 1–3 in pairs or small groups. It doesn't have to be a novel; it could be a biography, autobiography, reference work, magazine or even comic. For questions 2 and 3, they could briefly sum up what it was about.

2   Before you play the recording, ask your students to highlight the key words/phrases in sentences A and B (A: *try not to be put off … Books … hard to read.* B: *waste of time*). Then play the recording twice and ask them for their answer (We know the answer is B because she says … *it's useless stuff … you don't … get anything out of it*).

3   In pairs, students decide what the key words/phrases are in sentences B–F. They must listen for words or phases on the recording that have the same, or very similar meaning. Play the recording twice and then let students compare their answers, and explain to each other why they chose them. Check their answers (if possible, give them a copy of the tapescript so they can tell you exactly what they heard on the recording that helped them to identify the answers).

▶ Tapescript p.100

4   This personalises the theme of this section. Students discuss in small groups.

ANSWERS

Ex. 2
1 B
2 'it's useless stuff really, you don't actually get anything out of it.'

Ex. 3
1 B   2 F   3 A   4 C   5 D

Speaking: asking for and reacting to opinions (Parts 3 and 4) p.34

Aim:
• **to focus on useful expressions for reacting to what somebody says**

Exam information ▶ Cbk p.5

In Paper 5, Part 3, students are given a task to perform together. They are expected to take about three minutes to do this task, and need to work together without input from the examiner. Consequently, language of interaction such as giving opinions, asking for opinions, agreeing, disagreeing, etc., is very important and interaction is one of the criteria on which they are marked. Students should also consider other aspects, such as maintaining eye contact, nodding their head, making the right noises, and general body language.

Point out that they may be penalised in the exam if they try to dominate the conversation and not give their partner a chance to speak. They should remember that they are being marked on how they work **together** in this section.

Teaching tips and ideas

When students work together in pairs or small groups (especially when discussing something), it is helpful if they turn their chairs so that they are facing their partner(s). This makes verbal communication and interaction much easier than if they face forward.

1   Ask your students to work individually and think about the questions, then discuss them briefly with a partner. Questions 1 and 2 are typical of those that they might be asked in the FCE Speaking test.

2
1 Play the recording once and ask your students for their answers to 1 and 2. When discussing question 2 in Exercise 1, the two students use expressions of agreement and disagreement. There is good interaction between these two students – they are clearly working together and responding to what the other says.
2, 3 Before you play the recording again, ask your students if they know what the word *intonation* means (the rising and falling of tone as you speak). Play the recording again while your students listen for the phrases. After each phrase appears, pause the recording and ask your students to repeat the phrases, paying particular attention to the intonation. Then allow them a few moments to work in pairs and practise the phrases again.

▶ Tapescript p.101

3 Monitor your students while they do this to make sure they are working together, and that they are both giving each other the chance to speak.

Less forthcoming students might like to learn a few useful interrupting expressions that they could use if partnered with a particularly domineering student. These could include *Sorry to interrupt, but …, Can I interrupt you for a moment?*)

4 These questions are typical of those that students might be asked in Part 4 of the FCE Speaking test.

Exam information ▶ Cbk p.5

Part 4 of the FCE Speaking test is a three-way discussion between the examiner and the students. The topics discussed are loosely based on the topic in part 3. The examiner asks them some questions, and the students answer them. At this point in the exam, many students just respond to the examiner and ignore their partner, whereas they should still be working **together**.

ANSWERS

Ex. 1

1 **From left to right, top row:**
   a cookery book; a text book; a letter; a sign
   bottom row: a page on the Internet; a novel

Ex. 2

1
1 The cookery book and the page on the Internet
2 They work together well
2
That's right.   Yes, I agree …   But on the other hand …   I suppose so.   Right.   Well, yes, but …
OK, but …   What do you think? Yes, that's true.

Grammar 2: adverbs p.35

Aim:
- **to review the form and position of adverbs**

1, **2** Students underline the adverbs/adverbial phrases and circle the adjectives individually and then compare their answers with a partner. After they have copied and completed the table, they should then work together to choose the correct adverb form in Exercise 2. Students usually learn that adverbs are formed by adding -ly to the adjective, but this shows them that in some cases this can change the meaning (e.g. *hard* and *hardly*)

3 Your students can do this exercise with a partner, using a dictionary to check their answers. In a good monolingual dictionary, students will find adverbs contextualized so that they can see where they come in a sentence.

ANSWERS

Ex. 1

1
1 harder (adjective); badly, worse (adverbs)
2 well (adv); good (adj); more (adv)
3 fast (adv); dangerous (adj)
4 in that silly, unfriendly way (adv phrase)
5 still straight (advs)
6 harder (adv)
7 new (adj); automatically (adv)
8 early (adj); late (adv)

2
Adjective/Adverb/Adverbial phrase
interesting/interestingly/in an interesting way
bad/badly
worse/worse
good/well
more/more
fast/fast
dangerous/dangerously
(un)friendly/in a(n) (un)friendly way
still/still
straight/straight
new/newly(built etc.)
automatic/automatically
early/early
late/late

Ex. 2
1 a) *hard*   b) *hardly*
2 a) *lately*   b) *late*
3 a) *highly*   b) *high*
4 a) *free*   b) *freely*

Ex. 3
1 Does she *usually* get the bus to college?
2 He's not *often* late.
3 She's *never* been happy there.
4 You'd better go *straight* to the house.
5 I'll *certainly* be seeing her tomorrow.
6 I *nearly* didn't make it on time.
7 *Perhaps* she's missed her flight.
8 *Luckily*, I managed to get his number from Judy.
9 You are *probably* right.
10 I'm *definitely* not free next week.

▶ Photocopiable activity 3 *Find the mystery word* p.165

See also: *NEW FCE Gold exam maximiser* p.28

Exam Focus

Paper 3: Use of English: error correction (Part 4) p.36

Aim:

- to provide a procedure for completing the error correction task

Exam information ▶ Cbk p.5

There are five sections in this Paper, giving an average time per section of 15 minutes. Some sections may take longer to do than others. Students don't have to do them in order, so it may be a good idea to do the ones they find easiest first.

For this task, you might need to emphasise that the mistakes are by **line**, not by **sentence**, although your students will have to read the whole sentence to identify which word(s) should not be there. Sometimes, the extra word appears at the beginning or end of a line, which effectively places it in a 'blind spot'.

Begin this section by taking your students through the procedure, then telling them to close their books and asking them if they can remember the various points in that procedure.

1 Tell your students to skim the text for general meaning and to find out how the writer felt. At this stage they should not try to identify the extra words (although in many cases they will focus on these automatically, as the 'flow' of some of the sentences will seem strange or awkward).

2 Before they attempt the task, ask your students to look at the example, and to tell you what is wrong with the word *was* (the sentence is not passive, so we cannot use a passive voice construction).
Working individually, your students should then try to identify all the extra, unnecessary words. They can then compare their answers in small groups and explain why those words do not belong there.

> **Teaching tips and ideas**
> Students often seem to enjoy identifying mistakes like these, especially if they are made 'by accident' by their teacher. You could occasionally include 'mistakes' when writing sentences on the board, and wait for one of your students to identify them.

ANSWERS

Ex. 1
a)

Ex. 2
1 the   2 of   3 for   4 ✓   5 it   6 ✓   7 to
8 had   9 ✓   10 like   11 a   12 been   13 as
14 very   15 would

Listening 2: multiple-choice questions (Part 4) p.37

Aim:

- to provide a guided introduction to answering multiple-choice questions

1 Before your students do the task in Exercise 1, ask them to look at the three pictures and tell you what is happening in each one. What do they think has just happened? What do they think is going to happen? They should then look through the questions and match these to the pictures. At this stage, they could also highlight the key words in each question.

Exam information ▶ Cbk p.5

Point out to your students that the words in the answers are not usually heard on the recording; they are expected to listen for synonyms and parallel expressions in order to get the correct answer.

2, **3** Play the recording once through without stopping, then play it again, and ask your students for their answers. How did they decide on these answers? Check that your students haven't been misled by the distracters (for example, the word *shopping* appears in the answer options to number 1, and we know that the speaker's aunt was doing some shopping (key words: *stalls*, *shop*), but that was not the reason *why* she went to Paris. She went there for her *honeymoon*).

▶ Tapescript p.101

4 Discuss these questions with your class. Remind them that they hear the passage twice, so they shouldn't panic if they don't hear the answer the first time. If they don't get the answer on the second playing, they can guess, as they are not penalised for getting an answer wrong.

5   Put your students into small groups and ask them to tell one another any similar stories they have. Each group can then choose the best story, and get the teller to relate it to the rest of the class.

ANSWERS

Ex. 2

1 A   2 B   3 B   4 B   5 C   6 A   7 C

Ex. 4

1 Yes.

2 No – so students should look at all three options as they listen

3 b)

See also: *NEW FCE Gold exam maximiser* p.27

Vocabulary 2: modifiers/intensifiers p.38

Aim:

- **to focus on the use of modifiers with gradable/non-gradable adjectives**

Students often misuse intensifiers, especially *very*, which they tend to apply to all adjectives (~~very~~ *amazing*, ~~very~~ *starving*) regardless of whether or not they are correct.

1   In pairs, students look at the sentences and choose the adverbs which can be used. Explain that *pretty* and *totally* can sound fairly colloquial when used as intensifiers in some situations (*I did pretty well, It was totally cool.*) and are often used by younger people. They should check their answers in the **Grammar reference** on page 201, which explains the difference between gradable and non-gradable adjectives.

2

1 Students can do this in pairs, one student reading the prompt sentence (e.g. *I thought the film was quite good.*) and the second student responding with an intensifier (*Did you? I thought it was absolutely brilliant!*). Monitor the student pairs to check that they are using appropriate modifiers, and placing the stress in the correct place.

2 Play the recording, stopping it after each sentence and getting your students to repeat what they hear. Point out that more than one combination is possible, though some combinations are more likely than others (see ANSWERS).

Teaching tips and ideas

After your students have done this exercise, write the words *absolutely, very, really, quite, fairly, pretty, utterly, extremely, completely, totally, terribly, a bit* and *rather* on one side of the board, and *amazing, good, hard, impossible, boring* and *fantastic* on the other side of the board. Divide your class into small teams. Ask each team to choose one of the adjectives, and then give the class five minutes to write as many different sentences as possible, using that adjective and a variety of intensifiers. Stop them after five minutes. Award each team one point for each sentence that correctly uses an intensifier, and remove a point each time an intensifier is used incorrectly.

---

3   This can be a lively and entertaining exercise, especially if you have students who are able to do things that others can't (e.g. wiggle their earlobes), and are able to demonstrate them to their classmates.

4   This personalises the target language from this section, and can be extended into a piece of written text for homework.

ANSWERS

Ex. 1

1 ~~an absolutely~~ narrow escape (gradable adj)

2 ~~totally~~ good (gradable adj)

3 ~~utterly~~ hard (gradable adj)

4 ~~extremely~~ impossible (non-gradable adj)

5 ~~terribly~~ amazing (non-gradable adj)

6 ~~completely~~ boring (gradable adj)

7 ~~fairly~~ fantastic (non-gradable adj)

8 ~~totally~~ good (gradable adj)

Ex. 2

1 absolutely / totally / really / utterly wonderful (non-gradable)

2 extremely / really difficult (gradable)

3 absolutely / totally / utterly superb (non-gradable)

4 absolutely freezing (non-gradable)

5 totally / utterly wrong (non-gradable)

6 absolutely / really great (non-gradable)

See also: *NEW FCE Gold exam maximiser* p.29

Grammar 3: narrative tenses p.38

Aim:

- **to review narrative tenses in preparation for writing a story in the next section**

1

1, 2 First, check that your students know what a *parakeet* is (a small, brightly coloured bird with a long tail). Your students should then read the first paragraph of the story and answer the questions. Then ask them to focus on the verbs *was walking* (past continuous) and *had been clipped* (past perfect passive) and their function.

2

1, 2 After your students have read the second paragraph, they should discuss the questions with a partner. Refer them to the **Grammar reference** on page 204. Question 3 again focuses on the past perfect, because the parakeet found a home **before** the speaker's sister forgave her.

3

1, 2 Focus your students' attention on the note about over-using the past perfect. Students tend to over-use this structure, when in many cases the past simple works just as well.
In pairs, your students should then complete the text with the correct form of the verb, before discussing the questions in 3.2.

4

This exercise provides students with the opportunity to practise narrative tenses in their own story, using the picture as visual stimulus

---

ANSWERS

Ex. 1

1
1 In 1956 in Arizona.
2 She was walking around the house.
3 Because his wings had been clipped.
4 Perky flew off.

2
1 past continuous, past perfect passive
2 a) past perfect b) past continuous

Ex. 2

1
No.

2
1 A long period.
2 Past simple. In the order they happened.
3 had … found; past perfect; b)

Ex. 3
1 were sitting **2** had had **3** announced
4 explained **5** was standing **6** flew **7** landed
8 examined **9** matched **10** had been
11 phoned

2
1 They were telling stories about pets.
2 The bird had flown down and landed on his finger.
3 The dates, places and descriptions of the bird all matched.

See also: *NEW FCE Gold exam maximiser p.29*

Writing: story (Part 2) p.40

Aims:

- **to focus on narrative tenses and sequencing expressions**
- **to focus on the stages of planning and writing a story**

1

Individually, students complete the text with the sequencing words, then compare their answers with a partner or in small groups. Point out that in gaps 3, 8 and 9 more than one option will fit. They should use each word once only.

2, 3

After your students number the stages in Exercise 2, ask them to work in small groups and brainstorm ideas for Exercise 3. They should then decide on the best ideas and make a note of these. They now have a basic plan for their story.

4

1, 2, 3 After your students do Exercise 4.1, ask the whole class for ideas for 4.2 and their thoughts on which sentence would be the best ending in 4.3.

5, 6

This can be done as a homework task. Your students should allow themselves 30–35 minutes to write the story, and 5–10 minutes for checking and editing.

UNIT 3 Review p.41

ANSWERS

Ex. 1

1 After a while   2 At first   3 finally/eventually/ then   4 As soon as   5 before   6 After
7 While   8 Then/Eventually   9 finally/eventually

Ex. 2

1 background information
2 first events and/or a problem
3 later actions or results
4 final outcome

Ex. 4

1 It contains background information and the first event.
3 B – It is the most dramatic.

Ex. 5 Sample answer

Emma could not believe what she saw in front of her. She had been sitting in the classroom for the last two hours, not thinking about anything except finishing her history exam. Then suddenly, feeling that something in her surroundings was not right, she had raised her eyes from the exam paper. The classroom had completely disappeared.

Emma found herself standing in a cold damp castle. She was frightened but decided to take a look around. All the rooms were empty, but eventually she came to big hall and found an old man sitting on his own.
'Welcome Emma,' he said. 'Is there something you want to ask me?'
The only thing Emma could think of was the questions in her history exam, so that's what she asked him. The old man smiled and began talking while Emma closed her eyes.

When Emma woke up she was back in the history exam, but for some reason she knew all the answers. Emma knew that she wasn't going to fail her exam after all!

(173 words)

See also: *NEW FCE Gold exam maximiser* p.30

ANSWERS

Ex. 1

1 glimpse   2 carry on   3 nerve   4 unsteadily
5 severe   6 investigate   7 give   8 trip

Ex. 2

1 I came across   2 a waste of time   3 no sign of
4 going on   5 found out   6 made her way

Ex. 3.1

1 spelling   2 pronunciation   3 noun   4 verb
5 phrases   6 means

Ex. 4

1 My brother has the same colour hair *as* me.
2 You look unhappy – what's the matter?
3 *What's* the weather like where you are? Is it raining?
4 That outfit suits you – you look *like* a model or a film star.
5 I'm studying very *hard* for the exams.
6 he spoke to him *in a friendly way*, and he felt better at once.
7 It was *absolutely* freezing on the mountain top.
8 Your exam result was *very* good.

Ex. 5

1 once / after   2 eventually   3 then   4 When
5 As soon as / When   6 before   7 When / As soon as   8 While / As / When

▶ Photocopiable Unit 3 test p.116

UNIT
4 Food for thought

Vocabulary 1: food p.42

Aims:
- **to review/introduce words related to food and diet**
- **to provide a lead-in for Listening**

Before your students open their books, ask them about their favourite foods. *Is there anything they are particularly fond of? Is there anything they don't like or can't eat (perhaps because they are allergic to it)?*

1 Before students do this quick quiz, you might want to check they understand the following words: *protein* (a substance that exists in meat and eggs, which helps your body to grow and stay healthy); *carbohydrate* (a substance which gives the body heat and energy, found in rice, bread and potatoes); *cholesterol* (a chemical found in fat, which can cause heart disease);
They can do the quiz in pairs. Tell them some of the sentences 1–8 can be matched with more than one sentence in a)–h). When they have finished, tell them to close their books, and ask them questions about the foods, e.g. *What can you tell me about milk and cheese? Milk and cheese are dairy products. They're high in cholesterol and have a high proportion of fat,* etc.)

2, **3** When your students have matched the people to the speech bubbles in 2.1, they should work with a partner to discuss the sorts of food that should be eaten by the people in 2.2 They could extend this by writing a breakfast/lunch/dinner menu for one day for one or more of these people. They can then go on to discuss the question in Exercise 3.

ANSWERS

Ex. 1
1 f) 2 c) 3 h) 4 a) 5 b) 6 e) 7 d) 8 g)

Ex. 2
Footballer: I eat lots of protein ...
Celebrity: I mostly eat fruit ...

See also: *NEW FCE Gold exam maximiser* p.32

Listening: sentence completion (Part 2) p.42

Aim:
- **to provide a guided introduction to Paper 4, Part 2**

1 Discuss the photos, which introduce the topic of the Listening. (The man is Jamie Oliver, a popular TV chef. Cookery programmes have become extremely popular in Britain in the last few years, and some of the presenters have become very famous.)

Exam information ▶ Cbk p.5

In the exam, students are given a minute to read through the questions for each part before they hear the recording. They should use this time to highlight key words and, for Part 2, to think about the type of word that is missing (noun, adjective, verb, number, etc.).

2
1, 2 This exercise takes students through the pre-listening process that will help them to complete the gaps. Students should do this individually, and then compare their answers with a partner.

Exam information ▶ Cbk p.5

When the required answer is a number, this can be written as a numeral or a word (e.g. *8* or *eight* for gap 2).

---

3 Play the recording twice. Remind your students that they should not write complete sentences, just 1–3 words.

▶ Tapescript p.102

4 These questions personalise the theme of this section.

Teaching tips and ideas

Conduct a class survey to find the students' favourite foods or dishes. Each students writes a list of their top ten favourite foods/dishes, and the information is collated. Your students could also recommend their favourite restaurant and say why they like it.

ANSWERS

Ex. 2

2

a) 2   b) 1   c) 3   d) 5   e) 10

Ex. 3

1 a restaurant   2 eight/8   3 model   4 (TV)
programme   5 simple   6 lifestyle   7 cookery
book   8 wedding   9 unemployed   10 drums

See also: *NEW FCE Gold exam maximiser* p.33

Vocabulary 2: prepositions p.43

Aim:

- **to focus on dependent prepositions**

1   Ask your students to do this in small groups. Then tell them to close their books and read out the sentences to them, leaving a gap where the preposition goes. They can tell you what that preposition should be. Alternatively, read them out, sometimes using the correct preposition, and sometimes using the wrong one. Your students should tell you whether you are right or wrong.

2   This practises the target language in a personalised context. After your students have discussed these questions in pairs, they could tell the rest of the class about their partner, making sure they use the correct prepositions (e.g. *Thomas has a talent for playing the guitar, but he says he can never find time for it. He used to play the saxophone, but he lost interest in it.*)

ANSWERS

Ex. 1

1 for   2 in   3 on   4 to   5 as   6 in   7 on
8 for / in   9 to   10 of

See also: *NEW FCE Gold exam maximiser* p.33

Exam focus

Paper 1 Reading: multiple-choice questions (Part 2) p.44

Aim:

- **to introduce and practice a procedure for Paper 1, Part 2**

Introduce this section by asking your students if any of them have ever eaten anything strange, unusual or disgusting. *Are there any foods in their country that would seem strange to*

people from other countries? (e.g. snake, dog, etc) *Why do we eat some animals and not others*? (e.g. religion, squeamishness, some animals are considered as pets, some animals are too 'cute' to eat, etc)

Take your students through the **About the exam** and **Procedure** sections in the usual way (see Units 1–3).

1   Students skim the text and answer questions 1 and 2. You could first explain the word *tickle* and the title of the text: if something *tickles your taste buds*, it is something you like eating. You may also need to pre-teach some of the animal names in the text, e.g. *scorpions, grasshoppers, worms.*

2   Working individually, students answer questions 1–8, then compare their answers with a partner, explaining why they chose them. Remind them that in many cases, the key words in the answers are not in the text itself – they must look for synonyms and parallel expressions.

3   These questions could promote a lively discussion on what we would and wouldn't eat, and why.

ANSWERS

Ex. 1

1 Because it helps people to understand other cultures, it's good for you and it's environmentally friendly.

2 She is more reluctant.

Ex. 2

1 A (line 6: *a nine-year study of entamophagy, the eating of insects, which has taken them all over the globe.*)

2 C (line 13: *I came across a magazine called the Food Insect Newsletter and I just became fascinated*)

3 A (line 22: *I knew that I couldn't refuse or they'd be terribly offended.*)

4 B (line 25: *so I had to crunch down on it so it didn't get away*)

5 C

6 A (line 33: *it has juicy white meat inside, like a crab.*)

7 B (line 37: *'I know it makes sense in environmental terms'*)

8 D (line 45: *I think we gain more understanding of their culture.*)

See also: *NEW FCE Gold exam maximiser* p.34

Grammar 1: countable and uncountable nouns p.46

Aims:
- **to review countability of nouns**
- **to review quantifiers used with countable and uncountable nouns**

1 Allow your students a few minutes to decide on the countability of these words, and then tell them to look in their dictionaries. A good dictionary will tell them if a noun is countable, uncountable or both, and provide them with sample sentences of both.

Note that, in certain contexts, some words are uncountable in British English, and countable in American English (e.g. *accommodation* in certain situations). Again, a good dictionary will show this.

2 Introduce this activity by writing the word *glass* on the board, and asking your students to give you a sentence using the word as a countable object, and a sentence using it as an uncountable object, e.g. *Be careful with those **glasses** – they cost a lot of money. Look out! There's **glass** all over the floor.*)

3 The mistakes in these sentences are typical of those made by students at this level.

4 Your students probably often make mistakes with these quantifiers in their productive English.

5

1, 2 These tasks help students practise the target language in a personalised context. As a possible homework task, ask them to write more sentences about themselves using the quantifiers from this exercise.

Watch Out! *few and little*
These sentences highlight the importance of the correct use of the indefinite article, as its use changes the overall meaning of the sentence.

ANSWERS

Ex. 1
a) countable: book, meal, knife, plate, potato, series, spider
b) uncountable: accommodation, advice, aerobics, information, luggage, maths, news, progress, traffic, transport
c) countable or uncountable: chocolate, food, fruit, meal
d) always plural: clothes, scissors, police, trousers

Ex. 2
1 a) countable   b) uncountable
2 a) uncountable   b) uncountable

---

3 a) countable   b) countable
4 a) uncountable   b) countable
5 a) countable   b) uncountable
6 a) uncountable   b) countable

Ex. 3
1 luggage   2 These scissors aren't   3 *have* been informed   4 Maths *is*   5 trousers/don't
6 information   7 isn't   8 *some* advice
9 Traffic/has   10 *was* the best

Ex. 4
+ uncountable nouns: not much, no, very little, some
+ plural countable nouns: lots of, hardly any,

Watch Out! *few and little*
1 b   2 a   3 d   4 c
few/little have a negative meaning, *not much/many* and *not enough; a few/ a little* are more positive and mean *not much but some/enough*.

See also: *NEW FCE Gold exam maximiser* p.35

Use of English: open cloze (Part 2) p.47

Aims:
- **to introduce a technique for completing cloze texts: identifying the grammatical function of words (e.g. articles, prepositions, etc.)**

Exam information ▶ **Cbk p.4**

The items tested in this task are usually 'grammar' words. Students should read the whole sentence, and not just the words around the gaps. Sometimes there may be more than one possible answer for each gap, but they should only write one of these (if they write two answers, and one is right and the other is wrong, it will be marked as incorrect).

---

1 This introduces the theme of the text that students are going to complete. You could ask any students who are carrying a bottle of water if the label on the bottle is important to them, and why. This could lead into a brief discussion on designer goods and why some brand names are more important than others.

2 Students should skim the text, but at this stage should not try to complete the gaps.

3 The words and grammatical functions here provide students with a large range of the words that are typically removed from an FCE gapped text.

4 Your students should do this individually, and then compare their answers with a partner.

Reading 2: gapped text (Part 3) p.48

Aims:

• to provide further practice of the gapped text task
• to focus on lexical links between parts of a text

1, **2**   After your students have discussed the
questions in pairs or small groups and then read the main
part of the article, **not** the missing sentences, you could tell
them that Daniela suffers from something called Total Allergy
Syndrome, which many people believe is a modern disease
resulting from human changes to the environment (such as
chemicals in food, clothes, petrol fumes, etc.).
If you didn't do it at the beginning of this unit, you could
have a brief discussion on food allergies and the way they
affect some people's lives.

3

1 Before your students look at box 1, ask them why
  sentence H fits in gap 0, the example (*them* refers to *red
  spots* in the sentence before the gap. We can also assume
  that when she first showed the symptoms, she went to a
  doctor. Sentence H says that she went to several doctors –
  I went to see another, then another –, and the sentence
  after the gap says *Finally I saw a specialist)*. Remind
  students that to complete this task, they will often need to
  refer **forwards** in the text as well as **backwards**.
  Working individually, students then decide which sentence
  fits gap 1. Compare their answers as a class and ask them
  to explain (the highlighted phrase *the news* summarises
  the information in the previous sentence, i.e. the doctor's
  instructions).
2 Working individually, students then do the rest of the task.
  Allow them about ten minutes for this, before checking
  their answers and asking why they chose them.

4   This personalises the theme of this section, and
provides a useful platform for reviewing the use of *would* and
present conditionals.

5   Students can do this exercise in small groups, then
compare their plan for Daniela with other groups in the class
(if your classroom allows it, they can get up and walk around
comparing their plans). As a possible follow-on, the whole
class can then choose the best parts from their different plans
and form a new plan that everyone approves of.

Grammar 2: future forms p.49

Aim:

• to review future forms

1

1 Your students should underline the future forms
  individually and then compare their results with a partner.
2 Ask your students to continue to work in pairs and discuss
  the differences between the different future constructions.
  Compare answers as a class.

2   Your students should try to do this in pairs without
looking at the **Grammar reference** first. Then ask them for
their answers. Ask what is the function of each future form
they chose. They can then look at the **Grammar reference**
on page 204.

3   For this exercise, divide your class into three groups,
and ask each group to do one of the dialogues. When they
have finished, they can tell the rest of the class their answers.
The other students should decide if those answers are right or
wrong, and why.

4

1, 2 This exercise practises the target language in a
  personalised context. Alternatively, ask your students to
  write future sentences about themselves on a sheet of
  paper, then hand their paper to you. Read out the
  sentences to the class, and let them decide who wrote
  them.

2 will break.
3 I'm going to apply
4 will rain
5 I'll have
6 will you have finished
2 See Grammar reference pages 204–5.

Ex. 3
1 1 Are you going   2 'll give   3 'm leaving
    4 'll be
2 1 are you going to do   2 's   3 is   4 lands
    5 aren't going to have
3 1 won't be going   2 'll have done   3 'll be
    finished   4 Won't you be having

See also: *NEW FCE Gold exam maximiser* p.36

Vocabulary 3: body and health p.50

Aims:
- **to review words related to the body, illness and health**

1 While students are doing this exercise in pairs, write the missing letters on the board in random order. When they have tried to complete all the words, refer them to the board, which should help them complete those they haven't yet done. They can refer to their dictionary if they are not sure.

2 This activity demonstrates how words depend on one another to express meaning. It also shows how important it is to record vocabulary in context using sample sentences. A good dictionary will show which words work together (e.g. we can *clench* our *fist* and our *teeth*, but we can't clench our *eyebrows*).
Ask your students to do this in pairs, and then check their answers with another pair, referring to a dictionary to see if they are right or wrong.

3 Students could do this in small groups. One student in each group mimes what he/she does in the situations, and the others make sentences using the verbs from Exercise 2, plus any other verbs of body movement that they are familiar with.

4 This is just a small selection of many body-related idioms and colloquial expressions. The *Longman Dictionary of Contemporary English* lists over 25 idiomatic expressions for *hand* alone! Your students will be able to find other expressions by looking in their dictionary under the main word (i.e. the part of the body).

5 Many of the options in these sentences have similar meanings to one another, are related to one another by topic or are words often confused by students. Again, a dictionary will help your students.

Teaching tips and ideas
When your students have finished these exercises, ask them to write the words/expressions that they didn't know **before** they did this section on a sheet of paper, and tear/cut the paper up into individual word slips, which they give to you. Put these in an envelope. At the end of the lesson, if you have a few minutes, take these slips at random from the envelope, and give your class the definition of the word. They should tell you what the word/expression is.

6 This personalises the theme of this section.

ANSWERS

Ex. 1
1 throat   **2** ankle   **3** wrist   **4** cheek   **5** stomach
6 thigh   **7** heart   **8** thumb   **9** finger   **10** knee
11 elbow   **12** forehead   **13** mouth   **14** eyebrow
15 shoulder

Ex. 2
1 arms, legs   **2** legs   **3** arms, eyebrows, hands, fist   **4** shoulders   **5** head   **6** fist, teeth   **7** arms, back, legs

Ex. 3 Sample answers
1 stretch your arms   **2** stretch your arms   **3** bend your legs   **4** clench your fists   **5** clench your teeth
6 nod your head   **7** shrug your shoulders   **8** cross your legs   **9** rub your back   **10** shrug your shoulders

Ex. 4
1 mouth   **2** heart   **3** tooth   **4** hands   **5** back

Ex. 5
1 prescription   **2** surgery   **3** heal
4 temperature   **5** injections   **6** sore   **7** pain
8 hurt   **9** over   **10** bruised

▶ Photocopiable activity 4 *What do you think?* p.166
See also: *NEW FCE Gold exam maximiser* p.37

Speaking: advantages and disadvantages (Parts 3 and 4) p.51

Aims:
- **to focus on language for discussing advantages and disadvantages**
- **to practice the language in a collaborative Paper 5 task**

Before your students look at this section, ask them to imagine that the school they are studying at has decided to develop its facilities. Working as a class, they should decide on eight things that the school could do (e.g. a swimming pool, a snack bar, a video centre or cinema, etc). Write these on the board.

Then divide them into pairs, and ask them to work together to choose **three** of these things. Which would be of most benefit to the students? Why? Allow them about three minutes for this.

1

1, 2 Tell them to look at the discussion topic in 1.1, and think of words or expressions that could fit in the gaps in 1–6. Then play the recording once and let them complete the table in 1.2.

3 Working in their same pairs, they should tell each other about their opinion, using some of the expressions from their table.

2 , 3 Still working in pairs, students do Exercise 2. Monitor them to make sure that they are answering both parts of the task (1. talk about the advantages and disadvantages, 2. decide which thing the gym should choose.). Also make sure that one student in each pair is not dominating the discussion or doing all the work. Remind them that they should be encouraging each other to speak, and showing that they are listening to their partner.

Exam information

Although students are expected to work together to do this section of the Speaking test, they don't have to reach the same decision. They can agree to disagree.

---

4 Your students should spend about three to four minutes doing this.

ANSWERS

Ex. 1

1

1 good idea   2 drawback   3 problem
4 advantage   5 benefit 6 disadvantage

2

Positive: good idea, advantage, benefit
Negative: drawback, problem, disadvantage

Writing: article p.52

Aim:

- **to focus on the elements that make a good article**

Ask your students to read through the information on writing an article, then tell them to close their books and tell you about the features of a good article. Also ask them to tell you about any magazine articles they have read recently, either in English or in their own language. *What were they about? Why did they enjoy reading them?*

1 This exercise focuses students' attention on the 'audience' for the article. At this stage, they should not start writing it.

2 This takes students through the planning stage of writing an article, and focuses their attention on some features that make an article interesting. They should discuss the possible title in pairs and then extend this to the rest of the class. Title B is the best, because it is more 'upbeat' than the others, and is more likely to make someone want to read the article. It also reflects the content of the article that has been written here. You could also point out that the article begins with a question. This challenges the reader to think about the topic and makes them want to continue reading. It is a common way of beginning an article.

3

1, 2 Students can work in pairs or small groups to complete and extend the notes here. When they have finished, they will have a workable plan that will make their article far easier to write.

Exam information ▶ Cbk p.4

Students will lose marks if their work is badly organised, and/or if it lacks coherence and cohesion, or repeats something that has already been said. A simple plan like that in Exercise 3 only takes a few minutes, but will make a big difference to their final written piece.

---

4 , 5 Your students can do this for homework. They should allow themselves about 30–35 minutes to write it, and 5–10 minutes for checking and editing.

ANSWERS

Ex. 1
1 c)   2 b)

Ex. 2
Title B

Ex. 3
2 more nourishing food
3 more intensive and varied exercise
4 medical advances

Ex. 4 Sample answer
Healthier than ever before!

(As Exercise 2)

The most important difference between us and the older generation is education. There is so much information about what is healthy and what is not that it's easy to know what you should and shouldn't eat. My parents certainly didn't learn about this at school as my generation all have.

As well as that, food now is produced to a much higher standard than it used to be. Farming is more efficient and restaurants are cleaner. Most towns also have a gym where it is possible to exercise in many different ways. Finally, there have been more advances in medical technology in our lifetime than at any time in history, which means that we will live longer than any generation before us.

(As Exercise 2)

(176 words)

See also: *NEW FCE Gold exam maximiser* p.38

UNIT 4 Review p.53

ANSWERS

Ex. 1
1 books   2 information   3 produce   4 transport
5 research   6 climates   7 progress   8 experts
9 health

Ex. 3
1 of   2 am   3 a   4 a   5 going   6 to   7 being
8 the   9 to   10 be   11 of

Ex. 4
1 cooking   2 vitamin   3 allergic   4 habitat
5 swallow   6 high   7 dairy   8 ingredients
9 nutritious   10 advances   11 potato
12 catering   missing word = carbohydrate

▶ Photocopiable Unit 4 test p.118

Reading: multiple-choice questions (Part 2) p.54

Aims:
- **to introduce the theme of the unit**
- **to give further practice in Paper 1, Part 2**

Before your students open their books, ask them if they have bought any luxury products recently (e.g. perfume, video games, mobile phone with lots of gadgets, etc.). *Why did they choose this product? Do they think it was worth the money?*

1, **2** Ask your students to look at the photo, read the title and introduction, and discuss the questions with a partner, before skimming the whole article. This should take them about two minutes. At this stage, they are just reading for general information, although they will probably focus on a few of the details while they are doing this. When they have finished skimming, ask them to close their books and tell you what they can remember about the text.

3 This should be done as a whole class activity. Write your students' suggestions on the board. They can then check these on page 44 of their Coursebook.

4 Do number 1 with the whole class. The answer is D because the company wanted to **market** their new product – in other words, they wanted to interest people in their new video game. Working individually, students answer the other questions and then compare their answers with a partner.

5 This extends the theme of the article, and makes an interesting discussion topic, which could be done as a whole class activity.

ANSWERS

Ex. 1
1 They are 'the coolest kids' in a school or neighbourhood.
2 They can use alpha pups to market their products

Ex. 4
1 D (The introduction and the first paragraph talk about marketing the game)
2 C (line 10: *the young boys who set the trends in fashion among others of their age.*)
3 C

---

4 B (line 31: *Unknown to any of the boys, market researchers from Hasbro were sitting behind a one-way mirror ... secretly watching their reactions.*)
5 B (line 43: *you could be in one room and he could be in another room and you could be battling .... The boys were immediately enthusiastic.*)
6 A (line 50: *The adults behind the mirror were excited too. 'Get the name of the kid who said it's the best game ever ...'*)
7 C (line 53: *Nino gave each alpha pup ... to pass on to his friends.*)

See also: *NEW FCE Gold exam maximiser p.40*

Speaking 1: advertising. p.56

Aim:
- **to talk about the power and influence of advertising**

1, **2** Ask your students to discuss the questions in small groups, and then extend this into a whole class discussion.

ANSWERS

Ex. 1
The photos show: an advert on a hoarding for a car insurance company; a travel brochure advertising holidays; a poster in a shop window advertising reductions; a young woman handing out promotional leaflets on the street; a TV advert for soap powder

---

Vocabulary 1: consumer society p.56

Aims:
- **to review/introduce vocabulary connected with shopping and the consumer society**
- **to focus on word stress**

1   This exercise contains examples of words that students typically confuse or misuse. They should work in pairs and decide which word fits each sentence best, before checking their answers in a dictionary.

2

1, 2 This exercise highlights the stress and pronunciation changes that take place when some words change their form. Your students should work in small groups and take it in turns to say the words. You could refer them to their dictionaries for this, and ask them how stressed syllables are shown in the dictionary. Note that the pronunciation of *advertisement* is different in British and American English.

Play the recording, stopping after each word for your students to repeat them. They should pay particular attention to the unstressed vowel sound (the *schwa*), as this does not exist in many languages.

3   After your students have completed these sentences, ask them to read the sentences out to a partner. Their partner should listen carefully to their pronunciation, and decide if it is right or wrong.

4   This question extends the theme of this section. Your students can discuss this in small groups.

ANSWERS

Ex. 1
1 consumer   2 advertisements   3 commercials
4 advertising   5 marketing/agency
6 launch/campaign/publicity
7 promotions/discounts   8 logos

Ex. 2
1 an<u>nou</u>ncer an<u>nou</u>nce an<u>nou</u>ncement
2 <u>a</u>dvertiser <u>a</u>dvertising ad<u>ver</u>tise ad<u>ver</u>tisement
3 <u>co</u>mmerce com<u>mer</u>cial com<u>mer</u>cialisation
4 pro<u>mo</u>ter pro<u>mo</u>te pro<u>mo</u>tion
5 pub<u>li</u>city <u>pu</u>blicise
6 eco<u>no</u>mics e<u>co</u>nomy eco<u>no</u>mical
a) The stressed syllable changes in 2, 3, 5, 6.

Ex. 3
1 consumption   2 markets   3 promoting
4 launched/campaign   5 advertise
6 campaigned

See also: *NEW FCE Gold exam maximiser* p.39

Use of English: multiple-choice cloze (Part 1) p.57

Aim:
• **to introduce and practise Paper 3, Part 1**

Exam information ▶ Cbk p.4

This is mainly a vocabulary exercise, testing students' knowledge of word collocations, general vocabulary and phrasal verbs. Idiomatic and colloquial English expressions are **occasionally** tested (the sample answer in the text here is an example – *to spend a fortune*).

The alternatives for each gap are all related in some way. It is therefore very important that students read the words **before** and **after** the gap very carefully.

---

1   This prepares students for doing the task by giving them a general understanding of the text.

2   Before your students do the task, ask them to look at the example. Why is *fortune* the correct answer? (Because it works with the phrase *to spend a*.)

Your students should do the task individually, then compare their answers with a partner, and use a dictionary to see if their answers are correct.

As a brief follow-on, have a quick class discussion on brand names which are currently popular. What brand names are your students currently wearing or carrying? Why are these so popular?

ANSWERS

Ex. 1
c)

Ex. 2
1 C   2 B   3 D   4 B   5 D   6 A   7 C   8 A
9 C   10 A   11 D   12 B   13 A   14 B   15 C

Listening 1: radio adverts p.57

Aim:
• **to focus on the language of radio commercials**
• **to prepare for Speaking 2**

1, **2**   Before your students listen to the recording, ask them to look at the list of products and decide how each one could be sold. Also ask them to predict some of the key words and phrases they would expect to hear for each product (e.g. for the penknife: *sharp/cut/useful/good value*). Ask them to think about products such as cars, make-up, ice cream, etc. How do advertisers usually try to sell these? Are some products geared more to a male market than a female market or vice versa?

Play the recording twice. After the first playing, ask your students what is being advertised. What were the key words or expressions that helped them to decide? During the second playing, ask them to tick the boxes on the table and compare their answers with a partner.

▶ Tapescript p.102

3 Do this as a whole class discussion, and hold a class vote on the most effective and the least effective advert.

4 Play the recording a third time, while students tick the phrases they hear. There may be some words which are unfamiliar to your students in these advertisements; while they are listening again, they could also write down any words they didn't understand. Then ask them to think of what they **might** mean from the **context** in which they are being used.

Teaching tips and ideas

Cut out some advertisements from magazines, but remove the name of the product (or choose advertisements where the product advertised is not immediately obvious). Give these to your students and ask them to decide what they are advertising and whether or not they are effective.

ANSWERS

Ex. 1
1 b 2 a 3 e

Ex. 2
Who could use it 1, 2
What it can do 1,2
Effect of the product 2,3
Size 1
Convenience 1
Price 1

Ex. 4
You'll never again be without something to ...
You'll wonder how you ever managed without it.
Take advantage of our special discount.
This offer won't last long.
You won't regret it.
A price that suits your pocket.
Pop in to see our wide selection.

Vocabulary 2: describing objects p.58

Aims:
• to focus on language for describing objects
• to prepare for Speaking 2

1

1, 2 Students work in pairs to match the adjectives and adverbs with the nouns in 1.1. They should check their answers with you before doing Exercise 1.2.

2

1, 2 After they have completed the sentences with an appropriate preposition or participle and matched these with one of the products in 2.2, ask your students to think of some other expressions that could be used for the products. They could also choose one of the expressions from Listening 1, Exercise 4 on page 57 to add colour and interest.

ANSWERS

Ex. 1
1 1 b) 2 d) 3 e), g) 4 a) 5 f), h) 6 e), g)
7 f) 8 c)
2
1 incredibly compact
2 wide selection
3 amazing discount
4 total control
5 free sample
6 special price

Ex. 2
1 1 for 2 for 3 in/for 4 as 5 for 6 to
7 to
2 1 a) 2 d) 3 b) 4 c) 5 f) 6 d), e) 7 f)

See also: *NEW FCE Gold exam maximiser* p.41

Speaking 2: product presentation p.58

Aim:
• **to practice key language from the unit through a communicative activity**

1 Use this exercise to brainstorm and introduce useful adjectives and adjectival phrases (e.g. *confident, persuasive, aggressive, determined, friendly, honest/dishonest, creative, prepared to bend/distort the truth*, etc.)

2

1, 2 Your students can choose one of the objects on the board, or they can choose their own object and plan how they are going to sell it. Allow them about 10–15 minutes to prepare their presentation. While they are preparing, monitor them to make sure they are using some of the key language from this unit, and help them to choose appropriate words and expressions.

Grammar 1: indirect speech p.59

Aims:
• **to review tense changes in direct – indirect speech transformations**
• **to review word order in indirect questions**

Note: *Indirect* speech is also known as *reported* speech.

1

1, 2 Before your students do this exercise, ask your students to think of a direct speech sentence that could prompt an indirect speech sentence using *said*, *told* and *asked* (other reporting verbs are looked at later in this unit). They should also give you the indirect sentence (e.g. *I'm hungry – He said he was hungry. Be quiet – He told us to be quiet. What's your name? – He asked (me) what my name was.*) They should then do 1.1 individually before comparing their answers with a partner. Allow them a few moments to look at the **Grammar reference** on page 199, and to ask you any questions about points they are unsure of.

2   Ask your students to correct these in pairs without looking back at the **Grammar reference**, and then compare their answers with another pair of students.

3   The first part of this exercise should be done by matching key words and other reference devices in the two sets of sentences (e.g. 1: *suitcase* can be linked to c) *customs, airport* because we use a suitcase when we travel. The question *Could you open your suitcase please?* is often asked by *customs officials* at an *airport*). For the second part, you could ask your students to cover up sentences 1–8 and see if they can complete sentences a)–h) from memory.

4

1, 2 Students discuss these in small groups, before extending question 2 to a whole-class discussion. A *bad hair day* is a modern, humorous expression we use when we are unable to make our hair look nice, tidy, etc. (*Oh dear, I'm having another bad hair day*). Your students might like to learn some of the other expressions we use with *hair* (e.g. *to tear* or *pull your hair out, to let your hair down, keep your hair on, to get in somebody's hair*, etc.).

ANSWERS

Ex. 1

2 got   3 saw   4 found   5 wanted   6 asked
7 where   8 was   9 him I was going
10 following   11 would take   12 he couldn't

Ex. 2

1 Jane asked her mother if she could borrow the car.
2 Nobody told us why the manager had left.
3 I asked whether she had bought the jacket she wanted or not.
4 I asked my friend to come to the cinema.
5 Can you tell me where the library is?
6 Has anyone found out how much it costs?
7 Tim said he would meet me the following day.
8 John said he had seen the film last week.
9 I told him that I would be late.

Ex. 3

1 c) me to open my suitcase
2 e) not to worry – it would be fine
3 h) if he would slow down
4 d) him there were some good shops in the town centre
5 f) how much it cost
6 a) her to hurry up
7 b) John if he would give me a hand
8 g) he didn't have time

Ex. 4

1 Because he believed the advert, and thought it would give him smooth, manageable hair.
2 The claims were false – the man's hair looks terrible after using JollyGel.

See also: *NEW FCE Gold exam maximiser* p.42

Listening 2: multiple matching (Part 3) p.60

Aim:

• **to provide further practice in Paper 4, Part 3**

1   Students discuss the statements in small groups. They should try to give as many reasons as possible for their attitudes towards shopping.

2   Before your students look at the task, ask them briefly to describe the services and facilities in the town in which they are studying now. This gives them a chance to brainstorm/preview some useful vocabulary (e.g. *library, sports centre, hospital, shopping centre*, etc.) that they will meet again later in this unit. *Do they have any favourite shops? What do they sell? Why do they like them? Are there any shops they dislike and/or avoid? Why?*
Play the recording, then check their answers. *Why did they choose them? What words or expressions did they hear that helped them to decide?*

▶ Tapescript p.102

3   Do this as a whole class discussion.

ANSWERS

Ex. 2

1 F   2 B   3 D   4 A   5 C

See also: *NEW FCE Gold exam maximiser* p.43

Grammar 2: reporting verbs p.60

Aim:

* **to focus on other patterns after reporting verbs**

1

1 Tell your students to quickly look through the sentences and answer options and check that they understand what the reporting verbs mean (they can check these in a dictionary). They can then work in pairs to complete the sentences.

2 Your students would probably find it helpful to copy this table into their notebooks when they have completed it so that they have a useful reference source for the future.

2 After your students have done this in pairs, check and correct their answers, then tell them to close their books. On the board, write the **indirect** sentences (e.g. *She refused to go.*) and ask them to change them back to direct speech. In some cases, more than one direct speech sentence may be possible. (*I'm not going to go/I won't go/I refuse to go.* etc.).

3 Exercise 3.1 practises the target language in a controlled context. Exercise 3.2 allows for less controlled practice. Your students could do this for homework and compare their answers with a partner in the next lesson.

ANSWERS

Ex. 1

1

1 C – *offered* is followed by infinitive + pronoun (*offered to buy her*)
2 A – *told* must be followed by an object
3 B – *demanded* is followed by a *that* clause
4 B – *advised* is not followed by the infinitive
5 A – *remind* is not followed by an *–ing* form
6 C – *accused* is followed by object + *of* + *-ing*
7 A – *apologised* must be followed by to (*someone*)
8 C – *explained* is followed by to + object (*explain to someone that*)

2

verb + infinitive: *agree, explain, promise, offer*
verb + object + infinitive: *tell, invite, persuade, advise, remind*
verb + *that*: *suggest, accept, realise, recommend, demand*
verb + object + *that*: *promise, tell*
verb + *-ing*: *admit, deny*
verb + object + preposition + *-ing*: *remind, forgive, blame*
Watch Out! *suggest*
d) is not possible

Ex. 2

1 I refused to go.
2 He reminded Jake to buy some bread on the way home.

3 Mum congratulated Kerry on passing her exam.
4 Clare apologised for forgetting Sally's birthday/aplogised to Sally for forgetting ...
5 I warned Mary not to sit on that chair as it was broken.
6 Brad suggested meeting at the beach.
7 She threatened to give me a parking ticket if I didn't move my car.
8 She invited me (to come) round for dinner on Saturday.

Ex. 3

1 In Wilkinson's they told me they had just sold their last copy. They apologised and explained that it was very popular. They said I might find one in GamesRUs, as it is/was a bigger shop.
2 In GamesRUs they said they were out of stock, but would be getting some more in next/the following week. They offered to give me ring when the games came in, if I left/gave them my name and a contact number.
3 In VHM they told me they weren't sure if they had any left. The assistant offered me a seat while he went to the stockroom to look. They told me I was in luck as they had one copy left. They asked me if I wanted it.

▶ Photocopiable activity 5A *Spend, spend, spend!* p.167
See also: *NEW FCE Gold exam maximiser* p.44

Exam Focus
Paper 3 Use of English: key word transformations (Part 3) p.61

Aims:

* **to present and practise a procedure for completing the key word transformation task**

Take your students through the **About the exam** and **Procedure** in the usual way.
Students do the task individually or in pairs. Monitor them to check that they have used the correct form of the key word, and that they have not exceeded the word limit. When they have finished it, put them into groups of two or three pairs and ask them to compare their answers.

Exam information ▶ Cbk p.5
Key word transformations carry two marks each, as they are usually testing two language points.
Occasionally more than one answer may be possible, but students should only give one of these.

ANSWERS
1 had never been/gone 2 was brought up by
3 sings as well as 4 going to India appeals to
5 it sounds like 6 if he would like to
7 had been very confused by 8 was made up of
9 not made many appearances 10 on luck as well

Vocabulary 3: shopping and leisure facilities p.62

Aim:
- **to review vocabulary connected with shopping and leisure**

1

1 Students should do this in pairs, referring to a dictionary where necessary.

Teaching tips and ideas

After your students have done this exercise, tell them to work in the same pairs. One of them should write down the word options for numbers 1–3, the other should write down the options for 4–6. They should then close their books, and give each other the definitions of the words they have written. Their partner should try to remember/guess what the word is (e.g. *'You buy something very cheaply. It is usually quite expensive. What do we call this?' 'A bargain.'*)

2, 3 This practises the key language in a personalised context. Exercise 1.3 allows for less controlled practice – your students should try to think of as many questions for each sentence as possible (e.g. for sentence 4: *How do you usually pay for things? Do you prefer paying by cheque or credit card? Do you normally pay off your credit card bills in full each month? Do you think that it's too easy to get credit these days?* etc.)

2

1, 2 As an alternative to students matching the statements and places, tell them to close their books and read the statements to them. They should listen for key words and write down where they think you are. They should do this in pairs or small groups. This is quite a useful brainstorming activity and leads into the discussion.

3 Students should quickly answer these questions on their own and then discuss them in pairs or small groups, as in Exercise 2. Make sure they answer in full sentences and provide additional information where possible. If your

students all live in the same town, you could conduct a quick survey to see how much your students agree.

ANSWERS

Ex. 1
1 sales/bargains
2 receipt/exchange
3 bargain/discount
4 in cash/by cheque
5 budget/economical
6 queue/checkout

Ex. 2
1 e) 2 b) 3 d) 4 c) 5 a) 6 f)

▶ Photocopiable activity 5B *Shopping race* p.168

See also: *NEW FCE Gold exam maximiser* p.45

Speaking 3: expressing uncertainty (Part 2) p.63

Aim:
- **to focus on ways to express uncertainty when describing a photo**

Exam information ▶ **Cbk p.5**
In Part 2, students not only have to compare and contrast their pictures, but also give a personal reaction to them (as in Exercise 4.2). Some students are so focused on their pictures that they don't take in the examiner's question – as a result, they fail to complete the task properly. Make sure that your students are aware this is a two-part task, and to listen carefully to the question. (This is looked at in more detail in Unit 6.)

1 This quick vocabulary review will provide students with some useful key words for when they do the next exercise.

2 At this stage, students do not have to use complete sentences to describe the pictures. They could just point out the similarities and differences (and possibly make a quick note of them).

3 Play the recording while your students listen for the expressions of uncertainty.

▶ Tapescript p.103

4 The language from Exercise 3 will be useful for this.

5 Remind students to talk about the second part of the task (i.e. Student A must say where the advertising is most effective, Student B must say which activity is most enjoyable).

ANSWERS

Ex. 1
Photo A: checkout, cashier, shelves, trolley, shopping bag, special offers, bargains, advertisements
Photo B: fitting room, rail, special offers, bargains, assistant, department store

Ex. 2
Similarities: In both photos people are shopping and both the shops are indoors.
Differences: In the first photo the adults are with their children, whereas in the second photo they're shopping alone. In the first photo they are shopping for food, but in the second photo they are shopping for clothes. In the first picture they are buying something whereas in the second picture they are browsing.

Ex. 3
I'm not sure, but they might be …,
it's not very clear, but probably/I think …,
Perhaps …, It looks as if …, They seem to be -ing

Writing: letter of complaint (Part 1) p.64

Aim:
• **to plan and write a formal letter of complaint**

Before your students look at this section, ask them about the last time they complained about something. What did they complain about? Did they do it verbally or on paper? What was the outcome?

1 , 2   Ask your students to work through the exercises in pairs. Remind them to highlight the main points in the task, as effectively this will be their plan.

3   *Claimed, promised, said* and *stated* are useful reporting verbs when complaining (especially if the complaint is about an advertisement), as are conjunctions of contradiction (*but, however*, etc.). Students should note that *However* usually comes at the beginning of a sentence. We do not usually begin a sentence with *but*. *Actually* and *in fact* have the same meaning here.

4

1, 2 One problem with students' letters of complaint is that they often sound too demanding and, consequently, a bit rude. The assumption is that if you are angry about something, your language should reflect this. Letters of complaint should be firm but polite – a register which is quite difficult to achieve.

5 , 6   Your students can do this for homework. They should do this in about 35–40 minutes (including time for checking their answers for mistakes, omissions, etc.).

Exam information

Your students should write on alternate lines on their paper. This makes it easier to insert something later that they might have missed out. If they make a mistake in their writing, they should cross it out clearly - then it will not be looked at by the examiner.

ANSWERS

Ex. 1
1 Say why you are writing.
2 Explain the problem.
3 Say what you want the person to do.

Ex. 2
1 The local newspaper.
2 To complain about a misleading advertisement.
3 Six.
4 To withdraw the advertisement.
5 Formal.

Ex. 3
1 c)   2 d)   3 a)   4 b)

Ex. 4
1
Dear Sir/Madam
(1) *I am writing* **(2)** *an advertisement which appeared*
(3) *it was misleading in several ways.*
2 b)

Ex. 5 Sample answer
Dear Sir or Madam,
I am writing to complain about an advertisement which appeared in your newspaper yesterday. The advertisement was for CDs Incorporated. I thought it was misleading in several ways.

First of all, the advertisement stated that the doors would open at nine o'clock, but we did not get in until ten o' clock. Secondly, it claimed that prices would start at £2, but in fact nothing was less than £5. Thirdly, they promised that there would be huge discounts on everything, whereas there was only a small discount on some products. Finally, the advertisement also stated that all the CDs were up-to-date and included the latest singers and bands. However, the newest CD was already six months old, and I could not find any of my favourites.

Therefore, I would be grateful if you could remove the advertisement from the newspaper as soon as possible.

I look forward to hearing from you.

Yours faithfully
Andrea Campos
Andrea Campos   (156 words)

See also: *NEW FCE Gold exam maximiser* p.46

UNITS 1 – 5 Progress test p.65

ANSWERS

Ex. 1
1 combine = *combination*
2 finishing = *ending*
3 close = *close-up*
4 emotion = *emotional*
5 irritating = *irritated*
6 have place = *take place*
7 made = *caught*
8 impossible to me = *impossible for me*
9 fall = *sink*
10 with = *in*
11 feed = *eat*
12 revolted = *revolting*
13 living = *alive/live*
14 used = *spent*
15 broad = *wide*

Ex. 2
1 He *has* known her since he was a child.
2 How many times *do* you phone your sister every day?
3 I*'ve* had a car since I was eighteen.
4 Have you *been* running? You look hot.
5 My sister is *a* lot better at Maths than I am.
6 This ride isn't *as* exciting as the one we went on in Disneyland.
7 Tom is not much taller than I am – only about one centimetre.
8 I'm going to *the* Canary Islands for my summer holiday.
9 My father drives *more* slowly than my bother.
10 He *had* already finished the work when the teacher returned.
11 I usually just have *a* piece of toast for breakfast.
12 I'm watching *a* very interesting series about dinosaurs on TV.
13 The police told me *to* go away.
14 Brad asked Vicky *if* she wanted a drink or not.
15 They advised me not *to* worry as everything would be alright.

Ex. 3
1 A 2 B 3 D 4 B 5 A 6 C 7 B 8 D
9 D 10 B 11 A 12 C 13 B 14 C 15 B

Ex. 4
16 who 17 into / in 18 the / that 19 off
20 at 21 before / until 22 example / instance
23 how 24 each / every 25 it / this 26 for
27 despite 28 have 29 less 30 are

Ex. 5
31 admitted breaking / admitted having broken / admitted that he had broken
32 very few copies
33 going out with him
34 have much to eat
35 doesn't play tennis as well
36 haven't / have not discovered the cause
37 blamed me for (having caused)
38 have not worked together for
39 promised to come with us
40 would rather watch football than

Ex. 6
41 of 42 to 43 although 44 ✓ 45 myself
46 for 47 was 48 ✓ 49 more 50 though
51 it 52 have 53 that 54 so 55 ✓

Ex. 7
56 equipment 57 noisy 58 easily 59 unable
60 identified 61 threaten 62 exploration
63 catastrophic 64 generally 65 broken

▶ Photocopiable Progress test 1 (Units 1–5) p.120

UNIT
6 It's your call

Vocabulary 1: technology p.68

Aims:

- **to focus on some common words related to modern technology**
- **to introduce the theme of the unit**
- **to provide a lead-in to Listening 1**

Before your students open their books and look at this unit, ask them to think about some advances in technology over the last 30–50 years. *Are there any things they take for granted that their parents (or grandparents) would have been unfamiliar with when they were the same age?* Write their suggestions on the board, and then ask them what, in their opinion, the most important object is. *Why? Could they live without this? How would their lives be different if this didn't exist?*

If your students have come up with *computer*, *camera* and *telephone* (or *mobile phone*), ask them to work in small groups to brainstorm words connected with these objects.

1 Students work in pairs or small groups to do Exercise 1. Point out that a lot of words related to technology are the same in many languages, or have been adopted by other languages with small changes in spelling and pronunciation.

2
1 Your students could cover up Exercise 1 before they do this. Alternatively, tell them to close their books, and read the sentences out aloud to them, leaving gaps where the missing words go. Can they tell you what these words are?
2 This extends the topic in a personalised context. Students should do this in pairs or small groups.

3 In addition to discussing the **benefits** of these objects, students could also talk about the **disadvantages**. *Have there ever been moments when they wish the telephone hadn't been invented? What annoys them most about computers? Do they have any embarrassing photographs of themselves?* (This last question would lead them nicely into the next section of the unit.)

ANSWERS

Ex. 1
computer: battery, cable, CD, cursor, email, file, hard drive, keyboard, line, monitor, mouse, plug. screen, scanner
camera: battery, film, focus, negative, snap, zoom lens, (screen)
telephone: battery, engaged tone, handset, keypad, line, plug, ring tone, screen, text message

Ex. 2
1 negatives   2 battery   3 keyboard
4 zoom lens   5 cursor   6 scanner   7 keypad
8 ring tone   9 film   10 screen

See also: *NEW FCE Gold exam maximiser p.47*

Listening 1: multiple matching (Part 3) p.68

Aims:

- **to provide further practice of Paper 4, Part 3**
- **to focus on idiomatic expressions in the text**

Before your students look at this section, ask them about the **disadvantages** of being famous? *Can they think of any people who are frequently in the newspapers because they are famous?* You could also ask your students if **they** like being photographed. Why? Why not? (You could teach them the expression *camera-shy* for someone who doesn't like having their picture taken.)

1 In pairs, students discuss the photographs. Ask them for their ideas.

2 Allow your students a few moments to read through the list of statements and to highlight the key words in each one. Ask them to focus on statements A–F and briefly discuss whether they agree or disagree strongly with these.
Play the recording twice, and then ask your students for their answers. Why did they choose these? What key words or expressions on the recording did they match with key words in the statements?

▶ Tapescript p.103

3 After your students have matched the phrases to their meanings, play the recording again so they can check if they were right.

4 This extends the theme of this section. Students should discuss these in pairs before it is extended to a whole class discussion.

ANSWERS

Ex. 1

1 Photo A shows a man and woman being photographed by a lot of paparazzi. (The man is the singer Rod Stewart). He is joking with the photographers. In photo B the man, probably a friend, is trying to take a photo of the woman. The woman is putting her hand in front of the camera

2 The man is happy. The woman is annoyed or shy.

Ex. 2

1 F   2 C   3 D   4 B   5 E

Ex. 3

1 f)   2 e)   3 g)   4 c)   5 b)   6 d)   7 a)

See also: *NEW FCE Gold exam maximiser* p.48

Use of English: word formation (Part 5) p.69

Aim:

- **to provide practice of Paper 3, Part 5**

1 Allow students about one minute to skim the text for general meaning.

2 Students complete the text individually, and then compare their answers with a partner.

3 This personalises the theme of this section. You could also ask your students if they have ever met anyone famous. *Who? What were they like? Was the person they met the way they imagined them to be, or were they completely different?*

ANSWERS

Ex. 1

No, the writer doesn't want to be famous.

Ex. 2

1 actually   2 disadvantages   3 enjoyable
4 financial   5 photographers   6 journalists
7 completely   8 relationships   9 decision
10 personal

Grammar 1: certainty and possibility p.70

One of the best ways of explaining modals and other expressions of probability to students is in terms of percentage. *Must* expresses 100% certainty, *may, might* and *could* express (about) 40–50% certainty and *can't* expresses 0%. *Could* and *might* are also used to make suggestions ('*I'm hungry.*' '*Well, you could make yourself a sandwich.*')

1, **2** Students work in pairs to match the sentences and descriptions in Exercise 1 before completing Exercise 2. They should note that sometimes the degree of probability depends not only on the modal verb, but on other expressions in the sentence (e.g. *I suppose the report could be true, but I doubt it*. The use of *I doubt it* reduces the degree of probability)

3

1, 2 After your students have matched the statements and responses, and listened to the recording, tell them to close their books and read the statements 1–8 aloud to them. Working in pairs, they should write a response using a modal verb. They can either try to remember the responses from their books or think of their own example.

3 While your students practise the mini-dialogues, monitor them to check they are using appropriate stress and intonation. If necessary, play the recording again and stop after each dialogue, then choral drill the expressions.

4, **5** The basic structure is *modal + have + past participle* (active voice), *modal + have + been + past participle* (passive voice), and *must + have + been + -ing verb* (continuous aspect). Exercise 4 only has active voice examples. Exercise 5 has one passive voice example (number 1) which students should be careful with. Ask your students to work individually to do Exercise 4, then cover it up and do Exercise 5 with a partner.

Note that passives are covered in a later section in this unit.

6 Ask, or tell, your students what *CV* stands for (*curriculum vitae*). We also sometimes use the word *résumé*, and the American expression *bio data* is also becoming more common.

After your students have made sentences with the CV, you could ask them what other information should be included in a CV, e.g. personal details such as address, phone number, email, age, nationality; education and qualifications; skills (computer competence, driving licence, languages spoken, etc.); interests (if relevant to the job being applied for); references. Note that modern CVs do not usually include things like marital status, profession of parents, religion and other items which are considered too personal or irrelevant)

ANSWERS

Ex. 1

1 d 2 a 3 c 4 d 5 b

Ex. 2

1 may / might come

2 can explain

3 may / might stay

4 must remember

5 can't be

6 may be able to

7 must be feeling

8 may / might find

Ex. 3

1 e) 2 d) 3 a) 4 g) 5 c) 6 h) 7 f) 8 b)

Ex. 4

1 must 2 can't 3 must 4 could 5 must
6 may

Ex. 5

1 can't *have* been chosen

2 couldn't have *been* taken

3 can't *be* trusted

4 might have *been* watching

5 can't *have* seen

6 may have *wanted*

7 might *have* been

8 may *have* been intending

9 can't still *be* doing

▶ Photocopiable activity 6A *Modal hit and miss* p.170

See also: *NEW FCE Gold exam maximiser* p.48

Listening 2: song. p.71

Aims:

• **to practise listening for specific information**

• **to focus on some common collocations**

Tell your students the song *We are the Champions* is a classic rock anthem which is famous in a lot of countries – people know the chorus even if they don't know the whole song or the group who sings it. (It is often chanted at football matches, for example.) The original song was by the British rock group Queen. They were very popular in the 1970's and 1980's. Their lead singer, Freddie Mercury, died in 1991.

1 , **2** , **3** Exercise 1 can be done as a whole class discussion. You could ask your students to name some people, dead or alive, who they consider to be 'champions'. Why are they champions?

Play the song, while students complete the collocations in Exercise 2.

Your students can then discuss Exercise 3 in small groups. Monitor them and encourage them to use the modals and

structures from the previous section, as these will be very useful in answering some of the questions.

ANSWERS

Ex. 2

1 time 2 done 3 crime 4 made 5 share
6 taken 7 calls 8 fortune 9 cruise 10 race

Ex. 3

1 *I've done my sentence, sand kicked in my face, no bed of roses, No pleasure cruise*

3 c)

4 He is grateful (*I thank you all*)

....

Teaching tips and ideas

Your students could work together to compile a list of 'Top 10 heroes' and/or 'Top 10 villains'. These people can be dead or alive. This could be followed by some Internet research on these people, and a class project to write about them.

....

Reading: multiple matching (Part 1) p.72

Aims:

• **to provided a guided introduction to Paper 1, Part 1**

• **to focus on idiomatic expressions in the text**

Exam information ▶ **Cbk p.4**

In Paper 1, Part 1, the words in the headings are not normally found in the paragraphs – instead, students have to look for synonyms and parallel expressions. In many cases, the answer will be found by combining various ideas in the paragraph, so it is important that your students read the whole of the paragraph before choosing their answers. There is always one heading that does not match any of the paragraphs.

1 Students can work in small groups to answer these questions, and then compare them with another group. Questions 3 and 4 could prompt a lot of discussion – short-form text messaging is so common with young people in Britain that it is now possible to buy a dictionary of them! You could give your class some common English expressions and ask them to make short text messages with them (e.g. *How are you? Do you want to go out later? Where are you?* etc.).

2

1 Before your students look at the question, ask them about the advantages and disadvantages of text messaging and emails. This is extended in Exercise 5, so keep this short.

Instead of the students looking at the title/subheading of the article in their book (where they might be tempted to start reading the article), write them on the board and hold a whole class discussion, asking students to tell one another about their personal experiences with texting and emails. For example, do they find it easier to text someone than talk to them face to face?

2   Students then look at the first paragraph and discuss if this is true in their case.

3   This exercise takes students through the progress of identifying the main message of each paragraph. This will help them when it comes to doing the multiple matching task. They should do this with a partner before you ask the whole class for their ideas.

4   Look at the example with your students and ask them how heading H relates to the first paragraph (people thought that one thing would happen, but something else happened instead. In other words, something **unexpected** happened. As a result of using email and text messages, people are expanding their network of friends – this is a **benefit** of using such technology).

Students then work individually to complete the task. They should then compare their answers with a partner and explain how they chose those answers.

5   This extends and personalises the theme of this section.

6
1, 2 This exercise gives students a chance to expand their vocabulary and exploit the text.

ANSWERS

Ex. 3
1 *we don't have to spend ages planning a night out*
2 *I don't feel nervous.*
3 *old school mates*
4 *They can take their time planning their message and they can be a bit more playful; they can choose when they want to respond*
5 *to keep in touch with her students*
6 *they have started using these abbreviations in their normal writing*

Ex. 4
1 D   2 G   3 E   4 B   5 F   6 A

Ex. 6
1 b)   2 e)   3 c)   4 a)   5 d)

See also: *NEW FCE Gold exam maximiser* p.50

Grammar 2: passives (1) p.74

Aim:

• **to focus on forms and functions of the passive voice**

Note: The photos show a telegram being delivered in 1935; a family listening to the radio in 1945; an early personal computer in 1977.

1
1, 2 After your students do the quiz in pairs and underline the passive verbs, ask them if they can tell you when/why we use passives: (a) we don't know who did the action or (b) we don't need to know, or are not interested in, who did the action, or (c) it is obvious who did the action from the context of the sentence. Passives are also used to make something sound more formal e.g. *Passengers* are requested *not to talk to the driver*.

2   This exercise reviews the use of the passive voice with different tenses and forms. Your students should note that we do not normally use the passive voice for perfect continuous tenses (e.g. *The mechanic has been repairing my car* = *My car has been being repaired* in the passive, but we would not say this – it sounds rather strange).

3
1   Before your students look at this exercise, ask them to think again of some of the most important/useful inventions of the last 30 years or so. Then ask them to think of something, no matter how silly or trivial, that they would like to see invented to make their lives easier (e.g. a device that does all their homework for them, a machine that cleans the gap between the oven and the sink, etc). After they have read the article, ask them what they think about the iCEBOX; would they find it useful, do they think it will be a successful product, etc.
2   Your students should try to do this without referring back to Exercise 2. When they have finished, ask them to work in pairs. One of them should read their completed text to the other, who should decide if it sounds right.

4
1   In their same pairs, students complete the sentences and compare their answers with others in the class.
2   Play the recording and focus on intonation and stress. Students should then work in pairs, asking and answering the questions.

Teaching tips and ideas

If you have internet access, your students might like to use a search engine to look up *W. Heath Robinson* (a British artist who specialised in drawing bizarre machines) and *Chindogu*, (a Japanese concept of inventing useful devices that would probably never be successful despite their practicality). They could choose one of the devices and explain how it works, using the passive.

ANSWERS

Ex. 1
1 1844   2 1876   3 1895   4 1971   5 1975
6 1992

Ex. 2
1 are allowed
2 are sent
3 will be finished
4 to be made
5 were being followed.
6 should have been finished
7 are going to be cut
8 been given

Ex. 3
1 You can send emails, surf the web, watch TV or DVDs and listen to CDs or the radio, all from one piece of equipment. The Keyboard is wireless and washable.
2
1 has been installed   2 may be fitted
3 is concealed   4 is flipped open
5 could also be used   6 is accompanied
7 can be dealt with   8 will be left behind

Ex. 4
1
1 is spoken   2 's been offered   3 be treated
4 was written   5 have to be pulled down
6 are caused   7 wasn't invited
2
2 No, Rose was played by Kate Winslett.

▶ Photocopiable activity 6B *Imperfect passive* p.171
See also: *NEW FCE Gold exam maximiser* p.51

Use of English 2: open cloze (Part 2) p.75

Aim:
• **to provide further practice of Paper 3, Part 2**

1, **2**, **3**   Ask your students if there have been any occasions when they were really glad they had their

mobile phones with them (e.g. when their car broke down, when they were going to be late for an important appointment, etc). Then ask them to discuss the title of the text in pairs before reading the text and completing it. Remind them that the words that are missing are usually grammatical. In some cases, more than one answer is possible, but they should only write one of these (if they give two alternative words, and one is right but the other is wrong, it would be marked as incorrect in the FCE exam).

4   This extends the theme of this section. Your students could also discuss people who have come to a bad end as a result of technology. You might like to tell them about the *Darwin Awards* – these are awards for people who have managed to kill themselves by doing something incredibly stupid, and many of them involve the misuse of technology.

ANSWERS

Ex. 1
1 He became stranded on a piece of ice while trying to walk to the North Pole alone.
2 He was able to send a photo of where the air rescue team could land.

Ex. 3
1 which   2 as   3 was   4 been
5 making / taking   6 himself   7 be   8 for
9 would / might   10 them   11 against   12 took
13 it   14 the / this   15 spite

Vocabulary 2: communicating with others p.76

Aims:
• **to focus on the difference in meaning between say, speak, talk and tell**
• **to review prepositions used with expressions related to communication**

1
1 Your students should refer to a dictionary to make sure they are using the correct words. They should also make sure they use the correct form of the verb.
2 This practises the key language in a personalised context. For 4a) you could teach them the idiomatic expression *to put your foot in it* and extend this into a light-hearted discussion. Ask them if they have put their foot in it recently. What happened? What was the outcome?

2   When they have done this, tell the students to close their books. Read the sentences out to them, sometimes using the correct preposition and sometimes using the wrong one. Can they tell when you have made a mistake and correct that mistake?

3   This practises the target language in a semi-controlled context.

4   Allow your students about ten minutes to complete the sentences, and then compare their answers in pairs or small groups. A good dictionary will show them the collocations for some of the key words (e.g. **reach** a compromise, **make** or **give** a presentation, etc).

ANSWERS

1 a told   b telling   c tell   d telling
2 a speak   b speaks   c speak   d speak
3 a talk   b talking   c talked
4 a saying   b said   c say

Ex. 2
1 in   2 by/in   3 by   4 with   5 through
6 with

Ex. 4
1 have a word with   2 give a presentation
3 reach / come to / arrive at a compromise
4 done enough preparation
5 having a chat with   6 have a discussion about

See also: *NEW FCE Gold exam maximiser* p.52

Exam focus

Paper 5 Speaking: long turn (Part 2) p.77

Aims:

- **to introduce and practice a procedure for Paper 5, Part 2**

Take your students through the **About the exam** and **Procedure** sections in the usual way. Focus in particular on the fact that the task is in two parts – students must give a personal reaction to the photos.

1   The connection between the photos is that they both show young people interacting with older people. Ask your students for their ideas.

2
1, 2 Play the recording with the examiner's instructions, then stop it and ask your students what the task is. Then play the recording with the candidates doing the task, and ask your students for their opinions on questions 1–3.

▶ Tapescript p.103

3, **4**   Students enjoy doing these examiner-candidate activities. In larger classes, the students taking the candidates' roles find they can do the task with more confidence, as they are not the focal point of the whole class. The activity also helps the student playing the examiner to become more

aware of what is required in the exam – he/she is obliged to listen more carefully to what the others are saying, and this makes him/her think about his/her own English.
Allow about four minutes for Exercise 3, and another two to three minutes for Exercise 4. You could then ask a more confident group to re-enact their role-play for the rest of the class.

Exam information ▶ Cbk p.5

Students each have one minute to compare, contrast and give a personal reaction to their photographs. If they speak for too long, the examiner will stop them by saying 'Thank you'. Students should not be alarmed by this sudden interruption – it is not an indication that they have done badly or the examiner doesn't understand them; the Speaking test follows strict time limits, and the examiner may need to move on to the next part.

Your students should also note that at no time in the Speaking test are they given any indication of how well or badly they have performed. At the end of the test, the examiner simply says 'Thank you. That is the end of the test'.

ANSWERS

Ex. 1
They show young people interacting with older people.

Ex. 2
1 'I'd like you to compare and contrast these photographs, and say how you think these people are feeling.'
2
1 Yes   2 Yes   3 Yes

Writing: report (Part 2) p.78

Aim:

- **to plan and write a report**

Before your students look at this section, ask them what a report is. *Who might write a report? Who would they write it to? What sorts of things might a report be about?*

1
1, 2 Ask your students to read the report and to comment on the questions in 1.2. Then ask them to close their books. *Can they remember the key points of the report, and the order in which they came? Can they remember any of the key expressions? Is this, in their opinion, a good report?*

2

1, 2 In both parts of this exercise, students are drafting a plan for the report they are going to write. An effective way of doing this is to think of the main arguments they want to give and write down a few key words (*brainstorming*). They should then decide which of their arguments are the most important or relevant, and extend the key words into sentences. Finally, they decide in which order these sentences should come. This process should take about 15 minutes, by which point they will have a thorough, workable plan from which to write their report. (Note: this planning process can be applied to other writing tasks in the FCE)

3

1, 2 Guide your students through the task in 3.1 and the main points of 3.2. They can then apply the planning skills outlined above to planning the main points of their composition.

4

Students can write the report for homework. This should take them about 25 minutes, using the plans they have made. They should make sure that they check carefully for omissions, style, word count, etc.

ANSWERS

Ex. 1

1 A bad thing.

2

1 It mentions where the information came from.

2 No student *should* be allowed to bring a mobile phone to school

Public phones *should* be regularly checked.

Ex. 4 Sample answer

Introduction

This report explains why mobile phones are important for students, and makes recommendations about their use in the school. The information comes from a survey of students and their parents.

Benefits

1 Mobile phones are the best way for students to stay in contact with their parents. Students need them to inform their parents of changes to the times of activities such as sport or music. Also if a student is ill or has an accident, a mobile is the quickest way of contacting their parents.

2 Modern mobile phones are more than just a phone. They also have diaries, calendars, calculators, etc. and students need these to organise their lives.

Recommendations

Because of these benefits, we recommend that students should be allowed to bring their mobile phones to school, but they should check that

---

phones are switched off before classed start. We also recommend that students should only be allowed to use their phones in special 'phone zones', where they will not disturb anyone else.

(167 words)

See also: *NEW FCE Gold exam maximiser* p.53

UNIT 6 Review p.79

ANSWERS

Ex. 1

1 predictions **2** communication(s)
3 conversations **4** attractions
5 abbreviations **6** interruption

Ex. 2

I want to see you today
Talk to you later
Love you
can you wait for me?
text me before you go

Ex. 3

1 was so intensively advertised
2 was quickly dealt with
3 must have been seen
4 carried on with
5 is possible that
6 can't have been

Ex. 4 Examples only

1 She could / might be ill / very busy.
2 You could / must be getting a cold / flu.
3 He can't have studied hard enough. He may / must have been nervous on the day of the exam.
4 You could / might have dropped them somewhere
5 You can't have paid / must have forgotten to pay the bill.

Ex. 5

1 I made the order by phone.
2 In his letter, he told me he missed me.
3 Can I contact you by email?
4 He's constantly on the move.
5 All in all, it was an enjoyable experience.
6 Could I have a quick word with you?
7 If you're worried, we can talk it over tomorrow.
8 We arrived at the station just in time
9 I found it on the internet.
10 You have to speak to him in person – you can't phone.

▶ Photocopiable Unit 6 test p.123

UNIT
7 Back to the future

Listening 1: multiple-choice questions (Part 4) p.80

Aims:
- **to provide further practice in Paper 4, Part 4**
- **to focus on alternative ways of expressing ideas**

1 Your students could discuss the advantages and disadvantages of life now and then, or the things we take for granted that did not exist then (often quite basic things like running water, detergent, books, simple medicines, etc.). This question also provides an opportunity to review language of comparison and contrast (*however, but, whereas*, etc.). Ask your students to use complete sentences to answer this section.

2 When your students have read through the questions, ask them for the key words they underlined. *Can they think of any synonyms or parallel expressions for these key words?* (These may be in the listening passage itself.)

3
1, 2 Play the recording twice, and then let your students compare their answers in pairs. They should tell each other why they chose their answers (i.e. what they heard on the recording that matched the answer they chose).

▶ Tapescript p.104

4 Students can discuss these questions in small groups, and this can then be extended into a whole class discussion. Your students might like to compile a list of the Top Ten worst things about being involved in a project like this, or a Top Ten list of the things they couldn't possibly live without.

5 This transformation exercise focusses on useful language in the recording.

ANSWERS

Ex. 2
1 B 2 C 3 B 4 C 5 C 6 A 7 A

Ex. 5
1 dropped out   2 didn't matter what
3 had to do it   4 never forget what

Vocabulary 1: general nouns p.81

Aims:
- **to develop/review specific vocabulary related to general subject areas**
- **to focus on word stress**

This section provides useful training for the Reading and Listening papers of the FCE, as it helps students to identify and develop an awareness of the use of parallel words/phrases in these papers. For example, they may have the word *luxury* in a question and specific examples of luxuries in the text itself.

Before your students look at this section, write the word *luxuries* in the middle of the board, and ask them to brainstorm as many luxuries as possible. Write their ideas around the main word on the board. This could prompt a discussion as to what they consider 'luxuries', e.g. many students think that television is a necessity – they couldn't live without it. What we consider necessities now would have been luxuries 20 or 30 years ago.

1, **2** Working in pairs, students match the sentence halves and underline the general meaning words/specific examples. Ask them to think of some other words that could be added to the general meaning words (as in the brainstorming activity above). You could focus on sentence halves 6b and have a brief discussion on skills that are useful or essential now, but wouldn't have been a few hundred years ago (e.g. driving a car, speaking a foreign language, literacy and numeracy, the ability to use a computer or mobile phone, etc.).

3
1, 2 After your students have done the task, focus on the word *chocolate*. Many words in English have silent letters, with the result that they have fewer syllables than they appear to have. *Chocolate* is **normally** pronounced as having two syllables in English (tʃɒklət). Words like this can be a particular problem for students if a similar word exists in their language (in French, for example, the word *chocolat* is spoken with three syllables).
Ask your students if they can think of any other examples (e.g. *library, February*, etc.).

4, **5**   These exercises provide considerable scope for vocabulary development. Students could do Exercise 4 individually, then work in pairs or small groups for Exercise 5. You can then photocopy their mind maps so that every student has a copy of one. They should then be encouraged to store these in a vocabulary file, or develop another system for easy reference.

ANSWERS

Ex. 1

1 d)   **2** f)   **3** a)   **4** h)   **5** g)   **6** b)   **7** c)   **8** e)

Ex. 2

1 luxuries – cakes, chocolates
2 facilities – central heating, hot showers
3 problems – cold, hunger
4 weapons – swords, spears
5 materials – wool, leather
6 skills – hunting, farming, cooking
7 electrical equipment – televisions, computers
8 advantages – lack of pollution, closeness to
   nature

Ex. 3

O: skills
Oo: weapons, problems
Ooo: luxuries
oOo: equipment, advantages
oOoo: facilities, materials

Ex. 4

1 facilities   **2** creatures   **3** inventions
4 disasters   **5** Cosmetics   **6** subjects   **7** vehicles
8 equipment

See also: *NEW FCE Gold exam maximiser* p.54

Grammar 1: relative clauses p.82

Aim:

• **to review forms and function of defining and non-defining relative clauses**

1

1 After students have done Exercise 1.1, and discussed the questions in Exercise 1.2, you could ask them to close their books and work in pairs. Give them a series of relative pronouns (*who, which, that, when, where, whose, who, whom*) and tell them to write their own sentences using these words.
Note that *whom* (number 8) is rarely used in spoken English, and is becoming less common in written English.

Watch Out! *which, that*
Discuss the difference between sentence 1 and sentences 3 and 4: in sentence 1, the relative clause is non-defining and the information inside commas is extra; in 3 and 4, the

information defines which car is being described.

2   Students can do this in pairs. One student should close their book, and their partner should read the sentences out aloud. Can the first student identify the mistake? Alternatively, ask the whole class to close their books, and read the sentences yourself.

3   Ask your students to do this individually, then check their answers with a partner. They should then close their books. Ask them to tell you what they can remember about the history of the parachute.

4   This communicative exercise practises the use of defining relative clauses to describe what something does. This is a particularly useful skill in Parts 2 and 3 of the Speaking test (Paper 5).

ANSWERS

Ex. 1

1

1 who   **2** which/that   **3** when   **4** where
5 which   **6** whose   **7** Who   **8** whom
2
1 sentence 2   **2** sentence 2   **3** sentence 5

Watch Out! *which, that*
2 is not possible – this is a non-defining clause and *that* cannot be used after a comma in a relative clause

Ex. 2

1 The thing which I value ~~it~~ the most
2 He explained ~~all what~~ *everything that*
3 the house where I used to live ~~in~~
4 ~~Whose~~ *Who* does
5 everything ~~what~~ (*that*) you can.
6 Wales, where my grandfather was born ~~there~~
7 Students ~~which~~ *who* want to
8 Anyone who ~~he~~ wants to return
9 someone ~~whom~~ *who* I think
10 The girl, ~~that~~ *who* I'd seen before

Ex. 3

The idea was first demonstrated by a Frenchman called Lenormand, who jumped from a very tall tree carrying two umbrellas in 1763. A few years later, some adventurous people jumped from hot-air balloons using primitive parachutes which were made from strong cotton cloth. The first person to jump from a flying airplane (and survive the fall) was Captain Albert Berry, who jumped from a US Army plane in 1912.

▶ Photocopiable activity 7A *Relative matching* p.172

See also: *NEW FCE Gold exam maximiser* p.55

Exam focus

Paper 3 Use of English: open cloze (Part 2) p.83

Aim:

- **to present and practise a procedure for the open cloze**

Go through the **About the exam** and **Procedure** sections in the usual way.

Make sure that your students skim the whole text before attempting the complete the gaps. To avoid temptation, get the whole class to put their hands on their heads before they skim it! Allow them about one to two minutes for this. Your students should then complete the text individually. Allow them about ten minutes for this. Remind them that if they cannot complete a gap, they should go ahead to the next one, and then return to it afterwards. Also remind them that sometimes they will need to refer back to a previous sentence in order to identify the missing words (e.g. in this text, number 13 uses *this/that*, which refers back to *the 1860s* in the preceding sentence).

> **ANSWERS**
> **1** than   **2** who   **3** at   **4** of   **5** their   **6** been
> **7** by   **8** his   **9** then   **10** the   **11** or   **12** in
> **13** this / that   **14** have   **15** be

Reading: multiple matching (Part 4) p.84

Aim:

- **to practice an exam-style multiple matching task**

Before your students look at this section, ask them if they think the next 100 years will be better or worse than the last 100 years. *What good things do they think will happen? What bad things do they think will happen? Why? What could we all do to improve the future?*

1 , **2**   Students should discuss the questions in small groups, then compare their answers/ideas with the rest of the class.

3   The key words in text B are *latest technical advances* and *minute*. Note that *minute* is an example of a *homograph* (a word which is written in the same way as another word, but which has a different meaning and pronunciation).

4 , **5**   Working individually, students complete the task, then compare their answers with a partner, explaining which key words/phrases they used to identify their answers.

6   This exercise allows for further discussion of the topic.

7   Students should do this exercise individually and then check their answers with a partner. Encourage them to refer to a good dictionary.

> **ANSWERS**
> **Ex. 3**
> 1 the latest technical advances
> 2 minute
>
> **Ex. 4**
> **1** E   **2** A   **3/4** B/D   **5** B   **6/7** B/C   **8** A   **9** D
> **10** C   **11** D   **12/13** A/C   **14** C   **15** E
>
> **Ex. 7**
> **1** of   **2** of/in   **3** on   **4** of/on   **5** for   **6** on
> **7** on/for   **8** in

See also: *NEW FCE Gold exam maximiser* p.56

Grammar 2: conditionals (1) p.86

Aim:

- **to review past, present and future conditionals**

Note that mixed conditionals are dealt with in Unit 11.

1

1, 2 Your students can do Exercise 1.1 in pairs, then join with another pair to complete the information in Exercise 1.2.

2   Tell your students to cover up the previous exercises before doing this. The mistakes highlighted here are typical of student mistakes.

3 , **4** , **5** , **6**   These exercises practise the main conditional constructions in a semi-controlled context. Do them as a whole class discussion. You don't need to answer all the questions, but you should try to focus on at least one question from each exercise, ensuring that students use the correct conditional construction in each one.

> **ANSWERS**
> **Ex. 1**
> **1**
> 1 is/are
> 2 continues/we will need
> 3 inhabited/would be
> 4 were/would know
> 5 had spent/could have solved
> **2**
> 1 *if* + present + present
> 2 a) *if* + present + future
>   b) *if* + past simple + *would*
> 3 *if* + past perfect + *would / could have*

Ex. 2

1 if he *practises*   2 if you *take*   3 if I *had known*
4 you *get*   5 if I *had* worked   6 I *could* fix
7 I would never *have gone*   8 I *would* get

Ex. 3 Sample answers

2 If colonies are established on Mars, this may
solve the population problem.
3 If protein and vitamin pills replace … , meals will
be very boring.
4 If everyone speaks the same language, we will be
able to communicate better.

Ex. 5

1 have   2 take   3 go   4 wouldn't have had
5 wouldn't have wanted

See also: *NEW FCE Gold exam maximiser* p.57

Speaking: ranking; discussion (Parts 3 and 4) p.87

Aim:

- **to practice the language of conditionals in a Paper 5-style activity**

Exam information ▶ Cbk p.5
See TB Unit 3 p.24, Unit 4 p.34

1   Do this exercise as a whole class discussion. For
question 2, ask your students to decide on the most
important and the least important thing. Make sure that every
student gets the chance to voice an opinion – encourage the
quieter students to say something, and make sure that the
more confident ones don't dominate.

2

1, 2 After you have played the recording, ask your students if
they think the students on the recording did the task well
(e.g. *Did they both give each other the chance to speak?
Did they work with each other or against each other? Did
one of them dominate the conversation?*, etc.).

3   Rearrange your students so that they do not do this
exercise with the people they usually speak to. While they are
doing the task, monitor the pairs carefully to check they are
working together. Remind them that they do not have to
agree with each other on their choice of objects.

Exam information
In the Speaking test, your students may be paired with someone they know quite well. However, they are more likely to be paired with someone they don't often talk to, or even with a complete stranger. When doing pairwork exercises in class, try to get your students to work with different partners whenever possible.

4   This focuses on the final part of the Speaking test,
where the general theme in Part 3 is extended. Your students
do not have to answer all of these questions. They could
focus on one or two of them, and discuss them in detail.
Alternatively, divide your class into groups of three. One
student could take the part of the examiner, the other two
should close their books. The examiner could ask the students
the questions in Exercise 4, and maybe add some of his/her
own ideas.

ANSWERS
Ex. 2 **1** 1 shall we begin   2 don't you   3 comes first 4 me too   5 could manage   6 that's a good point 7 what about   8 Do you agree   9 suppose 10 That's true

Exam focus
Paper 4 Listening: extracts (Part 1) p.88

Aim:

- **to present and practise a procedure for Paper 4, Part 1**

Take your students through the **About the exam** and
Procedure sections in the usual way.

Remind your students to be aware of distracters here. We
hear in extract 1, for example, that there were usually people
to explain things in the museums. Initially, option A would
seem to be the correct answer. However, this does not refer
to the textbooks, but to the museums in general. The answer
is B, because the speaker is a teacher, and so the textbooks
are personally/professionally relevant to her. We don't learn
this until the end of the extract. Your students should
therefore listen to the **whole** extract before choosing their
answer.

If possible, make a copy of the tapescript to give your
students after they have done the task. Then play the
recording again, while they read the tapescript. Stop after
each extract, and ask them what they can see in the
tapescript that gives them the correct answer.

▶ Tapescript p.104

ANSWERS
1 B   2 B   3 C   4 A   5 B   6 C   7 A   8 C

See also: *NEW FCE Gold exam maximiser* p.58

Vocabulary 2: collocations p.88

Aims:
- **to focus on some common collocations**
- **to encourage dictionary work**

Exam information
This section provides useful preparation for Paper 3, Part 1 of the FCE. The options given are often synonyms – their meanings are the same or similar, but the words they work with are different.

1 Ask your students to do this exercise in pairs, then use a dictionary to check their answers. They should try looking under the subsidiary entries for *make* and *do*. If they cannot find the answers there, they should look under the key entries for the other words (e.g. for number 1, they could looking at the sample sentences for *arrangements*).

2
1, 2 Students should do this in pairs, then compare their answers with another pair before checking their answers in a dictionary. When they have done this, tell them to close their books. Read the adjectives in Exercise 2.1 out to your students, and ask them to give you any words that collocate with them.

3 This practises some of the key language in a personalised context.

ANSWERS

Ex. 1
1 made   2 do   3 do   4 make   5 make/do
6 making   7 make   8 has made   9 doing
10 doing

Ex. 2
1
1 spare   2 cookery   3 historical   4 latest
5 sunny   6 swift
2
a) cookery   b) sunny   c) swift   d) spare
e) historical   f) latest

▶ Photocopiable activity 7B *Collocations crossword* p.174
See also: *NEW FCE Gold exam maximiser* p.59

Use of English 2: multiple-choice cloze (Part 1) p.89

Aim:
- **to complete an exam-style Paper 3, Part 1 task**

1, **2** Students should do Exercises 1 and 2 in pairs, Allow them about ten minutes for this, then ask them for their answers. Focus on some of the incorrect options, and ask your students if they can think of any words these options collocate with, together with a sentence (e.g. 1C *installed*: *The new computer system is being installed. A drinks machine has been installed in the canteen.*).

ANSWERS
Ex. 2
1 A   2 D   3 B   4 B   5 C   6 A   7 B   8 A
9 D   10 A   11 C   12 C   13 A   14 B   15 D

Writing: composition (Part 2) p.90

Aim:
- **to plan and write a discursive composition**

1 This focuses students' attention on the main topic of their composition. In the FCE, students lose marks if they fail to answer the question correctly.

2
1, 2 This guides students through the essential planning process which will ensure that their composition has both cohesion and coherence. A piece of written text that has not been planned properly will lack 'flow', will contain repetitions (saying the same thing in two or more different ways in different stages of the text), and mistakes, crossings-out and insertions. A piece of written work that is difficult to read because of these features will lose marks in the FCE.
Persuade your students to avoid the common habit of writing a first draft of a composition, then rewriting it. This is not an effective planning strategy, not least because in the exam, they wouldn't have time to do this.

3 This is the most common structure of a discursive composition. Another common technique is to give an idea supporting an argument, and then an idea which gives a counter argument to that point (e.g. *On the one hand, it could be argued that museums are a waste of money because very few people are interested in them. On the other hand, museums are 'banks', keeping our heritage safe for future generations.*). This is then repeated for other arguments/counter arguments.
Asking a rhetorical question (paragraph opening D) is a good way of beginning a discursive composition. It gets the reader

personally involved, effectively 'challenging' him/her to think about the topic.

The composition here is in favour of museums – the arguments 'for' come after the arguments 'against', and so more closely support the conclusion.

4 , **5** , **6**   Students can write the composition for their homework. They should allow themselves about 35 minutes for this, including time for checking.

ANSWERS

Ex. 1
b)

Ex. 3
Paragraph 1: D   Paragraph 2: B   Paragraph 3: C
Paragraph 4: A

Ex. 4
1
a) However   b) To sum up
2
1 because of   2 therefore
3 Because/even though

Ex. 5 Sample answer
Most towns and cities have at least one museum, but how important are museums to people living in the 21st century?

Some people claim that museums use up money which would be better spent on other things. Museums are usually in very big old buildings in the city and that means they require a lot of maintenance. These buildings could be sold for a big profit and the money could be used for things like hospitals or the police: things that would have a positive impact on everyone's lives.

However, other people believe that if we understand how things happened in the past, we can improve the future. Museums play an important role in educating both the young and the old and they are centres for research. Also, museums are very important for tourism and they provide a peaceful place in the centre of busy cities, where anyone can go to relax.

To sum up, it seems to me that museums are a vital part of modern life and in no way a waste of money.

(176 words)

See also: *NEW FCE Gold exam maximiser* p.60

UNIT 7 Review p.91

ANSWERS

Ex.1
1 which   2 where   3 which   4 that   5 which
6 which   7 when   8 who

Ex. 2 Sample answers
1 … , I would go to Australia.
2 … will own my own company.
3 … would have lived in a cave …
4 … would take him to the old part first.
5 … can concentrate better …
6 … would take up horse-riding.
7 … would have been born in Roman times because …
8 … would turn it down because …

Ex. 3
1 although   2 However,   3 Despite
4 as a result of   5 therefore   6 however

Ex. 4
1 customer   2 thickness   3 returned
4 complaint   5 thinner   6 amazement
7 popularity   8 dramatically   9 unaware
10 confusion

▶ Photocopiable Unit 7 test p.125

We are family

Reading: multiple matching (Part 1) p.92

Aims:
- **to provide guided practice of the multiple matching task**
- **to focus on some common phrasal verbs**

1 Discuss the question briefly with the whole class. Ask your students if they have any friends or relatives in distant places. *Where do they live? What do they do? How often do your students see them?*

2 Students read the text quickly and choose the best alternatives. The title of the piece, *Steppe by Step*, should be explained before they do this. It is a pun on the expression *step by step* (to do things one stage at a time). *Steppe* (or *the Steppes*) is a large area of land without trees, especially in Russia, Asia and eastern Europe.

3 , **4** Before your students do this, remind them that they should read the whole paragraph before choosing the heading that relates to it, as there will often be a combination of ideas spread across each paragraph that links to the heading.
Your students should do this individually (allow about 10–15 minutes), and then compare their answers with a partner or in small groups. They should tell each other why they chose their headings for each paragraph.

5 Many phrasal verbs can have more than one meaning, e.g. *take off* in number 1. Most students at this level know that it means to leave the ground (for an aircraft), but may be unaware of its other meanings. Ask them if they can think of any other phrasal verbs that can have more than one meaning. Tell them to use a dictionary to find out if the phrasal verbs in the text can have another meaning.

6
1, 2 This provides a useful opportunity to review conditionals (especially Type 2 present conditionals) from the previous unit.

ANSWERS

Ex. 2
1 someone else's
2 how closely connected we all are
3 a stranger
4 successful

Ex. 3
1 H 2 F 3 C 4 G 5 B 6 D 7 E
Ex. 5
1 taken off 2 has gone on 3 find out
4 to test out the theory 5 get to
6 pass you on to

See also: *NEW FCE Gold exam maximiser* p.62

Speaking 1: quiz p.94

Aims:
- **to complete a quiz about friendship**
- **to introduce gerunds and infinitives (covered in the next section)**

1 Students discuss the sentences with a partner. Ask them if they can think of any other words connected with relationships, e.g. *classmate*, (*steady/ex-*) *boyfriend*, *girlfriend*, *partner* (used to talk about somebody you run/own a company with, but also used to refer to a boyfriend or girlfriend), *fiancée* (female), *fiancé* (male), *flatmate*.

2 , **3** You could follow up the quiz with a brief discussion on different aspects of friendship: what makes someone your best friend, describe your ideal friend or partner, why do friends fall out with each other, etc.

ANSWERS
1 colleague 2 acquaintance 3 stranger
4 relative 5 best friend

Grammar 1: gerunds and infinitives p.95

Aims:
- **to review verbs followed by gerund or infinitive verbs**

Before you do this section, write the words *agony aunt* on the board, and ask your students what they think this is. *What sort of things do people ask agony aunts about? Why do people confide in agony aunts instead of friends or family? Do they think it's right for newspapers and magazines to exploit people's personal problems in this way for financial gain?*

1 , **2** Divide your class into teams of four students, and then divide those teams into pairs (these are Group A and Group B). Allow each group 6–8 minutes to complete their letter. The two pairs in each group should then work together to compare their answers and give advice to the writers (they could use Type 1 and 2 conditionals here: *If you tell him the truth, he'll understand*, *If I were you, I'd give him the elbow immediately*, etc). The groups can then feed back their suggestions to the rest of the class, who can comment on the various suggestions and choose/vote on the best one.

Watch Out! *make/let/allow*
Focus on this while checking answers. *The teacher **made us to do** the exercise* is a common student mistake.

3 Number 3 (*remember doing something*) can be fairly difficult to understand, even by students at fairly high levels. If your students are still unsure about the difference, you could give them this example:
First I telephoned John. I have a very clear memory of this. Everybody tells me that I then telephoned Mary, but I have no memory of this. I remember phoning John, but I don't remember phoning Mary.

4 Ask your students to cover up the previous exercises before they try to do this. They can check unfamiliar words in their dictionary.

5 This practises the target language in a personalised context. Students can do this in small groups.

ANSWERS

Ex. 1
A
1 to be 2 to have 3 doing 4 to support
5 to keep 6 to move 7 to work 8 to accept
9 go 10 taking 11 to move on
B
1 to enjoy 2 doing 3 going 4 to spend
5 hearing 6 to watch 7 make 8 change
9 seeing 10 stay 11 telling 12 hurting

Watch Out! *make/let/allow*
1 *make* is followed by *to*-infinitive in the passive.
2 b) *let* is not used in the passive: we must use allow instead. *I'm not **allowed** to stay out late* (passive).

Ex. 3
1 I'd like to meet her b)
  I like meeting her a)
2 I stopped to talk to Rose b)
  I stopped talking to Rose a)
3 I remembered to phone Jack a)
  I remembered phoning Jack b)
4 He tried to write his essay in half an hour b)
  He tried writing his essay in half an hour a)

---

5 I regret to tell you that b)
  I really regret a)

Ex. 4
1 She keeps (on) interrupting me …
2 She insists on inviting …
3 The man pretended to be a government official.
4 She wanted him to explain everything to her.
5 I enjoy not having to get up early on holiday!
6 I regret having written the letter.
7 … the examiner let me take the examination
8 I hate relying on/having to rely on other people.

▶ Photocopiable activity 8 *Get it together* p.176
See also: *NEW FCE Gold exam maximiser* p.64

Vocabulary 1: adjective suffixes p.96

Aim:
• **to focus on how adjectives are formed**

1
1, 2 Encourage your students to develop a 'bank' of the most common adjective suffixes, and to pay attention to spelling changes (e.g. the final e is always dropped, *y* changes to *i*). After your students have completed the table, ask them to close their books, and then read out the words in the left-hand column in random order. Can they remember the correct suffixes to use, and any changes which take place in the spelling?

2 Students do this with a partner. Note that *value* has two positive forms (*valuable* and *invaluable*). *Invaluable* would not work in this sentence because of the intensifier *really*, which does not collocate (*absolutely* would collocate).

3 As an alternative to working in pairs, your students can walk around the classroom and talk to as many of their classmates as possible. When they have done this, they can take it in turns to tell the rest of the class about one of the people they talked to (e.g. *Marta's aunt is always very supportive of her. She is always encouraging her to do the things she wants.*).

ANSWERS

Ex. 1
1
1 f) dependable, lovable (*e* is dropped), washable
2 c) truthful, hopeful, harmful
3 b) active, creative (*e* is dropped), supportive
4 g) nervous (*e* is dropped), furious (*y* changes to *i*), famous (*e* is dropped)
5 d) natural (*e* is dropped), national, cultural (*e* is dropped)

---

6 a) friendly, cowardly, heavenly
7 e) funny (*n* is doubled), wealthy, healthy
2
+ *un*-: unlovable, untruthful, unsupportive,
unnatural, unfriendly, unhealthy
+ *in*-: inactive, infamous (= well known for being
bad)
+ *-less*: hopeless, harmless

Ex. 2
1 valuable   2 famous   3 hopeless   4 supportive
5 unhealthy   6 active

See also: *NEW FCE Gold exam maximiser* p.61

Use of English 1: word formation (Part 5) p.96

Aim:
• **to complete an exam-style word formation task**

1   Make sure your students skim the text first before deciding on the appropriate word forms.

2   Allow them about ten minutes to complete the task (although most students find this is the quickest part of the FCE Paper 3, and can complete it in about 7 minutes).

3   This personalises the theme of this section. When they have discussed this in small groups, your students could tell each other about **their** best friend. *How long have they known them? What sorts of things do they do together? What makes this person their best friend?*, etc.

ANSWERS

Ex. 1
a), c)

Ex. 2
1 personalities   2 natural   3 completely
4 nervous   5 unfriendly   6 development
7 generally   8 activities   9 truthful
10 supportive

Vocabulary 2: relationships p.97

Aims:
• **to review the terms for different members of the family**
• **to review/introduce some common adjectives of personality**
• **to preview some vocabulary needed for Exam focus Listening**

1   You could make Exercise 1.1 more communicative by telling your students to close their books and listening carefully while you read the sentences out to them. They can then work in small groups of three or four to decide if the definitions are correct or incorrect. They should write their answers down. The group with the most correct answers is the winner.
They can then discuss Exercise 1.2 in the same groups.

Teaching tips and ideas

Take in some recent photographs of your friends and family. Show these to your students and ask them if they can decide how they are related to you. You could also ask your students to bring in some of their own photographs in the next lesson, and show these to their classmates.

2
1 Students can do this in pairs.
2 In some cases, the opposite of the word will require a suffix or prefix (e.g. *unreliable, thoughtless*), and in others the word will change completely (e.g. the opposite of *stubborn = reasonable, flexible, open to reason*).
Many adjectives of character also have synonyms (e.g. *stubborn = obstinate, pig-headed, headstrong, wilful*). You could ask your students if they know of any other synonyms for the adjectives in the box.
3 Students discuss their family members in pairs. They should ask each other to elaborate as much as possible (e.g. *So why do you think you're so talkative? Did you inherit your stubborn streak from your parents?*, etc.)

3   With mixed-nationality classes, this could lead to some interesting cross-cultural discussion (e.g. in most western cultures, it is traditional for the bride's parents to pay for the wedding, whereas in China the groom's parents pay for it). With single-nationality groups, ask students if they know of, or have been to, weddings that are different from those in their own country.

ANSWERS

Ex. 1
1 Wrong – your nephew is your brother's or sister's son.
2 Correct – but your great-grandmother could also be any of the four combinations of your mother's/father's, mother's/father's mother.
3 Wrong – your aunt could be your mother's or father's sister or the wife of your uncle.
4 Correct.
5 Wrong – he's only your brother by marriage.
6 Wrong – he's the brother of one of your grandparents.
7 Correct.

8 Wrong – your brother-in-law is your sister's husband or your wife's brother.

9 Correct

Ex. 2

1 reliable   2 sociable   3 ambitious   4 generous
5 talkative   6 modest   7 sympathetic
8 sensible   9 thoughtful   10 stubborn

2

1 unreliable   2 unsociable   3 unambitious
4 mean   5 quiet   6 arrogant, proud
7 unsympathetic   8 impractical   9 thoughtless, selfish   10 reasonable, flexible

Ex. 3

1 got engaged   2 got married   3 wedding
4 bridesmaids   5 ceremony   6 reception
7 honeymoon

See also: *NEW FCE Gold exam maximiser* p.65

Exam focus

Paper 4 Listening: note completion (Part 2) p.98

Aims:

- **to present and practice a procedure for a Paper 4 note completion task**
- **to discuss celebrations in students' own countries**

Before your students look at this section, explain that they are going to hear a listening passage about weddings. Ask them to work in pairs or small groups to brainstorm words and expressions that they might expect to hear.
They should then look at the notes in their book, and decide what kind of information is missing.

1   Take the students through the **About the exam** and **Procedure** sections. Then play the recording twice, while students complete the missing information.

▶ Tapescript p.105

2   There is plenty of potential for cross-cultural exchange of ideas here. Ask them if they have any photographs taken at these events, and to bring them in the next lesson to show the others in the class.

ANSWERS

Ex. 1

1 (a) date   2 ceremony   3 guest list   4 flowers
5 (a) meal   6 accommodation   7 honeymoon
8 passport   9 photographs   10 speeches

Grammar 2: expressing hypothetical meanings p.99

Aim:

- **to review the use of *wish, if only, it's time, would rather, suppose, as if/though* for hypothetical situations**

1

1, 2 Students should work in pairs to match the sentences and discuss the questions.

Watch Out! *wish* and *would*

Note that we often use *wish* + *would* in situations where we are angry or frustrated with someone or something (*I wish you would be quiet!/I wish it would stop raining.*).

2   Number 4 could cause some confusion, because of the future aspect *next month*. You might need to point out that *If only* here refers to now, and not the exams next month. The speaker is angry/frustrated **now** about something that is going to happen **in the future**.

3   Your students could write their wishes on a sheet of paper and then give them to you. You can then read them out to the class, and they should decide who the wishes belong to. That student should then elaborate, explaining why they made those wishes.

4 , **5**   Students discuss Exercises 4.1 and 4.2 in pairs, then work with another pair to complete Exercise 5.

ANSWERS

Ex. 1

1 h) (present)   2 e) (present)   3 f) (future)
4 d) (present)   5 a) (present / future)   6 b) (past)
7 c) (past)   8 g) (past)

Watch Out! *wish* and *would*

1 a)   2 b)
1 b) A   2 a) B

Ex. 2

1 hadn't lost   2 would stop   3 could   4 didn't have   5 could   6 wasn't   7 would   8 was

Ex. 4

1

1 b)   2 b)   3 a)

2

Sentence a) in each case indicates the speaker thinks the situation is likely to be true. Sentence b) in each case refers to a hypothetical situation.

Ex. 5 Sample answers

1 Isn't it time we went to work?
2 Suppose I won the Lottery …
3 I'd rather go for a walk …

4 You look as if you are starving.
5 Would you rather we went to the cinema or watched TV?
6 It's high time you started to do some revision.
7 Suppose I lent you some money …

See also: *NEW FCE Gold exam maximiser* p.67

Listening 2: song p.100

Aim:

• **to listen to a song for gist**

1

1, 2 Students work in pairs to match the sentence halves and decide on the order for the chorus. Ask your students if they can identify a grammatical mistake that is quite often a feature of pop songs (line 5: *Even forever **don't** seem …*).

2, 3 Play the first part of the song and let students check their answers. Then play the whole song, and ask your students what it's about.

▶ Tapescript p.105

Teaching tips and ideas

As an alternative to Exercises 1–3, you might like to do a song dictation with your class.

1 Play the song once through, while your students listen and write down the key words they hear.

2 Play the song a second time. Students add to the list of the words they made in step 1.

3 Working in pairs, students use the words they have written down to recreate the lyrics of the song. As their key words will be mainly nouns and verbs, they will have to use 'grammar' words to complete the text (modals, articles, etc.). Allow them about ten minutes for this.

4 Play the song a third time while your students check their lyrics with the ones they hear.

ANSWERS

Ex. 1

1

1 e) 2 b) 3 a) 4 c) 5 d)

2

'Cause every time I breathe, I take you in and my heart beats again
Baby I can't help it, you keep me drowning in your love
Every time I try to rise above, I'm swept away by love

Baby I can't help it, you keep me drowning in your love

Ex. 3

a), c)

Speaking 2: how to keep talking/adding ideas (Parts 3 and 4) p.101

Aim:

• **to introduce and practise useful techniques for Paper 5, Parts 3 and 4**

1, 2 Allow your students a few moments to read through the task, then tell them to cover it up and ask them what they have to do. It is important for them to remember that the task is always in two parts (in this case, they must say how effective each idea is, and say which two they would recommend). Remind them that they don't have to agree with each other on the second part.

They should then work in pairs to complete the task. Monitor them to make sure that neither is dominating the conversation or letting their partner do all the work.

3

1, 2 The best way to keep talking is to think of other ideas that would be relevant to the topic. This is actually encouraged in the Speaking test – the pictures are merely a framework to provide stimulus. Providing they don't move away from the task, students should feel free to add their own ideas.

Play the recording, and ask your class how the two students keep the conversation going.

4, 5 The questions here are typical of the follow-on questions that students might be expected to answer in the final part of the exam. After they have discussed these questions in pairs, you could ask them to think of other questions that might be asked here (e.g. *Do people in your town go out a lot in the evenings, or do they tend to stay at home? Do families in your country live close to one another, or do they live in different parts of the country?*).

▶ Tapescript p.106

ANSWERS

Ex. 3

b) and c)

Ex. 4

3

another thing is that, as well as that

Writing: article (Part 2) p.102

Aim:

- **to plan and write an article**

Before your students look at this section, ask them if they can remember how to write an article. *What are the features that make a good article? What sort of language should they use?*

1, **2**　Allow students a few moments to read the task and highlight key words and phrases, then go through Exercise 2 with them. If the answers are false, they should say in which situation they would be true (e.g. number 2 would be relevant to reports, number 7 is for formal letters).

3

1, 2 This takes students through the planning process. This should take them about 5–10 minutes. They can either do this individually, or with a partner.

4

1, 2 Ask your students what the purpose of a title is (to make the reader want to read the article). Titles should be short and 'snappy'. In this case, title d) is the most effective – it is simply a list of key words that sum up the article. Your students should work in pairs to think of titles for their own articles, then feed back their ideas to the rest of the class, who should decide on the best ones.

5　Students often say that the beginning and ending of an article is the most difficult part to write. The best solution is for them is illustrated here – using questions. These stimulate the reader's interest, and make him/her want to read on. Another good way of beginning is by using a personalised anecdotal introduction (e.g. *I'll never forget my last birthday. It was one of the best days of my life.*).

6, **7**　Students can write their articles for homework. They should allow themselves about 30 minutes for this, including checking.

ANSWERS

Ex. 1

international magazine; one family celebration; reason for the celebration; what made it so enjoyable

Ex. 2

1 True.　2 False.　3 True.　4 True.　5 False.
6 True.　7 False.　8 True.

Ex. 4

1 b), d) – they give some information about the specific topic of this article.
a) and d) repeat the words of the question and are less interesting.

Ex. 5

1

A Christmas.

B National day. (In this case Bastille day in France, which marks the beginning of the first republic.)

C The birth of a baby.

2 They all ask a question which involves the reader.

Ex. 6 Sample answer

A wonderful wedding in New York

My family always celebrates birthdays and Christmas together, but once in a while something really special happens, something I'll never forget. Last month I went to my sister's wedding – in New York! My sister met her husband Sam in our home town five years ago. They were at a party and my sister says it was love at first sight. When Sam had to go home to New York two years ago, my sister went with him.

Their wedding ceremony took place in a small church surrounded by giant skyscrapers. It was only for close family and friends and of course my mother cried at the end! The reception was amazing. We went to a 5-star hotel next to Central Park and Sam has a friend who is a chef, who cooked the most delicious food.

For me it was the perfect wedding. Two families coming together and enjoying themselves. I miss my sister as she lives so far away, but I know she and Sam will be very happy.　　　(170 words)

See also: *NEW FCE Gold exam maximiser* p.68

UNIT 8　Review p.103

ANSWERS

Ex.1

1 forget to bring　2 let us take
3 interested in buying　4 get on well
5 wishes he had written to　6 it's time you went
7 not being able to　8 kept in touch
9 high time you bought

Ex. 2

1 D	**2** A	**3** A	**4** B	**5** C	**6** B	**7** A	**8** C
9 D	**10** B	**11** A	**12** B	**13** D	**14** C	**15** D	

▶ Photocopiable Unit 8 test p.127

Reading: gapped text (Part 3) p.104

Aims:
- **to provide guided practice of the gapped text task**
- **to practise word formation**

Before your students look at this unit, ask them how important they think looks are. *Are looks more important than personality? Are good-looking people more socially acceptable than those who aren't so attractive? Would any of your students consider having plastic or cosmetic surgery to change the way they look? What features would they most like to change?*

1, **2** After your students have discussed the people in the pictures, and read the title, sub-heading and main part of the article, ask them if they think these people are particularly attractive. Why?/Why not?

3

1 Remind your students that they are looking for ideas which follow on from the previous paragraph. We know the answer to gap 1 is H because the first paragraph tells us it is impossible to tell whether Miles has had a late night, and paragraph H goes on to give us more information about the difficulty of working out anything from his face.

2 Students can discuss these in pairs, then feed back to the rest of the class. Remind them that they should look at the paragraphs preceding **and** following the gap, as key information linking to the missing paragraph may be in both. As a class, they can then decide on the one piece of information that is most likely to be missing from each gap.

3 This focuses students' attention on the main meaning of each extracted paragraph. They should see if these main meanings match any of the ideas they came up with in Exercise 3.2.

4 Students do this individually, then compare their answers with a partner, explaining why they chose them.

5 Before your students put the words into their correct form, they should decide what kind of word is missing from each gap (e.g. noun, adverb, etc.). Go through these with your class before they decide on the correct word form (1 = verb, 2 = adverb, 3 = noun, 4 = adjective, 5 = adjective, 6 = noun, 7 = adverb, 8 = adverb).

6 As a follow-up, you could take in a selection of *Hello* and *OK*-type magazines, and students could look through these to choose facial features to create the 'ideal face'.

ANSWERS

Ex. 1
The small photo shows Miles Kendall before plastic surgery. The large photo shows him with Cindy Jackson after his 'transformation'.

Ex. 3
3
1 A   2 C, D   3 F, H   4 B   5 E

Ex. 4
1 F   2 A   3 E   4 D   5 C   6 B

Ex. 5
1 reshaping   2 pleasantly   3 appearance
4 facial   5 acceptable   6 encouragement
7 enthusiastically   8 Surprisingly

See also: *NEW FCE Gold exam maximiser* p.70

Grammar 1: present and past habit p.106

Aim:
- **to focus on language of past and present habit**

1

1, 2 Students work individually to choose the correct alternatives in each sentences, then compare their answers with a partner, referring to the **Grammar reference** if necessary.

3 Discuss this question with the whole class. Focus on number 10. *Do your students think that children have an easier time now than they did in the past, or do they think there's more pressure on them to excel at everything?*

Watch Out! *used to/be used to/get used to*
After your students have matched the sentence pairs and answered the questions, ask them to close their books and write sentences 1–3 on the board. They should work in pairs and try to remember the differences between the meanings of each one.

2 Students do this in the same pairs without looking back at Exercise 1 or the **Grammar reference**. They can then compare their answers with another pair before looking again at Exercise 1 to see if they are right.

3 This focuses on the past habit aspect of *used to* and *would*. Your students' sentences could be positive (*I used to/I would*) or negative (*I didn't use to*). When they have finished, ask them to read their sentences out to the rest of the class. Make notes, and when they have finished, ask your class questions to see if they can remember who did what (e.g. *Who used to deliver newspapers when he was 15 years old? Who used to steal apples from her neighbour's garden?*).

4 This focuses on the 'familiarisation' aspect of *used to*. If you are teaching this course at a school where students have come from other countries, they could focus on their experiences in the country in which they are studying (e.g. *I can't get used to potatoes for lunch every day, I can't get used to eating dinner so early every night, I've got used to the teacher's way of teaching.*).

5 Students can discuss these in small groups. Alternatively, they could think of some other situations. One fun idea is to tell them to imagine they have woken up as a member of the opposite sex. What things would they have to get used to, and would it be easy or difficult (e.g. *I will have to get used to putting make-up on every day, I'll find it difficult to get used to seeing my face in the mirror.*)?

ANSWERS

Ex. 1
1
1 lived/used to live   2 would walk/used to walk
3 never used to let   4 used to be
5 had/used to have   6 didn't have
7 didn't use to have   8 are taken
9 are always complaining   10 have
2
1 Past simple, *used to, would*
2 Present simple, present continuous
3 The main verb in sentence 2 describes an action. In sentence 7, it describes a state. *Would* cannot be used with state verbs.

Watch Out! *used to/be used to/get used to*
1 = I am accustomed to it.
2 = I am in the process of acquiring the habit.
3 = I had a different hairstyle in the past, and I had it for some time.

Ex. 2
1 ~~was~~ *used* to be   2 Did you *use* to live
3 ~~be~~ get used to   4 getting used *to*
5 He *gets* the bus   6 would ~~to~~ walk
7 I *enjoyed*   8 is always *trying*

See also: *NEW FCE Gold exam maximiser* p.69

Vocabulary 1: fashion p.107

Aim:
- **to review useful vocabulary related to clothes and fashion**

Before your students look at this section, ask them to work with a partner, and to look at what the other is wearing. They should describe the clothes their partner is wearing in as much detail as possible, brainstorming as many words as they know – types of clothes, pattern, colour, material and shade (e.g. *Moritz is wearing a pair of old trainers, a pair of light blue jeans with a hole in the knee, and a plain white sleeveless cotton T-shirt. He's also wearing a silver bracelet on his wrist.*).

1
1, 2 Before your students read the descriptions, ask them to work in pairs and try to describe what the man is wearing in each one. Again, they should try to give as much detail as possible. They can then match the description with the picture and complete the gap.
3 Students work in the same pairs to discuss these questions. Alternatively, focus on question 2 and involve the whole class in a brief discussion. *What is considered fashionable nowadays? Which shops/companies are considered fashionable or otherwise? Do you have to spend a lot of money to be fashionable? Can clothes be fashionable on some people but not on others?*

2
1 Students work in small groups to choose a new outfit for Stuart. If you have some clothing catalogues, bring these into class and let students choose the clothes from these (they should still describe the colour, material, etc.). Alternatively, they could choose a new outfit for somebody else in the class, and then describe this to the other students.
2 Working in the same groups, students write a description of the outfit they have chosen. They should take it in turns to each write one sentence. They should help one another with spelling, grammar, etc.

3 This personalises the theme of this section. Students should do this in pairs or groups, and try to keep talking for at least five minutes.

ANSWERS

Ex. 1
1 A 1   B 2
2
A 1 dark   2 wool   3 classic   4 pale   5 cotton
6 silk   7 leather   8 slip-on
B 1 bright   2 round-neck   3 matches
4 waterproof   5 looks   6 beige   7 brown
8 casual

See also: *NEW FCE Gold exam maximiser* p.71

Use of English 1: error correction (Part 4) p.108

Aim:

• **to complete an exam-style error correction task**

1, **2**, **3**   Do the task as a timed exercise. Allow your students about 12–15 minutes for this (including the pre-exercise tasks). They should do it individually, before comparing their answers with a partner. Remind them that there are usually between three and five lines which do not contain any mistakes.

4   Discuss this as a filler if you have time at the end of the task. Alternatively, ask your students if there is a particular period in time they would like to go back to because of the clothes that were worn at that time.

ANSWERS

Ex. 1
Good or fashionable clothes from a previous era, e.g. the 1920s or 1950s.

Ex. 3
1 of   2 ✓   3 there   4 such   5 the   6 that
7 be   8 so   9 which   10 also   11 in   12 been
13 ✓   14 it   15 ✓

Vocabulary 2: phrasal verbs with *up* p.108

Aim:

• **to focus on phrasal verbs with *up***

Up is a very common preposition – the *Longman Dictionary of Contemporary English* lists 30 uses of *up*, not including phrasal verbs or the use of *up* in compound nouns.

1

1 As an alternative to students working through these sentences, tell them to cover sentences a)–j), and then read them out yourself. Working in pairs, they should decide on the verb in 1–10 that supports each sentence.
2, 3 *Up* is often used in phrasal verbs to talk about finishing something, rather than upwards movement. In many cases, *up* can be removed – it is emphasising the 'completion' aspect (*Tidy up your room.* = *Tidy your room.*).

2   Students can work in pairs with a dictionary to look for examples of phrasal verbs that involve upwards movement, e.g. *pick up, lift up, look up* (referring to raising one's eyes), *climb up, walk up, run up.*

ANSWERS

Ex. 1
a)

Ex. 2
1
1 j)   2 b)   3 a)   4 i)   5 d)   6 e)   7 c)   8 f)
9 h)   10 g)
2
b)

See also: *NEW FCE Gold exam maximiser* p.73

Speaking 1: p.109

Before your students look at this section, ask them to think about their bedroom or their living room at home. *Is there anything they particularly like or dislike about it? If they could change anything about these rooms (apart from the size), what would they do? Do they think you can tell what a person is like by looking at their rooms?* Keep this brief, as it is the focus of an activity in the next section.

1, **2**   Ask your students to work in pairs to describe and compare the rooms. They should also give a personal reaction to the changes (e.g. *I'd really hate to have a room in that colour.*).

Exam focus
Paper 4 Listening: selecting from answers (Part 4) p.109

Aim:

• **to present and practise a procedure for Paper 4, Part 4, true or false task**

1   Take your students through the **About the exam** and **Procedure** sections before playing the recording twice.

▶ Tapescript p.106

2   The extracts are all colloquial expressions – they would be spoken rather than written (unless they were in a story or informal letter). After your students have decided what each comment refers to, they could try to rewrite the expressions in a more formal way (e.g. *It wasn't all plain sailing* = *It wasn't good or easy all the time. They'd definitely seen better days* = *They weren't in very good condition any more.*).

See also: *NEW FCE Gold exam maximiser* p.74

Vocabulary 3: things in the home p.110

Aim:

• **to review useful vocabulary related to things in the home**

1

1, 2 Some of the vocabulary in the box may need to be pre-taught (e.g. *blinds, upholstered, easy chairs, rug*) before your students attempt this.

3 Your students could discuss this in pairs. They could describe their room and the objects in it to their partner, who should draw a plan of the room showing where the objects are.
The question *Which would you like to have?* could be developed into an 'objects of desire' class survey – students work as a class to choose the ten most desirable things to have in a bedroom or ten things they would like to have in their classroom to make it a better place (e.g. comfortable chairs, computers, better lighting, air conditioning, etc.).

2

1 Students use a dictionary to check the meanings of these words. You could also introduce these other words, which can all be used to describe a room or a building: *airy, basic, bright, claustrophobic, cosy, damp, depressing, draughty, homely, pokey, practical, roomy, seedy, spacious.*

2 This is optional – if you already discussed this in the previous section, leave it out.

3 This provides lots of scope for discussion. Students work together to plan a makeover for their partner's room.

▶ Photocopiable activity 9 *Find the differences* p.177
See also: *NEW FCE Gold exam maximiser* p.74

Exam focus
Paper 3 Use of English: word formation (Part 5) p.110

Aim:

• **to present and practise a procedure for Paper 3, Part 5**

Take your students through the **About the exam** and **Procedure** sections.

> **Exam information ▶ Cbk p.5**
>
> Spelling must be accurate in all Paper 3 tasks.
>
> Note that American spelling and vocabulary are acceptable in all the Cambridge ESOL exams, provided they are used consistently.

1 Before your students put the words into their correct form, they should follow steps 1–2 in the procedure. Encourage them to cover up the words to the right of the text so that they are not tempted to start changing the words immediately. Allow them about 10–12 minutes to complete the task, then compare their answers with a partner.

2 This personalises the theme of this section. Number 2 could be followed by a class discussion on the most annoying noises (e.g. snoring, mobile phones ringing, etc.).

Grammar 2: participle clauses p.111

Aim:

• **to focus on the form and use of reduced relative clauses**

Reduced clauses are often used in written texts to add extra information without the need for complete relative clauses. These, when used too often, can make a text awkward to read. Removing the relative pronoun and any auxiliary verbs from the clause makes the text easier to read, simply because there are fewer words.

1 , 2 Ask your students to discuss Exercises 1.1 and 1.2 in pairs, and then to look at the **Grammar reference**. They should then do Exercise 2.

3 When describing homes, the best way to do this is spatially – beginning at the front and working through to the back, and in the case of houses, to describe the ground floor and then the first floor and so on. While one student describes his/her house, their partner should listen and make notes, then try to draw a plan of the different floors, adding any extra information to the rooms (e.g. if their partner tells them there are some pictures in the living room, they should write 'pictures' in the living room space on their plan).

4 Your students should do this exercise individually, then check their answers in small groups.

5 This practises the target language in a personalised context. Numbers 3 and 4 are particularly good subjects to extend into a whole class activity.

6 Students should work in pairs or small groups, and discuss both the good points and the bad points of the place where they live, before drawing a conclusion.

ANSWERS

Ex.1
Present participles have an active meaning, past participles have a passive meaning.

Ex. 2
1 leading into different rooms.
2 hanging from the ceiling.
3 collected by my grandfather.
4 decorated in different colours.
5 containing my grandmother's linen.
6 stretching down to a stream at the bottom.

Ex. 4
1 thought of   2 despised   3 competing
4 looking for   5 built   6 hidden   7 treated
8 considered   9 considering

See also: *NEW FCE Gold exam maximiser* p.74

Use of English 3: key word transformations (Part 3) p.112

Aim:

• **to complete an exam-style key word transformation task**

If you do this in class, allow your students about 15–20 minutes to complete it. Alternatively, set it as a homework task. It tests language from this and previous units.

ANSWERS
1 which starred   2 I used to walk   3 looks like/as though   4 was extremely bored by   5 wasn't as easy as   6 warned Eddie not to touch   7 might have left his glasses   8 haven't been surfing for
9 didn't deserve to be   10 the most interesting

Speaking 2: stressing key information (Part 2) p.113

Aims:

• **to do a Paper 5, Part 2-style task**
• **to focus on the importance of contrastive stress**

Exam information ▶ Cbk p.5

In the FCE Speaking test, students are assessed on their ability to use stress and intonation to convey the intended meaning.

---

1 , 2 Allow your students a few moments to read through the task in Exercise 1, and to complete the sentences in Exercise 2. They should then work in pairs and read the sentences aloud to each other.
Ask your students to decide on the words they think should be stressed, and to read the sentences to each other a second time. They should make sure that they don't over stress the words.
Play the recording, and then ask your students to read the sentences to each other a third time.

3 , 4 While your students are doing these tasks, monitor them to make sure they are placing stress on the key words, and also to make sure that they answer both parts of the question.

ANSWERS

Ex. 1

1 Compare and contrast the photos; say why ...

2 1 what is similar 2 what is different 3 why people might want to change the places

Ex. 2

1

1 private 2 being rebuilt / in 3 professional / amateurs 4 decorating 5 nervous / confident

2 1 large building, other, private house 2 being rebuilt, good 3 professional, amateurs 4 The couple, own 5 nervous, confident

Writing: report p.114

Aim:

- **to plan and write a report**

1 , **2** Discuss the questions with the whole class, and then ask them to work in pairs to brainstorm ideas for the report. They should each make a note of these ideas, as they will need them for their homework.

3 , **4** , **5** , **6** These can be done as a timed homework task.

ANSWERS

Ex. 1

1

1 You should begin a formal letter with *Dear Sir or Madam*, not a report.

2 You should use neutral or formal language.

3 You should give your own opinion in the conclusion.

4 You should use headings.

5 You should try to use vocabulary accurately.

2

Two things: say which room should be chosen and make suggestions for how the room could be made comfortable and attractive.

Exs. 3, 4 Sample answers

Introduction

This report is to ...

Location of the common room

It seems to me that the best place ...

Furniture and decoration

I suggest that there should be ... There could also be ...

Final recommendation

In my view, it would be best ...

Ex. 5 Sample answer

Suggestions for the new student common room

Introduction

This report is to recommend a room in the school for a student common room.

Location

The most popular choice is S1 next to the library. This room is big enough to be used as a common room and perfect for students studying in the library.

Furniture and decoration

Most of the furniture could come from the tables and chairs that are stored in S1 at present. Several students have also said that they have old furniture that they can give to the school.

The room needs painting, but students from the Art department have offered to paint during the summer holiday, if the school will pay for the paint. The floor is in good condition.

Additional facilities

There could also be a TV and video, as it is often not possible to watch any of the videos available in the library.

Recommendations

Therefore, I suggest that S1 be used as the student common room. A decision should be made quickly so the room can be ready for the new term.

(179 words)

See also: *NEW FCE Gold exam maximiser* p.75

UNIT 9 **Review** p.115

ANSWERS

Ex. 1

1 shoes, boots, trainers, slippers, socks

2 shirt, blouse, sweater, jacket, coat

3 football boots, trainers, pumps

4 sweater, winter coat, winter suit, scarf

5 suit and tie, ballgown, top hat

6 hat, scarf, hood

7 headscarf, skirt, sarong

Ex. 2

1 *had* a really late night 2 struck me *as*

3 got *to know* him 4 *social* life 5 *do* something

6 work *out* 7 *suits* you 8 keeping *up* with

9 *storage* space 10 burst into *tears*

Ex. 5

1 have 2 of 3 not 4 where 5 be 6 with

7 which 8 as 9 like 10 between 11 this

12 Although 13 goes 14 used 15 What

▶ Photocopiable Unit 9 test p.129

UNIT
10 Use your brain

Listening: sentence completion (Part 2) p.116

Aim:
- **to complete an exam-style sentence completion task**

Before your students look at this section, ask them to think of all the things that they have to remember every day. Give them a few examples to start them off (e.g. telephone numbers, email password, website addresses, cash machine card numbers, lesson times, etc.). *Do they find these easy to remember? Do they often forget any of these things?*

1

1, 2 Students discuss these in pairs. If any of them have ideas for remembering things, they can then share these with the rest of the class.

2 Allow your students a few moments to read through the task and the gapped sentences, and answer the questions. Discuss what kind of information they think is missing (e.g. number 2 must be an adjective or adjectival phrase).

3 This exercise focuses students' attention on the use of synonyms and paraphrasing in the listening task. The words they need to complete the sentences are all in the listening text, but the key words preceding them often aren't. For example, in number 3, the gapped sentence says *Dominic did not manage to complete his education.* The corresponding sentence on the recording is *He **started a course** at college, but he **dropped out** before finishing **the course**.*

4 Play the recording twice. Students complete the sentences, then compare their answers with a partner.

▶ Tapescript p.107

5 Students work in pairs to try the memory test.

ANSWERS

Ex. 2
1 No. He had to work out 'a way of training his memory.
2 He associates them with someone famous. He makes up stories.

---

3 He runs courses for people who want to improve their performance.

Ex. 3
b) 3   c) 1   d) 2   e) 5

Ex. 4
1 words   2 difficult   3 college   4 television
5 3,000   6 face   7 journey   8 casinos
9 athletes   10 age

See also: *NEW FCE Gold exam maximiser* p.76

Grammar 1: obligation, necessity and permission p.117

Aim:
- **to review/develop language of obligation, necessity and permission**

1 Do this as a whole class activity. Your students should decide together on the best answer for each sentence. Write these on the board. Give them a few moments to decide whether or not they want to change anything, and then review their answers.

2 Do this exercise as a cumulative collaborative task: with a partner, students discuss questions 1 and 2. They should then get together with another pair and check their answers, before doing questions 3 and 4 (in the same group of four). Finally, they should join with a third pair to compare everything so far, and to look at questions 5 and 6. When they have done this, write a selection of some of the words/expressions (e.g. *should, have to, mustn't*, etc.) on the board, and tell them to close their books. In their groups of six, they should try to use these words/expressions in sentences of their own.

3 For Exercise 3, you could add another option: *be a good English speaker.* This will not only help your students to review the target language, but will also provide an element of learner training.

4 Remind your students that contractions (e.g. *shouldn't, didn't*, etc.) count as two words in key word transformations.

5 This practises the target language in a personalised context. Do this as a weave drill (i.e. one student completes a sentence, then asks another student to do the same, and that student asks another one and so on: Student 1: 'This week I absolutely must tidy my room. What about you Concha?' Student 2: 'Oh well, this week I absolutely must practise some phrasal verbs. And you, Ahmad?' Student 3: 'Me? Well, this week I absolutely must call my father.' etc.

> **ANSWERS**
>
> **Ex. 1**
> 1 have to 2 I didn't have to 3 if we could
> 4 can't 5 don't have to 6 can 7 had to
>
> **Ex. 2**
> 1 c) as it expresses lack of obligation – a) and b) express lack of permission.
> 2 a) 2 b) 1 c) 3
> 3 d) as it expresses expresses obligation – a), b) and c) all express lack of obligation.
> 4 a) You *should* speak English in class.
>   b) You *shouldn't/should not* speak your own language in class.
> 5 b) – to express criticism of a past action, we use *shouldn't / should not have done*.
> 6 a) Probably not. b) Yes. c) Yes.
>
> **Ex. 4**
> 1 aren't allowed to 2 needn't have
> 3 aren't supposed to park 4 should have built
> 5 must carry 6 shouldn't have let him

See also: *NEW FCE Gold exam maximiser* p.76

Use of English: error correction (Part 4) p.119

Aim:
- **to complete an exam-style error correction task**

1 You could ask your students to close their books before doing this part of the exercise (so that they are not tempted to start reading the text straight away), and write the question *How can you improve your memory?* on the board. They can then discuss this in small groups before sharing their ideas with the rest of the class.
Students skim the text to see if their ideas are mentioned.

2 Before your students do this, remind them that there are between three and five lines which do not contain mistakes, and they should be particularly careful of extra words at the beginning and end of each line. Look at the

example 0 and ask them if they can tell you why *and* shouldn't be there (the next line begins with *which*). Your students should complete the task individually, then compare their answers with a partner.

> **ANSWERS**
>
> **Ex. 2**
> 1 the 2 as 3 ✓ 4 when 5 there 6 ✓
> 7 for 8 was 9 it 10 myself 11 ✓ 12 what
> 13 on 14 with 15 making

Vocabulary 1: expressions with *mind* p.119

Aim:
- **to focus on idiomatic language**

Before your students look at this section, write *mind* on the board, and ask them if they know of any expressions that use this word. (It is a very common word – there are at least 70 expressions that use it!)
Your students might like to make a note of the difference between *I don't mind* and *I don't care*. The first suggests that the speaker is fairly easy-going about something ('Would you like to go to the cinema or to the pub?' 'Oh, I don't mind. Either.'). The second suggests that the speaker is not interested, and can sound a bit rude ('Shall we go to the beach this afternoon?' 'I don't care.'). Students sometimes use *I don't care* when they really mean *I don't mind*.

1 Students work in pairs to match the sentences. Then tell them to close their books. Read out sentences 1–8, and ask them to respond using one of the expressions a)–h).

2 In their pairs, students take it in turns to ask and answer the questions. They should to keep talking for about four minutes. When they have finished, they could look in their dictionaries for other examples using *mind*.

> **ANSWERS**
>
> **Ex. 1**
> 1 g) 2 e) 3 a) 4 h) 5 b) 6 d) 7 c) 8 f)

See also: *NEW FCE Gold exam maximiser* p.77

Reading: multiple-choice questions (Part 2) p.120

Aims:
- **to complete an exam-style reading task**
- **to focus on word formation**

1 Your students should discuss the question in pairs, and this can then be extended to include the whole class. This could produce some interesting discussion (e.g. a lot of people have a successful career without being intelligent, and being intelligent does not necessarily help you to make friends). *Can they give any other examples of what an intelligent person is or can do? Do they think that looks are more important than intelligence?*

2 After they have read the beginning of the article and answered the question, ask your students to quickly skim the rest of the text for its general meaning.

> **Teaching tips and ideas**
>
> After your students have skimmed the text, tell them to close their books. Ask them to work in pairs, and on a piece of paper to write:
>
> 1 Five nouns that were in the text.
>
> 2 Five verbs that were in the text.
>
> 3 Five adjectives that were in the text.
>
> They should then check to see if the words they chose are there. This activity makes students aware of how much information they are taking in, even when reading a text very quickly. It therefore provides them with an example of why skimming a text before answering any questions is a useful technique.

3 Your students should do this individually. Remind them that they are looking for synonyms and parallel phrases in the text, and they should be careful of distracters which may fool them into thinking an answer is correct. You could do number 1 as an example with them, and ask why C is the correct answer (*improve the intelligence* in option C matches *boosting children's IQs* in the first paragraph of the text).

4 Before your students change the words, tell them to work in pairs and discuss what kind of word is missing from each gap. If it is a noun, is it countable or uncountable? If it is countable, is it singular or plural?
You could focus on sentence 2 and extend this into a whole class discussion; in what ways can modern life be stressful? In what ways can it be stimulating?

5 Students enjoy doing puzzles like these. Ask your students if they know of any other examples that they could give to the rest of the class. They could even spend a few minutes devising an IQ question of their own and giving it to the rest of the class.

ANSWERS

Ex. 3

1 C (line 3: *computer games, television and the Internet have become key factors in boosting children's IQs*)

2 D (line 8: *Over the past two decades … researchers have found that IQ scores can give a good indication of what children's future exam results will be.*)

3 C (this refers to the whole idea in the previous section)

4 C (line 20: *young people are required to interact constantly with electronic gadgets and equipment.*)

5 A (line 30: *children's IQ scores varies according to the type of intelligence being tested … No one knows why this is the case.*)

6 D (line 46: *But a recent study found no reliable evidence*)

7 A (line 51: *requires positive qualities such as perseverance*)

Ex. 4

1 accurately   2 complexity   3 popularity
4 aggressive   5 imagination   6 groundless

See also: *NEW FCE Gold exam maximiser* p.78

Grammar 2: *it is, there is* p.122

Aims:

- **to focus on the different uses if *it is* and *there is***
- **to use the target language to describe popular indoor games**

1

1 Students work in pairs and complete the exercise in their book.

2 Your students should complete the rules before looking at the **Grammar reference**. They should then check their answers to Exercise 1.1. When they have done this, tell them to close their books again, and read the sentences in Exercise 1.1 to them again. This time they must identify **and** correct the mistakes.

2 Briefly ask your students if they know the games in the photos (Scrabble, backgammon and Monopoly). *Can they name any other games or activities of this type that people play?* In small groups, they then complete the descriptions of different games using *it* or *there*.

3 This personalises the theme of this section. Students discuss in pairs or small groups.

4 As an alternative to giving their description to another student, they could read out their description to the rest of the class, who have to decide what the game is.

ANSWERS

Ex. 1

1
1 *It's* going to be   2 *There's* no need   3 Correct.
4 *There* once used to be   5 *It* was   6 Correct.
7 *There's* no point   8 Correct.   9 *There* is no charge   10 *It's* not worth

2
A there   B it   C it

Ex. 2
A 1 It   2 There   3 It   4 it
(Chess)
B 1 it   2 there   3 It   4 There   5 there
(Paper, scissors, stone)
C 1 There   2 It   3 there   4 It
(Crossword puzzle)

See also: *NEW FCE Gold exam maximiser* p.79

Vocabulary 2: education p.123

Aims:
• **to focus on some commonly confused words connected with education**
• **to talk about personal experience of education**

Before your students look at this section, write the word *education* in the middle of the board, and ask your students to brainstorm as many words as they know connected with this subject. They should try to categorise these words under sub-headings, so that you can build up a spidergram on the board. Possible subheadings might include: types of educational institute (e.g. *primary school, state school*); subjects; types of lesson (e.g. *lecture, seminar*); types of teacher (e.g. *lecturer, tutor*); common verbs (e.g. *enrol, register*); exam verbs (e.g. *pass, fail, sit, cheat*); miscellaneous (e.g. *uniform, play truant*). With a good class, you will probably fill up most of the board.

1 This exercise focuses on some words that students sometimes confuse. Ask your students to do this individually, then compare their answers with a partner, using a dictionary to check for meaning.

2 In their same pairs, students discuss the questions. They should try to give as much information as possible. For example, for the second question, they should say **why** they liked/disliked the subjects. For the third question they could focus on an actual exam they have done and what happened before/during/after they did it. You could also give them the

clichéd expression *'School days are the happiest days of your life.'* and ask if they agree or disagree with this.

3

1, 2 Before your students try to put the words in the correct place, ask them to focus on those words and ask one another what they mean. This exercise is useful, as it shows that it is difficult to understand words when they are taken out of their direct context. When seen in context, however, the meaning can usually be deduced without having to refer to a dictionary.

4 Students work in pairs or small groups to match the phrasal verbs with their meanings. Ask them if they can think of any other phrasal verbs that could connected to education (e.g. to **get down to** work, to **catch up with** work you have missed, etc.).

5 Students discuss the questions in groups, then feed back their ideas to the class.

ANSWERS

Ex. 1
1 primary   2 classes   3 teachers   4 subjects
5 marks   6 teach   7 revising   8 took   9 passed
10 retake   11 course   12 studying

Ex. 3
Archaeology: 1 courses   2 modules   3 lectures
4 seminars   5 field trips   6 examinations
Graphic Design: 1 practical   2 coursework
3 placement   4 projects   5 continuous assessment

Ex. 4
1 e)   2 f)   3 a)   4 c)   5 b)   6 d)

▶ Photocopiable activity 10A *Phrasal verbs bingo* p.178
See also: *NEW FCE Gold exam maximiser* p.81

Reading 2: multiple matching (Part 1) p.124

Aims:
• **to practise an exam-style reading task**
• **to focus on useful expressions in the text**

1 Before your students look at this section, ask them for their ideas on the best ways to study effectively. They then read the advice in Exercise 1 and compare their ideas.

2 Allow students about three minutes to skim the text. The text is humorous. Ask your students if they can recognise the style used here. *Is it a serious article giving advice? Is it a serious warning about the dangers of not studying properly? Is it humorous and/or ironic? How can they tell?*

3   Allow your students about 10–15 minutes for this. You could begin by looking at the first paragraph with them, and asking why H is the answer (the words 'carefully organises everything … everything in place … adjusts' refers to tidy and workspace in heading H).

Alternatively, divide the class into seven groups and give each group one of the paragraphs in the text. They should read their paragraph more carefully, and think of a suitable title for it – the title should summarise in a few words what the paragraph is about. They can then compare their ideas with the headings in Exercise 3. Are any of them similar?

4   Exercise 4 focuses on collocations and idiomatic expressions in the text. Students can do this individually or in pairs.

5 , **6**   You could develop the discussion into a class survey: the Top Ten tips for being an effective student. They can work in small groups to think of some useful tips, and write these up in complete sentences, either using imperatives as in the examples, or modals and other language of advice (You should … , It is important to… , Above all, you should never… , etc.). They can then share their ideas with the rest of the class, who can choose the best pieces of advice. Write these on the board.

ANSWERS

Ex. 2
1 All of it. It doesn't work because he uses each piece of advice as an excuse for not getting down to doing any work.

Ex. 3
1 F   2 C   3 E   4 G   5 D   6 A

Ex. 4
1 give myself *time*   2 plan for *a break*
3 leaf *through* the pages   4 *get* down to
5 *remove* an obstacle to studying
6 interfere *with* my concentration
7 get down to the task *in/at* hand
8 *fulfil* your social commitments

Exam focus
Paper 5 Speaking: collaborative task/discussion (Parts 3 and 4) p.126

Aims:
- **to present and practise a procedure for Paper 5, Parts 3 and 4**
- **to focus on the importance of interaction in the Speaking test**

Take your students through the **About the exam** and **Procedure** sections in the usual way.

1   When discussing the candidates' performance, your students should remember that interaction is one of the criteria on which they are graded.

▶ Tapescript p.107

Exam information

Students should be aware that if they don't understand or don't hear the examiner's instructions, they can ask him/her to repeat them. Expressions such as *I'm sorry, could you repeat that?*, *I'm afraid I didn't catch all of that*, *What was the second bit again?* are all acceptable. *What?* or *Eh?* should be avoided!

---

2   This provides more simulated practice, with one of the students role-playing the examiner. If possible, arrange the class so that students are working with classmates that they don't normally work with. Do the exercise twice, with new students in each group the second time they do it.

3   Students discuss this in their final group of three. The 'candidates' should say how they felt they did, before the 'examiner' gives his/her comments.

ANSWERS

Ex. 1
1 See tapescript on page 107.
2
1 Martin   2   Agna

Writing: article p.126
Aim:
- **to plan and write an article**

Before your students look at this section, briefly review the main points about writing an article. *What register should they use? What can they do to make their article more interesting?*

1 , **2**   After students have worked individually to read the task and answer the questions, you could guide them through the stages of planning, i.e. brainstorming, organising, thinking of a good introduction, writing the article, adding a good conclusion and checking the work afterwards. Write these up in point form on the board.
The plan should take them about ten minutes. They can compare their plan with a partner, and possibly borrow ideas.

3   The mistakes in this exercise are fairly small, possibly caused by carelessness rather than not knowing the correct structures. In many cases, it is an accumulation of small mistakes that cause a student to lose marks in the FCE, highlighting the importance of carefully checking their writing when they have finished it.

4   Students write their article for homework. As a possible follow-on in the next lesson, they could work in pairs to look at each other's work and comment on it.

ANSWERS

Ex. 1
1 Other students.
2 It can be quite informal as this is for young people.
3 Two: favourite ways of studying; things that help you to learn.
4 Personal information.

Ex. 3
1 vary *the* way
2 with other *people*, rather than *to study* alone
3 When we *discuss* ideas together
4 If I *am studying*/if I *study* … feel *relaxed*.
5 We *don't* need to … to see my *mistakes* and *correct them*.

Ex. 4 Sample answer
What are the best ways to learn?

When people think of studying, what's the first word that comes into their heads? Boring? Maybe they had a bad experience at school. But you know, studying doesn't have to be boring – there are lots of fun ways to learn! Here are a few ideas.
I find I can remember things if I've seen them written down. That's why, when I learn an interesting fact, I take a big piece of paper and then write it in big colourful letters and put it on my wall. When I need to remember, I just close my eyes and I can picture the piece of paper.
If I'm trying to learn a language, I like to listen to a radio programme in that language. I can do this while I'm cleaning my room. I don't have to concentrate 100 per cent, but I still find I can follow what's happening.
So you see, you can look and learn, you can listen and learn or you can find your own way, but don't let anyone tell you that studying is boring.

(179 words)

▶ Photocopiable activity 10B *Which writing task?* p.180
See also: *NEW FCE Gold exam maximiser* p.82

UNITS 6 – 10 Progress test p.127

ANSWERS

Ex. 1
1 recharging   2 journalists   3 make   4 tells lies
5 say bad things   6 what you look like
7 dropped out of   8 equipment   9 facilities
10 spectacular   11 carried out   12 supportive
13 confident   14 make up my mind
15 inaccurate

Ex. 2
1 to   2 with   3 been   4 they   5 have   6 it
7 in   8 will   9 have   10 to   11 has   12 were
13 which   14 to   15 for

Ex. 3
1 D   2 D   3 A   4 C   5 B   6 C   7 A   8 D
9 A   10 B   11 C   12 A   13 D   14 A   15 C

Ex. 4
16 themselves   17 by   18 its   19 to   20 over
21 in   22 someone / somebody / anyone / anybody
23 up   24 than   25 only / just   26 the   27 due
28 well   29 there   30 as

Ex. 5
31 to give up   32 made a big impression on
33 is capable of doing well   34 (really) wish I could
35 been a rise in   36 catches on to
37 you must have passed   38 don't need to
39 am getting used to it   40 was worn by

Ex. 6
41 this   42 is   43 only   44 ✓   45 ✓
46 which   47 they   48 by   49 a   50 ✓   51 to
52 ✓   53 one   54 about   55 such

Ex. 7
56 practical   57 difficulty   58 easily   59 healthy
60 artistic   61 creative   62 activities
63 thought   64 unusual   65 memorize

▶ Photocopiable Progress test 2 (Units 6–10) p.131

UNIT
11 Hard at work

Speaking 1 p.130

Aim:
- **to discuss the qualities that are needed for different jobs**

1, **2** Before your students do the quiz, ask them to read through the questions and answer choices, underline any words they don't understand and decide if they can work out what they might mean from the context.
Students do the quiz in pairs – they should take it in turns to ask and answer the questions – before working out their score and looking at the key on page 190.

3 Explain that students should use the information they learned about themselves in the Key to the quiz to help them do this exercise. You could also review some nouns that express the qualities needed for certain types of jobs (e.g. *commitment, energy, enthusiasm, ruthlessness, courage, creativity*, etc.).

Exam focus

Paper 4 Listening: multiple matching (Part 3) p.131

Aim:
- **to present and practise a procedure for a Paper 4, Part 3 task**

1 Before your students look at the task, you could discuss the advantages and disadvantages of living and working in a big city (e.g. *There is more crime in big cities, there are better job opportunities*, etc.). This could be extended to talk about the advantages and disadvantages of living in the *countryside*.
Note: The photo shows two Japanese girls in Tokyo, who have fallen asleep over their lunch in a fast food restaurant.
1 Before you play the recording, ask your students to read through the list of options and underline the key words. Ask your class if they can think of any words or expressions they might expect to hear on the recording that correspond to the options (e.g. for A *It's easy to travel around the city I live in*, words and expressions might include: *public transport, bus, train, underground, from one place to another, get from A to B, simple, good, excellent*, etc.). Remind them that they are unlikely to hear the actual words that are in the list – they will need to

listen for synonyms and parallel phrases instead. Play the recording twice, and then ask your students to compare their answers with a partner. What did they hear on the recording that corresponded to the list of options?

▶ Tapescript p.107

Sentences 1–7 contain idioms and other expressions connected with work. Focus on number 3 and ask your students what perks they would like to have in a job. Also look at number 7 and ask them to think of things that they could do in a big city at various times of the day.

3
1, 2 Tell your students to choose two of the people, and then play the recording again. Your students should complete their notes, then work with a partner to compare ideas.

4 This personalises the theme of this section. Do this as a whole class discussion, or students can work in small groups.

ANSWERS

Ex. 1
1 C   2 B   3 F   4 A   5 E

Ex. 2
1 c)   2 f)   3 a)   4 g)   5 d)   6 b)   7 e)

See also: *NEW FCE Gold exam maximiser* p.83

Vocabulary 1: employment p.132

Aim:
- **to focus on words and expressions related to work**

Before your students look at this section, ask them if any of them have ever applied for jobs. *What did they do when they applied? What were the different stages they went through?* Write any key words or expressions on the board. If your students are too young to have had any work experience, ask them what they would have to do if they found a job they wanted to apply for.

1
1 Students work in pairs to put the sentences in the correct order. When they have done this, ask them to highlight

any words they are not sure of, and to ask you what they mean. Then tell them to close their books, and read the sentences out to them in the correct order, leaving gaps for some of the key words and expressions. Can they remember what these are? (E.g. *You should enclose an up-to-date _____ with your letter.*)

2 Students can do this in pairs or small groups. Question 2 provides an opportunity to review modals and other language of obligation and prohibition (e.g. *You must arrive on time. You shouldn't talk too much. It's a good idea to prepare a list of questions to ask the interviewer.* Etc.).

2 Students can work in small groups to add other ideas to this list, then discuss which they think are the most important, and why.

3 Do this as a whole class discussion. The questions here provide plenty of scope for discussion, so you might like to focus on just one or two of them (questions 2 and 4 in particular could promote a lot of discussion and debate).

ANSWERS

Ex. 1

1 Look at jobs advertised in the newspaper ...
2 If you decide you want to apply, write ...
3 You should enclose ...
4 Make sure it includes ...
5 Send off your letter or application form ...
6 Once you get an interview, it's up to you!

See also: *NEW FCE Gold exam maximiser p.83*

Grammar 1: ability and possibility p.132

Aim:

- **to focus on modals to talk about ability and possibility**

A lot of students work part-time to support themselves or their studies. In Britain, most students take holiday jobs. Ask your students if this is the same in their countries. *If they work, what sorts of jobs do students do?*

1 , **2** The extract in Exercise 1 presents the modal verbs in context. Exercise 2.1 focuses students' attention on the modal verbs as they complete the notes. Students work individually to do these, then discuss Exercise 2.2. in small groups.

3 Check your students' answers to Exercise 3.1. Then ask them to write their own paragraph and check it carefully for mistakes. When they have done this, collect their work and read each passage out to the rest of the class (don't

emphasise any language mistakes – focus instead on the ideas and issues that the students raise). Ask the class to decide who wrote which passage. Pick up on any interesting points that are raised and extend these into a whole class discussion.

4 After your students have completed Exercise 4, ask them to look at the **Grammar reference** and check their answers. Discuss the answers as a class.

5

1, 2 Students discuss these in groups. They could also compile a list of Top Ten life skills that are essential in order to do well in life, and put these in descending order. As a class, they can then decide on the Top Five life skills, and explain why they are so important.

6 When your students do this exercise, they should pay particular attention to the tense of the first sentence, and make sure that their completed second sentence refers to the same time period.

ANSWERS

Ex. 1
The issue of students working part-time.

Ex. 2
In favour: Rudy, Andrew, Ahmad
Against: Fernando, Daeho-Choi

Ex. 3
1 can   **2** should be able to   **3** can't   **4** have to be able to

Ex. 4
   1 both possible; could (after *if*)
   2 won't be able to (*if* + present + future)
   3 both possible (*was able to* suggests a sense of achievement)
   4 both possible (both suggest difficulty/achievement)
   5 managed to (*could* is not used for a specific situation in the past)
   6 both possible (*couldn't*, i.e. the negative form is used for a specific situation in the past)
   7 could have become (unfulfilled ability in the past)
   8 couldn't have helped (before *if I'd*)
   9 can (general behaviour)
   10 could (typical behaviour in the past)

Ex. 5
1 could swim better than   **2** you'll / you will be able to   **3** could have helped me   **4** I could speak
5 didn't succeed in getting   **6** could be
7 was able to drive   **8** manage to catch

See also: *NEW FCE Gold exam maximiser p.85*

Reading: multiple matching (Part 1) p.134

Aim:

• **to do an exam-style multiple matching task**

1, **2** If your students do not know the story of Nick Leeson, this exercise could promote a lot of lively discussion using modals and other expressions of deduction (e.g. *He can't be a murderer because he doesn't look dangerous. He could be a con man because he looks friendly and honest.* etc.).

Background information

Nick Leeson was a trader for Barings Bank, a very old, established British family bank. He borrowed large amounts of money from the bank in order to invest in shares. He lost all the money, but kept this secret from his employers. Eventually the bank discovered what had happened, but by then it was too late, and Barings went bankrupt.

3 Before your students choose their headings, look at the example H, and ask them why this is the correct answer (Leeson got a job in a bank when *the world of high finance was doing well*, and *the City of London was the place to be* – he was in the *right place* at the *right time*).
Working individually, students complete the task, then compare their answers with a partner.

4 Do this as whole class discussion. Ask your students what punishment they think would be suitable.

5 Your students should try to complete the phrases without looking at the text, then check the text for the correct answers. Focus on one or two of the phrasal verbs in this exercise, and ask your students if they can think of any other phrasal verbs that use the same main verb.

ANSWERS

Ex. 1
1 He worked in a bank as a trader.
2 He had secretly invested a large amount of the bank's money and lost it all.

Ex. 3
1 F 2 D 3 G 4 B 5 E 6 A

Ex. 5
1 get 2 make 3 work 4 carry 5 run
6 break 7 turn 8 amount

See also: *NEW FCE Gold exam maximiser* p.86

Grammar 2: conditionals (2) p.135

Aim:

• **to focus on mixed conditionals and conjunctions**

1 These sentences introduce the idea of mixed conditionals. Your students should be familiar with the classic Type 2 and 3 conditionals), but may be less familiar with the use of the clauses in (a), (b), (e) and (f).
After your students have decided on the present/past aspects of these sentences, concept check their understanding by asking questions, e.g. for 1(a): *'Did Leeson lose £800 million?'* *'Yes he did.'* *'Is he still married to Lisa?'* *'No, he isn't.'* *'Why isn't he married to her now?'* *'Because he lost £800 million and went to prison.'* etc.

2
1, 2 Do number 1(c) with your students first, then let them work in pairs. (We know that 1 is past because it says *last year*, and we know that c) is present because it uses the present continuous.

3
1 Point out to your students that the sentences have time indicators (e.g. *last month, that Ann told me about*) that will affect the tense of the verb they choose in the main clause.
2 Students can work in small groups to discuss these. They should try to use both positive (*If I had …*) and negative (*If I hadn't …*) conditional clauses. Remind them that the conditional clause can also come in the second part of the sentence (*I wouldn't be learning English now if I'd been born in Australia.*) – the first clause of a conditional sentence is the part that the speaker considers most important.

4 *Unless* has the same meaning as *if not*. Other conditional conjunctions are stronger or more formal than *if*. *In case* suggests an unlikely situation. *Providing* is the same as *provided (that)*. Your students should use a dictionary to check how these are used, and/or look at the **Grammar reference** on pages 194–5.

5 Students work individually to complete the exercise, then compare their answers with a partner. Note that sometimes more than one option is possible.

6
1, 2 With the same partner, students unjumble the tips, and then think of some of their own. The main clause of their sentences should include an imperative, as in the examples.

ANSWERS

Ex. 1
1 (a) present   (b) present   (c) past
2 (d) present   (e) past   (f) past   (g) present

Ex. 2
1 c) past + present
2 f) past + past
3 a) past to present + future
4 d) present + past
5 b) past + present
6 g) future + present
7 e) past + future

Ex. 3
1 hadn't spent / would be able to
2 would be / had joined
3 was/were / would have risen
4 wasn't/weren't / would have asked

Ex. 4
1 unless   2 as long as   3 in case
4 on condition that   5 providing   6 even if

Ex. 5
1 unless / paid for
2 as long as/on condition that/providing
  that/provided that / promise
3 even if / had to   4 in case / lock
5 if / was raised 6 in case / don't accept

Ex. 6
1 Don't invest in shares unless you are prepared to
  take risks.
2 Never wear jeans to an interview if you want the
  job.
3 Don't carry lots of cash around with you in case
  you get robbed.
4 Never let anyone know your cashpoint PIN even
  if you trust them completely.

▶ Photocopiable activity 11A *Conditional connections* p.181
See also: *NEW FCE Gold exam maximiser* p.87

Vocabulary 2: numbers and money p.136

Aims:
• **to practise saying numbers**
• **to review vocabulary connected with money**

1

1, 2 Working in small groups, students discuss how to say
   these numbers. Ask them for their answers, but do not
   correct them at this stage.
3 Play the recording, stopping it after each number, and
   chorus-drill the numbers with your students.

▶ Tapescript p.108

Note that the shortened use of dates (23.12.05) differs
from country to country. In Britain, the date comes first,
then the month and then the year. In the USA, the month
comes first, then the date and then the year.
4 Play the recording, stopping it after each sentence to let
  your students decide how to write the number. They can
  discuss this in pairs.

2   Before your students look at this exercise, ask them to
brainstorm words connected with money. Write these on the
board, dividing them into groups of nouns, verbs and
adjectives. Then ask them to decide which of the words on
the board they might expect to see/hear in an advertisement
for a bank.
1, 2 Working in pairs, students complete the text in Exercise
   2.1 and discuss the questions in Exercise 2.2.

3   In the same pairs, students identify the odd one out.
They can then use the words that don't belong in sentences
of their own.

4   Do this as a quick game. Divide your class into small
groups, and ask each group in turn to choose a preposition
for each sentence. Award the groups 1 point for each correct
preposition they identify.

5   Students discuss the questions in small groups, before
it is extended to include the whole class. You could also teach
your class the expression *(Love of) money is the root of all
evil*. Ask them if they agree with this.

ANSWERS

Ex. 1
2
1 j)   2 d)   3 h)   4 f)   5 i)   6 e)   7 b)   8 k)
9 l)   10 a)   11 g)   12 c)
4
1 90 kph   2 0777 843 1905   3 5.15 p.m.
4 8 °C   5 €120,000   6 15/02/04

Ex. 2
1 debit card   2 cash points   3 credit card
4 statement   5 overdraft   6 foreign currency
7 travellers cheques   8 commission   9 cheques
10 current   11 deposit   12 savings   13 Interest

Ex. 3
1 receipt   2 tip   3 win   4 gain   5 worth
6 withdraw/pay for   7 cash   8 receive

Ex. 4
1 on   2 to   3 into   4 in   5 from   6 to

See also: *NEW FCE Gold exam maximiser* p.88

Listening 2: multiple choice (Part 4) p.138

Aim:

- **to complete an exam-style Paper 4, Part 4 listening task**

1   As an alternative to working in pairs, students could write their wish list on a piece of paper, and give it to you. Read these out to the class and see if they can decide who the lists belong to.

2, **3**   Allow your students a few minutes to read through the questions and underline the key words. Play the recording to the point where Ed says '… *people with a lot less money.*' and discuss the best answer for question 1. This can be done by a process of elimination (the first two options are not true, so the third option must be correct. This is confirmed when Ed says that having more money is not going to make a big difference to rich people. In other words, rich people do not become much happier with more money). Play the rest of the recording without stopping, and then let your students compare their answers with each other, explaining why they chose them.

▶ Tapescript p.108

ANSWERS

Ex. 2

1 C   2 B   3 A   4 B   5 B   6 C   7 A

Use of English: open cloze (Part 2) p.138

Aim:

- **to complete an exam-style open cloze task**

Before your students do this task, remind them that sometimes more than one answer may be possible but they should only give **one** of these.
Allow your students about 10–12 minutes to complete this. They should skim the text for general meaning first before attempting to fill in the gaps.

ANSWERS

1 with   **2** in / during   **3** why   **4** Apart   **5** more
6 it   **7** that / which   **8** into   **9** instead   **10** as
11 though   **12** a   **13** where   **14** ago   **15** the

---

Exam focus

Paper 5 Speaking: a complete test p.139

Aim:

- **to practise a complete FCE Speaking test**

By this stage of the course, your students should be familiar with the individual sections of the Speaking test. This is the first time that they will get the chance to do a complete test. This is very much a 'workshop' session, where you will be playing the role of facilitator and monitor rather than teacher. You should allow at least an hour to do everything (you may need to carry it over to your next lesson).

1, **2**   Guide your students through Exercises 1 and 2, focusing in particular on the interaction between the two students on the recording. Ask them to suggest some useful ways of increasing the chance of a better grade in the speaking test that are not specifically language-oriented, e.g. by working **with** their partner, asking questions, offering ideas, showing that they are listening, appropriate use of paralanguage (smiling, nodding/shaking their head, maintaining eye contact, etc.).

▶ Tapescript p.108

3   While your students are doing the tasks, monitor the groups to make sure they are doing it correctly. Gently correct any bad habits that may have a negative effect (e.g. mumbling, covering the mouth, talking to the table, repetitive phrases such as *you know*, etc.). Make sure during the 'examiner's' feedback that their comments are encouraging rather than critical. If you give any feedback yourself at the end of the session, emphasise the good points rather than the bad points.

ANSWERS

Ex. 2

grammar and vocabulary: satisfactory – variety of errors but not impeding communication.
pronunciation: good – errors but not impeding communication.
organisation: good – all points covered.
intereaction: good – asks questions (Athene). Satisfactory – keeps conversation going, but interrupts (Stefan).

▶ Photocopiable activity 11B *Useful expressions* p.182

Writing: letter of application p.140

Aim:

- **to plan and write a formal letter of application**

1 Working individually, students read the task and highlight key words, then work with a partner to answer the questions which follow it.

2 , **3** , **4** Let your students read though the letter and highlight anything that they think is bad about it, before discussing it with their partner and completing Exercises 3 and 4.

You should also ask them if there is anything **good** about it (e.g. it opens and closes well – *Dear Sir or Madam, Yours faithfully* – it is divided into paragraphs, and some of the information **would** be relevant – the writer says what she is doing now, why she wants to work on the course and when she is available).

5 Your students should work individually to write their plan – about ten minutes. Monitor their work, offering ideas if they seem unsure what information to include and where to put it in the letter, then ask them to compare their plans with a partner. Can their partner offer any suggestions or advice?

6 , **7** Students write the letter for homework.

ANSWERS

Ex. 1

1 Organising sports and social activities for a group of young people.

2 Telling us about yourself and saying why you think you would be a suitable person for the job.

3 Essential: able to speak English; interested in sports; experience of being with young people; interested in travel; enjoys being with people

Ex. 2

1 No – it doesn't answer both parts of the task.

Exs. 3, 4

2 ✗ (It doesn't specify **why** the writer thinks they would be suitable for the job.)

3 ✗ (It would be very clear to an examiner that the letter wasn't planned, and would fail in the exam. A more organised sequence would be: reason for writing; where you saw the advert; relevant information about yourself; relevant experience; reason why you would like the job; availability.)

4 ✗ (It is too informal; contractions, e.g. *I'm*, are not appropriate in a formal letter; the letter should be signed with the full name.)

5 ✗ (*I am available* is appropriate, but not the use of a contraction, *I'm*.)

6 ✓

7 ✗ (small mistakes: I *am writing*; I *have* just finished.)

8 ✗ (98 instead of 120–180 words.)

9 ✗ (not enough information to make a decision.)

Ex. 6 Sample answer

Dear Sir or Madam

I am writing to apply for one of the positions on the International Adventure Course advertised in yesterday's Daily Post.

I am eighteen years old and live in Spain. I have just finished my secondary education and in October I will be starting a university course in Business Administration. I have already studied English for six years and I like this subject very much.

I have quite a lot of experience of working with young people. I am the oldest of a family of five children, and in addition to this I have many younger cousins. I also enjoy sport and belong to our local sports centre as well as playing volleyball at school. In addition, I enjoy activities such as art and design, and I sing and play the guitar a little.

I would really enjoy the chance to use my English in Canada and to work in an international environment. I am available between July 13th and September 20th.

I look forward to hearing from you.

Yours faithfully
Antonia Martinez

(170 words)

See also: *NEW FCE Gold exam maximiser* p.89

Unit 11 Review p.141

ANSWERS

Ex. 1

1 could *have bought*   2 if I *could* / *was able to*

3 I *just managed to* catch it   4 *can* be bad

5 I *would* have   6 *unless*

7 providing that it *doesn't rain*   8 Even *if*

9 I *would be* fitter   10 *in case*

Ex. 3

1 D   2 B   3 A   4 B   5 D   6 C   7 B   8 A

Ex. 4

1 disgusting   2 dangerous   3 regulations

4 uncomfortable   5 boring   6 clearly

7 difference   8 imagination   9 decision

10 impossible

▶ Photocopiable Unit 11 test p.134

Reading 1 p.142

Aim:

• to read an extract from a novel for gist and detail

Background information

Rebecca is a novel by the British writer Daphne du Maurier. It tells the story of a shy young woman – we never learn her name – who marries an older man called Maxim de Winter. He had previously been married to Rebecca. Rebecca was extremely beautiful and popular. She drowned in a boating accident, but her body was not found. The young woman goes to live with Maxim in a beautiful old house by the sea. She is treated very badly by Maxim's housekeeper, Mrs Danvers. Mrs Danvers adored Rebecca, and hates Maxim's new wife. One day, Rebecca's boat is found, with her body inside it. Holes are found in the bottom of the boat. People begin to suspect that Maxim murdered Rebecca. The extract that the students are going to read takes place shortly after Rebecca's body has been discovered.

Du Maurier's novels *Rebecca*, *Jamaica Inn* and *The Birds* have all been made into films.

1   Discuss the film still as a class. This shows the *coroner's court*, where the extract students are going to read takes place. Pre-teach the words *inquest* and *coroner*, which are explained at the end of the extract, as understanding of the text largely relies on the students knowing these words.

2, **3**   Students quickly read the extract and answer the questions in Exercise 2. Check answers, then allow them about 5–7 minutes to read the extract in more detail and work in pairs or small groups to answer the questions in Exercise 3. Focus on question 1, and ask your students to highlight all the words and expressions that tell us how Maxim's wife feels.

4   Before your students discuss these questions, you might like to sum up what happens before the part they read. See the **Background information** box above.

ANSWERS

Ex. 2

1 Mr de Winter
2 Maxim's second wife
3 Maxim de Winter's first wife
4 The cause of death of Maxim de Winter's first wife

Ex. 3

1 Nervous: *a hurried, nervous meal ... I could not swallow ... It was a relief when ... my hands were very cold, my heart beating in a funny, jerky way ...*
2 Maxim de Winter has just given his evidence.
3 That it was an accident due to carelessness on Rebecca's part.
4 That someone had deliberately made three holes in it.
5 Maxim. The Coroner asks him about his relationship with his first wife.
6 Hot and faint – she's afraid of what might happen to Maxim.

Writing 1: making your writing more interesting p.143

Aim:

• to focus on ways of making a story more interesting to read

If you have a class set of the *Longman Language Activator*, bring these to class.

1   The numbers at the end of each question refer to the flagged paragraphs in the text where they will find their answers. Working individually, students look for the words, then compare their findings with a partner. Ask them to quickly brainstorm other words that they could use to add to their answers for questions 1, 2 and 3.

2

1 The verbs in the text give us a better idea of how something happens or how something is done. Ask your students to tell you in which situation they would *pace up and down*, or *slip into* (or *out of* a room). Can they think of any synonyms for these and other words in the text?

2 The words and expressions in 1–5 help to make the story more vivid. *We ate a hurried and nervous meal* gives us a far better idea of the situation than if we just said *We ate a meal.*

3

1, 2 When students have done this in pairs, and checked how the words are used in a dictionary, ask them to work in small groups to think of more words that could go under each general word.

4 This lets students practise the target language and some of the other ideas from this section. They should do this in pairs or small groups, and then read their completed story to the rest of the class.

ANSWERS

Ex. 1
1 hot, oppressive **2** white, dull **3** hot, stuffy
4 suffocated

Ex. 2
1
1 pace up and down **2** crept **3** paused
4 hammered **5** slumped **6** strike
2
1 meal **2** heart **3** boat **4** the holes in the
boat **5** the door and windows

Ex. 3
1
1 walk **2** eat **3** think **4** hit **5** breathe
6 look

Ex. 4 Sample answer
Maxim begged Frank to take me back home immediately, and so we left him in the courtroom. Frank drove very fast. For the first time since I had known him, he was at a loss for anything to say. That meant that he was very worried. Usually he was such a slow, careful driver, stopping at every crossroads, peering to right and left, blowing his horn at every bend in the road. Now he was driving incredibly fast.
When we finally arrived home, he left me at the front door and drove away at once, insisting that Maxim might need him. Wearily, I went upstairs and lay down on the bed. I kept thinking what people might say. 'Why should he get off? He murdered his wife – it's too late now. He will have to hang for it – that would serve him right. Let it be a warning to others.'

▶ Photocopiable activity 12A *Crossword race* p.183
See also: *NEW FCE Gold exam maximiser* p.90

Vocabulary 1: crime and punishment p.144

Aim:
• **to focus on some words connected with crime and punishment**

1 , **2** Treat this as a student-centred workshop. Set them a time limit of about 10–15 minutes for Exercise 1, and about eight minutes for Exercise 2. Monitor the groups to make sure that everyone is participating. When they have finished, ask them to close their book, and give them the definitions of some of the words. They should tell you what those words are.

3 Students work individually to complete the exercise, then compare their answers with a partner.

ANSWERS

Ex. 1
Criminals
arsonist blackmailer burglar forger hijacker
kidnapper mugger murderer pickpocket
shoplifter smuggler thief
Law courts
the accused/defendant defence
find innocent/guilty inquiry judge jury lawyer
prosecution trial verdict witness
Sentences and punishments
(release on) bail capital punishment
community service corporal punishment fine
prison sentence (put on) probation
suspended sentence

Ex. 2
1 A pickpocket; a mugger attacks people and steals their money.
2 A burglar; an arsonist sets fire to buildings.
3 A shoplifter; a hijacker takes over a plane or other form of transport.
4 A smuggler; a blackmailer finds out information about people and demands money to keep it secret.
5 The defendant; the judge decides how he should be punished at the end of the trial.
6 The prosecution lawyer; the defence lawyer tries to prove he is innocent.
7 The witness; the prosecution lawyer tries to prove the defendant is guilty.
8 The judge; the jury decides if someone is guilty or not guilty.
9 You can be released on bail; you may be given a suspended sentence after the verdict.
10 You will probably be put on probation; capital punishment is for murder, but not all countries allow it.

Ex. 3
1 robbed   2 stolen   3 burglary   4 make
5 suspect   6 give   7 pleaded   8 jury   9 convict
10 let off

See also: *NEW FCE Gold exam maximiser* p.90

Speaking p.145

Aim:
• **to discuss crimes and punishments**

1   Do this as a whole class discussion. Let them take control of the discussion, but make sure that everyone gets a chance to speak, and encourage/prompt students who are holding back.

2, **3**   The cases here are all examples of real crimes from Britain and the USA. Your students might find some of the punishments surprising, and there is plenty of scope here for a discussion/debate on different punishments for different crimes.

Listening 1: sentence completion (Part 2) p.145

Aim:
• **to do a sentence completion task**

This is a very entertaining listening passage which describes people who have tried to get compensation for incidents or accidents which are their own fault. Before you do this with your students, ask them if they have had, or have heard of someone who has had, an accident and claimed compensation. *What were the circumstances? Were they successful?*

1   After your students have read through the sentences, ask them what kind of word or words might be missing from each gap, and if they can think of any words that would fit and work in the context of the sentence.

2, **3**   Play the recording twice, and let your students compare their answers in pairs or small groups before discussing the questions in Exercise 3.

▶ Tapescript p.110

ANSWERS

Ex. 2
1 a coffee   2 leg   3 competition   4 garage
5 dog biscuits   6 own child   7 (front) teeth
8 (night)club   9 camper van / campervan
10 seventy / 70

See also: *NEW FCE Gold exam maximiser* p.91

Grammar 1: passives (2) p.146

Aim:
• **to focus on more advanced passive constructions**

1

1, 2 Students should work in pairs to complete the active sentences and find examples of the different constructions in Exercise 1.2. Ask them for their answers and write these on the board, then tell them to close their books. They can then work in small groups to change the sentences on the board back into the passive – give them the subject of the sentence in each case as a prompt (e.g. for number 1, write *He* on the board next to the active sentence already there).

2   Before your students do this exercise, ask them when we can omit the agent in passive sentences. This can be done when a) we don't know who the agent is, b) we don't need to know who the agent is, c) the agent has already been mentioned or d) the agent is obvious from the context of the sentence (e.g. *The man who robbed the bank was arrested last night* – we don't say *by the police* at the end because only the police can arrest someone, and therefore the agent is obvious from the context).
Ask your students to work in the same groups as in Exercise 1, and decide whether or not an agent is needed before they change the sentences to the passive. They should tell one another why or why not. They can then change the sentences to the passive.

3   These verbs are often used by newspapers and other media outlets when reporting stories – by not saying who the agent is, they cannot be accused of libel or misrepresentation. They are also useful when the writer wants to focus on the more important aspects of a story. In the sentences about Count St Germain, for example, we are interested in the count himself, and not in the people who reported, believed, said, etc., what he did.

4   When doing this exercise, tell your students to be particularly careful of the tense (newspapers mostly use the present perfect and the present simple, e.g. number 5 in Exercise 4 could be *are advised* or *have been advised*).

5   Ask your students to discuss the headlines in pairs and then work together to write their report, using some of the passive constructions in Exercise 5.2 (they can also add some of their own).

ANSWERS

Ex. 1
1
1 gave   2 read   3 telling   4 promoted
5 made   6 saw

2
verb + -*ing* form (gerund) = 2, 3
verb + perfect infinitive = 4
3
After *feel* and *see*, verb + infinitive with *to* is used in the passive, without *to* in the active.

Ex. 2
1 I hope to be chosen to play on the team.
2 I don't like being given lots of homework.
3 The defendant was awarded $1 m.
4 I can't remember ever being punished by my father.
5 He was heard to shout for help by several witnesses.
6 I hope I will be allowed to study abroad.
7 I was not very pleased that I was ordered/at being ordered to do jury duty.

Ex. 3
1 c) 2 f) 3 e) 4 g) 5 a) 6 d) 7 b)

Ex. 4
1 have been reported   2 are believed
3 has been suggested   4 is thought
5 are/have been advised

See also: *NEW FCE Gold exam maximiser* p.92

Listening 2: song p.147

Aim:
• **to listen for specific information**

Men in Black was a very popular science fiction/comedy film when it was released in 1997. The title song was a big hit around the world, especially with young people.

1
1, 2 Discuss the questions around the class, and ask your students if they have seen the film. *Did they enjoy it? What did they like about it? Do they like science fiction films? What is their favourite? What do they think is the appeal of such films?*

2 This is a rap song, and it can be difficult to understand the lyrics even for native speakers. Allow your students a few minutes to read through the lyrics, and ask you about any words or expressions they don't understand (e.g. *Ray Bans* – a brand of sunglasses; *yo* – yes, *ain't* – isn't, *right on* – all right/yes, *freezin' up all the flack* – dealing with all the criticism). They should then try to complete the lyrics using the words in the boxes.

3, **4**, **5** Play the song once and let your students decide on the two things the Men in Black ask people to do before extending the discussion to talk about crime prevention in Exercise 5. The lyrics to the last verse are

not printed. You could ask students to try to work them out themselves.

ANSWERS

Ex. 1
1 Tommy Lee Jones and Will Smith.
2 They are law enforcement officers, protecting the Earth from aliens.
3 To protect them from a special light which would make them lose their memory.
4 Tommy Lee Jones retires.

Ex. 2
1 dress 2 make 3 saw 4 see 5 gone
6 silence 7 shadow 8 list 9 fingerprints
10 back 11 enters 12 zoom 13 fill 14 talk
15 turn 16 only 17 worst 18 near
19 fearless

Ex. 4
a), c)

Exam focus

Paper 1 Reading: gapped text (Part 3) p.148

Aim:
• **to present and practise a procedure for the gapped text task**

Go through the **About the exam** and **Procedure** sections in the usual way.

1 Before your students look at this section, ask them to think about the town or city they live in, come from or are studying in. *Do they know any of its history? When was it founded? Why did people build a town there in the first place? What attracts people to a town or city?* (e.g. to work, to study, to be near family or friends, to get away from people elsewhere, etc.)? This is also discussed in Exercise 3 later in this section, so you might want to leave it until then. Your students should then look at the title and subheading, and discuss their ideas about the origins of city life.
Look at the example and ask them why I is the correct answer (the first paragraph tells us that people wandered the world or lived in tiny villages, and the third paragraph tells us that people gave up this lifestyle and began to live in cities. Therefore we need something that tells us about the sudden transition from one situation to another – *suddenly, all this changed … people started to build cities* gives us the answer.).
Working individually, students then complete the rest of the text (allow them about 10–12 minutes for this) before comparing their answers with a partner, and explaining why they chose them.

2, **3** Do these as an optional follow-on if you have time after students have completed the task.

4 This gap-fill task gives students a chance to recycle language encountered in the text. Students can do this individually and then compare their answers in pairs. Alternatively, it could be done as a game where students score points for guessing letters correctly.

ANSWERS

Ex. 1

1 C 2 G 3 E 4 H 5 A 6 F 7 D

Ex. 4

1 origins 2 remains 3 evidence 4 birth
5 proof

See also: *NEW FCE Gold exam maximiser* p.94

Vocabulary 2: nouns linked by *of* p.150

Aim:

• **to focus on/review collective nouns and collocations**

1

1, 2 After students have identified the word which does not belong, ask them to close their books, and then read out to them the words which **do** belong (e.g. *sheep, cattle,* etc.) in random order, and ask them to give you the word that works with it (e.g. a *flock* of sheep, a *herd* of cattle, etc.). They should then look at Exercise 2.2 and work with a partner to complete the sentences. You could ask them to cover up Exercise 2.1 before they do this.
Note that *a pack of lies* is idiomatic.

2 Students work individually to choose the correct words in Exercise 2.1, then work with a partner to correct the mistakes in Exercise 2.2. They should try to do this without referring back to Exercise 2.1.

ANSWERS

Ex. 1

1

1 papers 2 cowboys 3 dogs 4 apes
5 parcels 6 stones 7 information

2

1 collection/stamps 2 pack/lies 3 gang/thieves
4 panel/experts 5 bunch/flowers

Ex. 2

1

1 a pile 2 a row 3 a piece 4 a bar
5 a fragment 6 an item

2

1 *bar* of chocolate 2 a *block* of flats 3 in *rows*
4 *item* of clothing 5 *pile* of papers 6 *piece* of news

See also: *NEW FCE Gold exam maximiser* p.93

Grammar 2: *have/get something done* p.150

Aim:

• **to focus on the causative use of *get* and *have***

1 All the verbs must be in their past participle form. When your students have done the exercise, ask them if they can think of other things that they have done for them.

2 In addition to practising the causative *get*, this exercise also provides an opportunity to review modals and other expressions of advice (e.g. *You should/ought to … , You'd better … , Why don't you … , If I were you, I'd …* etc.). Students can do these in pairs before feeding back to the rest of the class.

3 Students work individually to put the questions in the correct order, then ask and answer the questions in pairs. They should try to give as much information as possible (e.g. *I had my purse stolen out of my rucksack a few years ago. I was on holiday in a small town on the coast, and was walking down the street when I felt … ,* etc.).

ANSWERS

Ex. 1

1 photocopied 2 painted 3 told 4 made
5 videoed 6 checked 7 framed 8 taken

Ex. 2 Sample answers

1 You'd better / You should get / have it cut.
2 You'd better get / have it fixed / replaced.
3 Why don't you get / have it developed?
4 If I were you, I'd get / have it cleaned.
5 You'd better get / have it checked / repaired / fixed / mended.
6 Why don't you get / have one taken?

Ex. 3

1 When did you last get your hair cut?
2 Have you had your photograph taken recently?
3 Have you ever had a tooth taken out?
4 When did you last get your eyes tested?
5 Have you ever had your hair coloured?
6 Would you ever get your nose pierced?

See also: *NEW FCE Gold exam maximiser* p.94

Use of English: multiple-choice cloze (Part 1) p.151

Aim:

• **to complete an exam-style multiple-choice task**

1, **2** Discuss the question in Exercise 1 with your students, then allow them about 12–15 minutes to choose the correct answers for the text.

ANSWERS

Ex. 1

The treasure was buried gold.

Ex. 2

1 D   2 B   3 D   4 A   5 C   6 C   7 D   8 B
9 D   10 C   11 A   12 C   13 B   14 D   15 C

Recently my grandmother bought a dog because she said she was lonely on her own. So I have decided I'm going to stop being afraid. Last week I went to visit my grandmother and I played with her dog. I had never felt so nervous in my life, but I knew that I had to do it.

(174 words)

▶ Photocopiable activity 12B *Key words risk 2* p.185
See also: *NEW FCE Gold exam maximiser* p.96

Writing 2: story p.151

Aims:
• **to plan and write a story**
• **to focus on interesting vocabulary**

As your students have already practised writing a story, and should by now be familiar with the process of doing an exam-style writing task, you could do this section as a workshop session. Divide your class into small groups, and let them work through Exercises 1, 2 and 3. They should **all** make notes. Allow them about 20–25 minutes to do all of this. For Exercise 5, they should work in small groups with a dictionary and, if available, a *Longman Language Activator*, to complete the tasks and finish the story.

As an alternative to doing the writing task in Exercise 6, students could write the story they planned in Exercises 1–3. They should do this for homework, making sure they check their work at the end.

ANSWERS

Ex. 1

1 students   2 Steve, a man/boy

Ex. 5

1
1 a)   2 b)   3 b)   4 b)   5 b)
2
1 aimlessly   2 oppressive   3 nervous
4 suddenly   5 frantically

Ex. 6 Sample answer

Ever since I was a little boy I have been afraid of dogs. I know that's quite common, but I'm not just afraid, I'm absolutely terrified of them.

It all started when I was two years old. I was playing in our garden when I heard crying. In the grass was a tiny puppy, staring at me. I picked it up to take it inside. Suddenly, from nowhere, a dog came running up to me and knocked me over, took the puppy and ran away.

Later, my mother explained that the dog was the puppy's mother and was just trying to protect her child. But it was no good, I refused to go near another dog.

UNIT 12 Review p.153

ANSWERS

Ex. 1

1 1 h)   2 f)   3 g)   4 j)   5 b)   6 l)   7 i)   8 k)
  9 e)   10 a)   11 c)   12 d)
2
A criminal commits a crime (1). The police arrest a suspect (9). The suspect and witnesses make statements (10). The judge may release the suspect on bail (5) before he stands trial (11).
The suspect pleads guilty or not guilty (2). Witnessses give evidence in court (6). The judge finds the suspect guilty (12) and convicts him of the crime (3), or finds him innocent. If he is guilty, the judge passes sentence (7). The judge may put the criminal on probation (8). If he is innocent, the judge lets him go free (4).

Ex. 2

1 with   2 off   3 into   4 over   5 up   6 in

Ex. 3

1 was made to feel   2 is said to have   3 have this tooth taken   4 is expected that   5 having my hair cut   6 weren't allowed to   7 to get this suit cleaned   8 discovery occurred   9 was built on   10 large/huge sums for

Ex. 4

1 great / fabulous   2 luxury / fantastic
3 beautiful   4 pleasant / friendly   5 delicious / tasty   6 wonderful / marvellous   7 thrilling / (an) exciting

▶ Photocopiable Unit 12 test p.136

UNIT
13 Natural wonders

Reading 1: multiple matching (Part 4) p.154

Aim:

- **to complete an exam-style multiple matching task**

Before your students look at this section, ask them if they have pets at home. *Do these animals have any unusual skills? Do they react differently to different people? Do your students think they can communicate with their pets? If so, in what way? Do they think that pets have a 'sixth sense'?* (E.g. they can tell when their owners are coming home, or know when something is wrong well before their owner does.)

1, **2** The discussion above will probably help your students to guess what the connection is between these animals. Allow them about 3–4 minutes to quickly read the text, and check their basic understanding by asking a few general questions, e.g. *How many animals are described? Where do/did they live? What do your students think is the most unusual case mentioned?*

3, **4** Focus attention on the example, and ask why it corresponds with paragraph C (*often in a different country = lengthy trips abroad*). Then allow them about 15 minutes to complete the task. They should do this individually, and then compare their answers with a partner, explaining why they chose them.

5 This exercise focuses on words and phrases that can be used to say something in another way. Once your students have found these, ask them to work in pairs and use them in sentences of their own.

6 This exercise can be extended in the same way as above. Ask your students if any of the phrasal verbs in the exercise can have more than one meaning (*run into* can also mean *to meet a friend or acquaintance by accident: I **ran into** Marie when I was out shopping.*).

7 This extends the theme of this section. Possible explanations could include the animal's sense of smell, or just coincidence.

ANSWERS

Ex. 1
They all have telepathic powers.

Ex. 3
1 B 2 D 3 A **4/5** B/E 6 B 7 A **8/9** B/C
10 E 11 D **12** A **13** E **14** B **15** E

Ex. 5
1 to humour 2 attached to 3 on one occasion
4 In his absence 5 all was well 6 ignored
7 couldn't take it any more 8 take time off
9 Occasionally

Ex. 6
1 looked after 2 grew up 3 deal with
4 run into 5 run around

See also: *NEW FCE Gold exam maximiser* p.100

Vocabulary 1: animals p.156

Aim:

- **to focus on nouns, verbs and idioms connected with animals**

1

1, 2 Working individually, using a dictionary if necessary, students complete the mind map in Exercise 1.1, then work with a partner to make mind maps for Exercise 1.2.

2 After your students have matched the sentence halves, ask them to think of other animals, and to work in pairs to write sentences about what they do, where they live, what you can do with them, etc.

3 After your students have worked out the meanings of the expressions in this exercise, you might like to ask them if they recognise or can work out the following expressions: *to take the bull by the horns/a little bird told me/a wolf in sheep's clothing /to do something at a snail's pace/to have butterflies in the stomach/to count your chickens before they've hatched/to be as stubborn as a mule/a white elephant/a bird in the hand is worth two in the bush.* You could then ask your students what the equivalents are in their own language.

ANSWERS

Ex. 1
1 DOG
Movement: bite, jump up, scratch
Parts of body: claw, fur, paw, tail
Sounds: bark, snarl
Where it lives: kennel

---

2 CAT
Movement: bite, jump up, scratch
Parts of the body: claw, fur, paw, tail
Sounds: miaow, purr
Where it lives: –
HORSE
Movement: bite, gallop,
Parts of the body: hoof, tail
Sounds: neigh
Where it lives: stable
BIRD
Movement: flutter, peck
Parts of the body: beak, feather, tail
Sounds: sing
Where it lives: cage, nest

Ex. 2
1 c) dog   2 e) bird   3 d) dog   4 a) cat/dog
5 f) dog   6 b) bird

Ex. 3
1 in a straight line   2 give help and protection to
3 a very complicated situation that causes a lot of
problems   4 The unpleasant situation in business
where people are constantly competing against
each other for success.   5 someone talks angrily
but would not behave violently   6 tell a secret,
possibly unintentionally

See also: *NEW FCE Gold exam maximiser* p.97

Speaking 1 p.156

Aim:
• **to discuss the topic of pets**

This extends the theme of this unit and is a topic that may
come up in Paper 5 of the exam.

1, **2** Students should discuss the questions in
groups of three. Allow them about ten minutes for this, then
extend it into a whole class discussion. Ask your students if
there is an animal they would really like to own, but probably
couldn't for practical or safety reasons. Alternatively, ask them
to write the kind of animal they would particularly like to
own, and the name they would give that animal, on a piece
of paper and hand it to you. Read these out and let your
class decide who chose which animal.

Exam focus

Paper 3 Use of English: multiple-choice cloze (Part 1) p.157

Aim:
• **to present and practise a procedure for Paper 3, Part 1**

Ask your students to read through the **About the exam** and
Procedure sections, then tell them to close their books and
tell you what they can remember.
Before your students do the task, ask them to look at the
picture of the dog and the title of the text. What do they
think the text will be about?
Allow them about two minutes to skim the text, then ask
them to close their books again. What can they remember
about the text?
Remind them that when they do the task, they should read
the whole sentence before choosing the words for each gap.

ANSWERS							
1 C	2 A	3 C	4 B	5 C	6 D	7 B	8 D
9 A	10 C	11 A	12 B	13 A	14 D	15 C	

Listening: sentence completion (Part 2) p.158

Aims:
• **to complete an exam-style task**
• **to role-play an interview with a famous conservationist**

Before your students look at this section, ask them if they
enjoy watching wildlife programmes on television. *Why? Why
not? Are there any television presenters in their country who
are famous for making wildlife programmes?*

1 Point out that the woman in the photo is Charlotte
Uhlenbroek. Students discuss the questions in small groups,
then feed back their ideas to the rest of the class.

2 Go through each sentence with your students, asking
them what kind of word is needed for each gap, and what
kind of information this word will give them. For example, in
sentence 1 we are told that Charlotte's mother is English. We
can therefore assume that the word in the gap is an adjective
that tells us the nationality of her father.

3 Play the recording twice while students complete the
missing information.

▶ Tapescript p.110

4 Do the discussion with the whole class. You could
extend this by asking your students if they have ever had any
bad/funny/unusual experiences with animals.

5 Before your students role-play the interview, ask them
if they have heard of Jane Goodall and why she is famous.

Background information

Dr Jane Goodall is considered to be the world's foremost authority on chimpanzees, and has been observing their behaviour in their natural environment for over 25 years. In 1977 she founded the Jane Goodall Institute for Wildlife Research. After they have done the role-play, your students might like to visit the Institute's website at www.janegoodall.org

Students work in pairs to role-play the interview. Student B's information is in note form, but they should try to answer using complete sentences, and making their English as natural as possible (e.g. childhood: *Well, I've always been interested in animals. I suppose it started when I was given a toy chimpanzee when I was two. Believe it or not, I've still got it.* etc). Your students should also face each other when doing this to encourage eye contact and more natural interaction.

ANSWERS

Ex. 2
1 Dutch 2 American 3 researcher 4 animal communication 5 friend 6 formal 7 killer bees 8 kicked 9 body language 10 pets

See also: *NEW FCE Gold exam maximiser* p.98

Grammar 1: *so, such, too, enough, very* p.158

Aim:
• **to review the use of intensifiers**

You could focus attention on the **Watch Out!** box before students do Exercise 1.

1 Ask your students to cover up the **Watch Out!** box and to complete the sentences individually before comparing their answers with a partner and then, if necessary, checking again with the rules in the **Grammar reference** section.

2 In their same pairs, students join the sentence halves together. In some cases, more than one possible combination is possible. If they choose a combination that is not in the answer key for this exercise, ask them to explain the situation they are referring to (e.g. *The day was so hot that I didn't want to go home. I was on the beach with my friends, and the thought of going back to my small apartment in the city didn't appeal to me at all.*).

3 Ask your students to do these in pairs or small groups, and then check their answers.

4 This exercise should be spoken rather than written, and students can discuss their ideas in small groups. Once they have discussed the four situations in the exercise, they should add some of their own ideas, using the adjectives in the box or some of their own choosing.

ANSWERS

Ex. 1
1 so 2 such a 3 enough 4 enough 5 Very 6 such 7 very 8 too

Watch Out! *very* and *too*
Sentence 2

Ex. 2
2 f) *too* big *to* fit 3 d) *such* a good time on holiday *that* I 4 a) *enough* money *to* pay 5 b) *so* hot *that* I 6 c) *enough* qualifications *to* get

Ex. 3
1 so frightened that he could 2 such a strong wind 3 were too complicated for me 4 never seen such an 5 was not well enough 6 such a lot of money

▶ Photocopiable activity 13A *First to 48* p.186
See also: *NEW FCE Gold exam maximiser* p.98

Speaking 2: quiz p.159

Aim:
• **to provide a lead-in to the Exam focus text**

1 Students work in small groups to answer the questions. Before they do this, they should quickly read through the questions and answers, and underline any words they don't recognise. They can then either use a dictionary to check for the meanings of unfamiliar words, or you could teach some of these using example sentences (e.g. for *hurricane*: *It lasted for almost six hours. Wind speeds exceeded 120 miles per hour. Hundreds of buildings were damaged or destroyed as a result.*).
The answer to question 7 is looked at in detail in the next section (Reading), so don't spend too long discussing this.

2 Play the recording once, and ask your students which answer they found the most surprising. (Most of them will probably say number 5.) You could briefly review vocabulary for alternative power sources here (e.g. *tidal power, wind farms, hydroelectricity, solar power,* etc.).

▶ Tapescript p.111

ANSWERS

Ex. 1
1 A 2 C 3 B 4 C 5 C 6 A 7 C

Exam focus

Paper 1 Reading: multiple matching (Part 1) p.160

Aim:

- **to present and practise a procedure for Paper 1, Part 1**

Take your students through the **About the exam** and **Procedure** sections in the usual way.

1 Tell your students to read through the list of sentences and check any words that they don't recognise in a dictionary if necessary.

Before they do the task, look at the example answer with them, and ask them why this can be used for the first paragraph (the first paragraph describes a simple *experiment* – throwing a stone in a lake or pond – which shows how a *tsunami* starts).

Working individually, students complete the task, then compare their answers with a partner.

2

1, 2 Exercise 2.1 helps students to summarise the key information about *tsunamis*. Students could write the paragraph for homework. They could also do the same for other natural phenomena, using their own knowledge.

3 This gives students a chance to use the vocabulary in a more light-hearted way, rather than discussing real disasters.

ANSWERS

Ex. 1

1 F 2 G 3 A 4 B 5 D 6 C

Ex. 2

1 What three things can cause a *tsunami* to start? *Earthquakes, volcanic eruptions, meteor/comet strikes.*

2 How far can *tsunamis* travel? *Several thousand kilometres.*

3 Why are *tsunamis* difficult to see in the open ocean? *Because most of a* tsunami *is below the surface.*

4 What can happen just before a *tsunami* hits land? *It slows down and becomes much taller. Sometimes the sea moves away from the shore, uncovering the shoreline; on other occasions the wave arrives suddenly, without warning.*

5 Where are *tsunamis* most common? *In the Pacific area around Japan.*

Grammar 2: emphasis with *what* p.161

Aim:

- **to focus on emphatic use of *what***

1 *What* is used in the second sentence in each pair to add emphasis to the subject of the sentence. Students work in pairs to rewrite the second sentence. They can then close their coursebook and try to rewrite their answers using *what* (in other words, to reproduce the original second sentences from their coursebook).

2

1, 2, 3 The use of the emphatic *what* in spoken English is fairly common, especially when giving advice. (*What you need is a good, long holiday.* is similar to saying *You should really take a good, long holiday.*).

Students work in pairs to match the sentences, then take it in turns to say them to each other. They should focus on the stressed words in the response, deciding which words are being emphasised.

Play the recording twice. The first time, students just listen. The second time, stop after each response, and choral drill the response with the class. Your students can then work in the same pairs to read the statements and responses again, this time stressing the appropriate words based on what they heard on the recording.

3

1, 2 This exercise practises the target language in a semi-controlled context. Students work individually to complete the responses using their own ideas, then work in pairs to practise their mini-dialogues.

ANSWERS

Ex. 1

1 Their unpredictability was the most dangerous thing about them in those days.

2 It collects information about conditions which …

3 Many people forget that, in certain weather conditions, avalanches may occur.

4 In fact, pressure between rocks on or under the Earth's surface causes earthquakes.

5 The way they are named is unusual.

Ex. 2

1 c) 2 e) 3 a) 4 b) 5 d)

See also: *NEW FCE Gold exam maximiser* p.99

Vocabulary 2: the natural world p.162

Aim:

- **to review/introduce language connected with the weather**

1   Students should put the words into groups based on features of the weather. Start them off by doing the first group of three (i.e. *climate, temperature, weather*, which are all **general** words about the weather) as a class. Then ask them to discuss/categorise the other words in pairs or small groups. When they have done this, ask them if they can think of any other words to add to their groups.

2   The words here are all collocations that can be used for different weather conditions. Students can refer to a dictionary for this.

3   Students can work in pairs or small groups of different nationalities to discuss the weather in their countries. Alternatively, each student could write a brief description of his/her country, then pass this to you. Read these out to the rest of the class, omitting the name of the country, and ask your class to decide which student's country is being described. (E.g. *In _____ we have mild summers and cool winters. It rains quite a lot, but we get a lot of sunny days too. It rarely snows in winter, and in summer the temperature rarely goes above … .* etc.)

4   After your students match the two halves of the sentences, discuss the questions with the whole class.

5

1, 2 After students have completed the idiomatic expressions in sentences 1–6, and discussed the meaning, ask them to close their books or cover up the exercise. How many of the expressions they can remember? Students should be careful when learning idioms that they learn the whole expression (including any necessary prepositions, etc.), as idioms sound strange or could be confusing if not used in their entirety.

ANSWERS

Ex. 1
breeze, gale, wind; climate, temperature, weather; cloud, fog, mist; drizzle, shower, rain;
frost, hail, snow; lightning, thunder, thunderstorm

Ex. 2
1 rain   2 weather   3 cloud, fog   4 wind
5 thunderstorm   6 snow   7 weather

Ex. 4
1 d)   2 b)   3 f)   4 c)   5 e)   6 a)

Ex. 5
1
1 snowed   2 rain   3 floods   4 sunny   5 cloud
6 storms

See also: *NEW FCE Gold exam maximiser* p.101

Speaking 3: individual long turn (Part 2) p.163

Aim:

- **to practise the language of the unit in a Paper 5, Part 2-style task**

1   This exercise introduces some useful expressions for describing what students can see in their pictures, and giving a personal reaction to it. The emphatic use of *what* is very useful here.
Your students can complete the sentences in pairs or small groups.

2   As an alternative to the procedure in the coursebook, read the instructions for student A out aloud, and then allow student A in each pair about one minute to describe his/her pictures to student B. At the end of the minute, say *Thank you* (and make sure that everyone stops speaking), then read out the question to student B. He/she should direct his/her answer to student A, and should take about 20 seconds to do this.

3   Students change roles and follow the instructions in the exercise.

ANSWERS

Ex. 1 Sample sentences
What's happening in photo A is that (a lot of cars are stuck in a snow storm).
What's different about photo B is that (it's summertime/the weather must be very hot/it is in the countryside, not a city).
What they seem to be doing in Photo A is (trying to push their car through the snow).
What I notice about the person in photo B is that (he is looking at something – maybe he's looking at the sky to see if it's going to rain).
What must be most difficult for these people is (that the weather makes it difficult for them to do their jobs).
What I'd find difficult in this situation is (the frustration – not being able to do anything about it).

Use of English 2: error correction (Part 4) p.164

Aims:

- **to complete an error correction task**
- **to discuss traditional stories and beliefs about natural phenomena**

1   This exercise introduces the theme of the error correction task (i.e. natural phenomena). Discuss the questions with your class, and then let them check their answers on page 188.

2   This should take your students about one minute to do. They should not start to correct the text yet. When they have read it, tell them to cover the text and to tell you what they can remember.

3   Working individually, students do the task. This should take them about ten minutes.

4   Discuss this as a class.

ANSWERS

Ex. 1
1 d)   2 c)   3 a)   4 b)

Ex. 3
1 to   2 ✓   3 there   4 must   5 yourself   6 ✓
7 enough   8 exactly   9 it   10 ✓   11 shape
12 of   13 when   14 ✓   15 out

▶ Photocopiable activity 13B *The wrong words* p.187

Writing: informal letter (Part 2) p.164

Aim:
• **to write an informal letter**

As with Unit 12, you might like to treat this section as an informal workshop session. At this stage of the course, you might also like your students to write the actual letter in the class as a timed task, so that they get a feel for the exam.

ANSWERS

Ex. 2
contractions, shorter sentences, colloquial expressions, phrasal verbs, connectors such as *and*, *but*, exclamation marks

Ex. 3 Sample answer
Dear Pat
Thanks very much for your letter – it was nice to hear from you. I'm really glad to hear that you're coming to visit my country. I hope you'll be able to come and spend some time with me.
Here are the answers to your questions. In my opinion, September is the best time to visit. It can rain a lot, but it's still quite warm. February is the coldest month, so it's not a good idea to come then. If you want to stay in the countryside, then the south-west part is probably the best place to go.

There are two very big nature reserves, where people are not allowed to drive a car. At the end of September the leaves on the trees turn brown – it's very beautiful.
I think the best way to get there is by train. It's cheaper and quicker than driving, especially if you buy a one-month travelcard.
Let me know what you decide to do and I'll come and meet you at the airport if you like.
Please give my regards to your family.
All the best
Jean   (183 words)

See also: *NEW FCE Gold exam maximiser* p.103

UNIT 13 **Review** p.165

ANSWERS

Ex. 1
1 *gallop* – the rest are sounds, but this is a movement, e.g. *horses gallop.*
2 *bone* – the rest are on the outside of body, but *bones* are inside.
3 *can* – the rest are places where an animal lives, but a *can* is a container.
4 *beak* – they are all parts of the body, but the *beak* is on a bird's head, and the rest are to do with feet.
5 *purr* – the rest are ways of flying, but *purr* is the sound a cat makes when it is contented.
6 *emotion* – the rest are examples of emotions.

Ex. 2
1 earthquake   2 Drought   3 volcanic eruption
4 *tsunami*   5 avalanches   6 Floods

Ex. 3
1 read   2 close   3 admitted   4 all   5 takes
6 tragic

Ex. 4
1 I've ended up working   2 have run out of oil
3 take place in all   4 slows down when   5 put
out a big forest fire   6 taken part in   7 keep on
going   8 phoned up directory enquiries   9 going
on next door   10 came across an old storybook
11 pick up new ideas   12 make up the answers

Ex. 5
1 while 2 having   3 and   4 What   5 hardly
6 more   7 so   8 every   9 their   10 when
11 unless   12 enough   13 could   14 After
15 the

▶ Photocopiable Unit 13 test p.138

UNIT
14 Getting there

Speaking 1 p.166

Aim:

- **to provide a lead-in to Reading 1**

1, **2** Students do the quiz individually, then compare their answers with a partner. In addition to saying which options they chose, they should try to give more details about each of their choices (e.g. if they choose C for question 1, they could say what they would do and why they would do it). Extend this to a whole class discussion.

Reading 1: multiple-choice questions (Part 2) p.166

Aim:

- **to complete an exam-style Part 2 task**

Before your students look at this section, ask them why people enjoy travelling to different countries around the world (e.g. to meet new people, to see different, unusual or exciting places, to eat unusual food, to escape from their everyday lives, to learn more about other cultures, to get away from people at home, etc.). Ask them to tell you about the most interesting/unusual/exciting/exotic place they have visited, or a holiday that they will always remember.

1 After your students have quickly read the text and answered the questions, you could focus on Exercise 1.2 and ask them to write a brief paragraph about one place they would really like to visit and why. They should give their paragraphs to you. Read these out to the rest of the class. They should decide who in the class chose which destination.

2 Ask your students to look at number 1 and to decide as a class what the correct answer is. They can do this as a process of elimination. The answer cannot be A because the text says *'aware of how tired they might be … He would see who was sucking a sweet …'*; it cannot be B because we know that *'his pupils continued to suck, gaze and scribble …Only Rowan … listened.'* It cannot be D because *'he could not bear to think that he was the cause of this boredom'*. The answer must be C. This is confirmed in the text where it says that *'instead of teaching, he would tell his pupils about his journeys.'* – his sympathetic response to his students' boredom.
Working individually, students then complete questions 2–7.

3, **4** Students can work individually or in pairs to decide how the story continues, then tell the rest of the class what they think. In groups of three, they then look at the different summaries on pages 187, 188 and 190. For 4.2, try to arrange the students so that they are working with people they do not normally work with.

ANSWERS

Ex. 1
1 Scotland   2 London
3 Africa, Patagonia, Peru, China, Australia, Sudan

Ex. 2
1 C   2 A   3 C   4 D   5 C   6 D   7 B

See also: *NEW FCE Gold exam maximiser* p.104

Vocabulary 1: hopes and ambitions p.168

Aim:

- **to focus on language used to talk about hopes, dreams, ambitions, etc.**

1

1, 2 Some of the words in 1–8 collocate with more than one of the words in a)–h) (for example, you can *score* a goal or *achieve* a goal), with a change in meaning. After your students have done 1.1, ask them to close their books and write the bold words from both sentence halves on the board. Working in pairs, students decide which words can collocate with which before doing Exercise 1.2.

3 This practises some of the key language in a personalised context. Your students could discuss the qualities that are needed to become successful or to achieve goals (e.g. determination, hard work, ruthlessness, ambition, single-mindedness). *Do they know of any famous people who have had to work hard to achieve their goals? How did they do this? Do they think it is necessary to sacrifice one thing in order to achieve another?* (E.g. when you become famous and/or rich, you often have to sacrifice privacy, the company of friends and family, etc.).

2

1 After your students have chosen the correct phrasal verbs for sentences 1–8, ask them to focus on the phrasal verbs that are wrong, and work in pairs or small groups to use these in sentences of their own. They should try to do this without a dictionary, then use the dictionary to check that they have used the phrasal verbs correctly.

2   Students discuss these in the same pairs/small groups, before comparing their ideas with the rest of the class.

ANSWERS

Ex. 1

1   1 f)   2 c)   3 a)   4 h)   5 g)   6 b)   7 e)
8 d)

2

1   You *score* a goal in a sport (e.g. football). You *achieve* a goal when you do something you really want to do.

2   You *hit* a target when you are shooting something. You *meet* a target in business.

3   You *take* aim with a gun. You *achieve* an aim when you do something you really want to do.

4   You *have* a dream if you want to do something. You *fulfil* a dream if you do something you want to do.

Ex. 2

1

1 get on   2 face up to   3 give up   4 comes up
5 deal with   6 talk through   7 bring up
8 finish up

See also: *NEW FCE Gold exam maximiser* p.105

Use of English 1: word formation (Part 5). p.168

Aim:

• **to complete an exam-style word formation task**

1   Working individually, students decide what motivates them, adding their own ideas to the list. They can then compare their ideas with a partner before sharing them with the whole class, who should try to decide what the biggest motivating factor is for most people.

2 , **3**   Potential problem areas in the text include: the spelling of *successful*; the plural use of *expectations*; the use of both a negative prefix and a suffix for *unpleasant*.

ANSWERS

Ex. 3

1 ambitious   2 successful   3 expectations
4 steadily   5 childhood   6 unpleasant
7 illness   8 greatest   9 believe
10 encouragement

Listening 1: multiple matching (Part 3) p.169

Aim:

• **to complete an exam-style Paper 4, Part 3 task**

1 , **2**   Ask your students if they can remember the procedure suggested in Unit 11, page 131.
Play the recording twice, then let your students compare and discuss their answers in small groups before discussing the quotations in Exercise 2. These focus on idiomatic expressions from the text.

▶   Tapescript p.111

3 , **4**   Do Exercise 3 as a whole class discussion before students get into pairs to do Exercise 4. This provides a good opportunity to review language of suggestion and advice (*Why don't you … ? You should … . You ought to … . If I were you … . It might be a good idea to … . Have you ever thought about … ?* etc). There are more words and expressions for advice later in this unit.

ANSWERS

Ex. 1

1 F   2 A   3 D   4 E   5 C

Ex.2

1   His uncle showed him round his Royal Air Force base – this encouraged him to pursue a career in aerospace.

2   She is waiting to find something she is really good at.

3   He is talking about his first child, who has given him a purpose in life.

4   When she fell out with her coach, she had to stop her training in America. But she has continued with her skiing.

5   This refers to his dream of going round the world to extreme places.

See also: *NEW FCE Gold exam maximiser* p.106

Reading 2: gapped text (Part 3) p.170

Aim:

• **to complete a gapped text task**

1

In pairs or small groups, students look at the pictures and discuss the questions.

Background information

Oman is a sultanate on the southeast of the Arabian peninsula. It shares borders with Saudi Arabia, Yemen and the United Arab Emirates. Arabic is the main language, but English is often spoken as the *lingua franca*. Its main religion is Islam. It is rapidly becoming a popular tourist destination. It has an excellent website at www.omanet.com.

2 Before students do this, look at the example with them, and ask them why the answer is H. (We are told in the first paragraph that Louise Hose is a *geologist* and she has an unlikely *task*. In paragraph H we are told that she has been asked to examine the cave systems. *Geologists* relates to *caves*, and *task* relates to the job she has been given of examining them. We also see in paragraph H that *the authorities* want her to examine them. In the paragraph which follows this, the expression *planners in the country* is a synonym for *authorities*).

3 Students can do this in pairs or small groups.

4 Rather than do all the questions, you might prefer to focus on one or two and discuss these. Question 3 would be particularly good for a mixed-nationality class, as your students could share information about their countries. Question 5 would work well for a single-nationality class, especially if they all come from the same area. *Has tourism had a positive/negative impact on their area? How do local people feel about tourists? Do they think there should be a 'quota' of tourists allowed into their country?*

ANSWERS

Ex. 2
1 B 2 D 3 A 4 G 5 E 6 C

Ex. 3
1 wealthy 2 spectacular 3 unlikely 4 amazed
5 harmful 6 attractive 7 watchful

Vocabulary 2: holidays and travel p.172

Aim:
• **to review vocabulary related to holidays and travel**

1 As an alternative to your students reading sentences 1–8, ask them to close their books. Dictate the words for different types of holiday (backpacking, a cruise, an expedition, etc.) and check that they understand what these mean. Then read sentences 1–8 out to them. In pairs, they should decide which holiday you are describing. Ask them for the key words and expressions that helped them to decide.

2 , **3** In pairs, students decide which things they would take on the different holidays, then complete the sentences in Exercise 3.

4 For question 2, students could write their one essential thing on a piece of paper and give it to you. Read these out. They should try to guess who chose what.

ANSWERS

Ex. 1

1
1 a cruise 2 a package holiday 3 a holiday course 4 a guided coach tour 5 an expedition
6 backpacking 7 a city-break 8 trekking

Ex. 3
1 insect repellent 2 phrasebook 3 sleeping bag
4 guidebook 5 hat/smart clothes
6 sea-sickness pills

See also: *NEW FCE Gold exam maximiser* p.107

Grammar: ways of giving advice p.173

Aim:
• **to focus on overt and implied language of advice**

1 , **2** After your students have found the different phrases in Exercise 1, they should work in small groups to do the key word transformations in Exercise 2. They should be particularly careful with the negative constructions in 2 and 4 (*It is wise not to drink; She advised us not to stay*; students will often get the order of *not* and *to* wrong – *It is wise **to not** drink* is a common mistake).

3 Again, students can write their pieces of advice down and give them to you. You can then read these out and they should try to guess which country is being described.

4 After doing the task, students could work in pairs to think of three more problems Chris had, then read these to another pair, who can give suitable advice (e.g. *'I got terrible food poisoning.' 'You shouldn't have eaten from the roadside stalls.'*, etc.).

5 Students should try to talk for about four minutes. Remind them to interact using techniques looked at earlier in this course (e.g. asking questions, maintaining eye contact, showing that they are listening, responding, etc.).

ANSWERS

Ex. 2

1 me it was advisable
2 unwise/not wise to drink
3 not attempt to climb
4 was advised not to stay
5 are reminded (that) they
6 not miss seeing
7 ought to visit the cathedral
8 are recommended to leave

Ex. 4 Sample answers

2 He should have put on some suncream. He shouldn't have stayed out in the sun for so long.
3 He should have studied the language before he went. He should have asked the people to speak more slowly.
4 He should have left his passport in the hotel safe. He shouldn't have carried his passport around with him.
5 He should have phoned or written to his parents.
6 He shouldn't have gone without her. He should have called her while he was away.

See also: *NEW FCE Gold exam maximiser* p.108

Speaking 2: prioritising (Parts 3 and 4) p.174

Aim:

• **to practise the language of the unit in a Paper 5, Part 2-style task**

1, **2** Ask your students to work in pairs or groups of three, to read the task and discuss the objects they would take. They should take about three minutes to do this, before extending the discussion to compare their ideas with others in the class.

3 Your students could do this in groups of three, with one of them taking the examiner's role and asking the questions. They should try to keep the conversation going for about four minutes.

Use of English 2: open cloze (Part 2) p.174

Aim:

• **to complete an exam-style open cloze**

1, **2** Students explain what they know about Mount Everest, then read the text quickly and decide in pairs what kind of word is missing from each gap. They should then work individually to complete the text.

3 Students work in small groups to discuss these qualities and decide on the greatest challenge in the world. This could be a major physical feat, or it could be something less dramatic – raising a family, for example.

ANSWERS

Ex. 2

1 it 2 had 3 as 4 since 5 their 6 least
7 on 8 When 9 but / although 10 There
11 must / should 12 long 13 Despite 14 every
15 does

Listening 2: song p.175

Aim:

• **to listen to a song for specific information and gist**

1, **2** Your students should be able to identify the positive aspect of this song from some of the key words in the extracts (*faith, shine, dream, spell, high, bright, alive*). There are some 'negative' words (*alone, poor*) but the overall tone here is positive. Ask your students to think of some other 'positive' words and to make a list of these (e.g. *joy, happiness, love, success,* etc.). They can then try to decide where the extracts go in the song.

3 Play the recording and let your students check their answers.

4 After your students decide which sentence summarises the song best, ask them if they have their own 'philosophy' for life – what do they believe is the key to happiness, and how can they achieve this?

ANSWERS

Ex. 1
Positive

Ex. 2
1 f) 2 k) 3 h) 4 a) 5 l) 6 j) 7 b) 8 c)
9 e) 10 i) 11 g) 12 d)

Ex. 4
b) *you should keep on aiming high*
   Just seek yourself and you will shine
   you … can build a bridge …

Writing: composition (Part 2) p.175

Aim:

- **to plan and write a discursive composition**

You might like to do this section as a student-centred workshop.

1 – 5   Ask your students to work through these exercises in small groups. Monitor the groups, only helping them if they have problems. Encourage them to ask each other for help rather than turning to you.
They can then write their composition individually for homework.

6   Students should note that number 3 is inadvisable in the exam – they may run out of time. Good planning should negate the need for this.
Number 4 would not be possible in the exam, as dictionaries (bilingual or monolingual) are not allowed.

ANSWERS

Ex. 3

1 However   **2** For example   **3** as a result
4 As well as this   **5** Finally

Ex. 5 Sample answer

In today's busy world holidays are a very important way to relax, but how should you spend your time? Some people feel that the best way to relax is to do something new and challenging, like visiting another country. What often happens when the holidays start is that people get ill, for example they catch a cold. Then, when they go back to work, they find it very difficult to get used to the fast pace of life again. If people go abroad or do an adventure holiday, they remain active and so don't experience those problems.
Other people feel that they spend the rest of the year doing difficult things and that they need to spend time doing very little. If you go to familiar places and do familiar things it means you can relax more as you don't have to think so hard about what you're doing.
In my opinion, people should be encouraged to try new things all the time, but above all they should relax and enjoy themselves.   (172 words)

▶ Photocopiable activity 14 *First to zero* p.188
See also: *NEW FCE Gold exam maximiser* p.110

UNITS 11 – 14 Progress test p.177

ANSWERS

Ex. 1

1 references = referees
2 promoted = promotion   **3** go = run
4 with = of   **5** for = in   **6** percent = percentage
7 from = of   **8** mystery = mysterious
9 Tools = Weapons   **10** herd = gang
11 analysis = analysed   **12** under = in
13 foggy = fog   **14** in the move = on the move
15 filled = achieved

Ex. 2

1 I don't know *how* to   **2** should *be* able
3 succeed *in* passing   **4** phone *in* case
5 If I *had* stayed   **6** Even *if* I
7 like *being* told   **8** made *to* wait
9 Alexander the Great *is* believed
10 get *my* eyes tested   **11** good *enough* at
12 studied for *such* a long time   **13** What you mustn't forget *is* that   **14** but *what* I really hate
15 they *should / must* not leave

Ex. 3

1 B   **2** D   **3** A   **4** C   **5** D   **6** D   **7** A   **8** B
9 A   **10** C   **11** A   **12** C   **13** A   **14** D   **15** D

Ex. 4

16 been   **17** for   **18** of   **19** which/that
20 does   **21** soon   **22** if/though   **23** his   **24** on
25 and   **26** one   **27** as   **28** between
29 what/the   **30** their

Ex. 5

31 should have been warned about   **32** to get my hair cut   **33** ended up staying   **34** to avoid paying for   **35** was responsible for taking
36 come up with   **37** were you I'd take
38 make him out   **39** have died out
40 hadn't been snowing

Ex. 6

41 have   **42** become   **43** ✓   **44** so   **45** are
46 be   **47** they   **48** ✓   **49** than   **50** ✓   **51** up
52 ✓   **53** for   **54** those   **55** since

Ex. 7

56 extremely   **57** unexpectedly   **58** arrival
59 argument   **60** Unluckily   **61** completely
62 knowledge   **63** athletic   **64** successful
65 amazement

▶ Photocopiable Progress test 3 (Units 11–14) p.140
▶ Photocopiable activity *First Certificate in English Quiz* p.190

Recording scripts

UNIT 1
page 7, Listening 1: note completion, Exercise 2

Katy: In today's edition of *Film Now* we're looking at what makes your all-time best-ever films. Gavin Stevens is with us now to tell us about the results of one survey that's been done, and to ask for your own views.

Gavin: Thanks Katy. Well, a couple of years ago an Internet company did a survey about people's film preferences. The survey was carried out in the year 2000 and they were trying to find out about the most popular films of the 20th century. They put a questionnaire on the web and 50,000 people answered.

K: Really? What sorts of things did they ask about?

G: Well, they asked for people's favourite films and then they analysed that list to find the most popular types of films – for example, romance, science fiction, action and so on – and they found out that most people's favourite sort of film was drama – out of the ten top films chosen, eight fitted that category. In fact the film that came out as the most popular of all time on the survey was … Can you guess? Made way back in 1972?

K: *The Godfather*?

G: Right. You've got it. And as well as that they looked at plot, and they found all the top films had a strong plot, building up to a climax, but there were two themes which seemed to come up again and again. One was boy meets girl.

K: And the other?

G: It's good versus evil – the struggle of the hero against the villain. Again, nothing new about that, I suppose. But in the most successful films you got a combination of both types of plot, so in *Star Wars*, for example, another big favourite, you got the romance between Han Solo and Princess Leia as your boy meets girl theme, and then you got the struggle of the rebels against the Empire, good versus evil.

K: Mmm. What else did they ask about?

G: They looked at the *settings* of the most popular films, and when they analysed the places where they were set, they found that people liked exotic locations – deserts, jungles and so on. But they also looked at setting in terms of time – whether people liked films about the past, present or future, and it turned out that some of the most popular films were those set in the future – things like *Star Wars* and *Blade Runner* and so on.

K: And presumably they looked at who were the favourite stars of the 20th century?

G: Well, from the really big stars three names came up again and again. Robert de Niro, Harrison Ford and Humphrey Bogart.

K: All men?

G: No, but the female stars were a bit less predictable. The names that came up were Diane Keaton, Jodie Foster, Marilyn Monroe and Carrie Fisher. So as well as glamour – the traditional idea of the Hollywood film star – character seemed to be important as well.

K: Was there anything else?

G: They found a couple of interesting things to do with film titles. Firstly, a lot of the most successful films seem to be made up of just two words – six out of the ten most popular films had two-word titles. And secondly, a lot of film titles included a name related to a place, like *LA Confidential*.

K: LA?

G: Los Angeles. Or a person – like *Saving Private Ryan*.

K: Right. So, listeners, what's your vote for the best films of the 21st century? And remember, they don't have to be American or English films. Let's have details of your favourite film types, plots, settings, stars and film titles by phone or email, and in our next programme we'll give you the results.

UNIT 1
page 14, Listening 2: extracts (Part 1)

1

Man: Well, it starts in New York in the 1950s, and then the setting changes to 19th century Europe. The plot depends heavily on flashbacks, and there are a lot of characters so it does all get a bit confusing at times. I don't think that seeing it on screen is as enjoyable as actually reading it – it really needs a narrator and I actually think it's one of those things that's better on paper than in the cinema, the film seems to lose a lot of what makes it different and unusual as a novel.

2

Woman: It was very well done I thought, didn't you?

Man: Yes. I've seen it on the stage before, but this was actually better. Not so much the individual performances, more the way the whole thing was put together. And of course the setting makes all the difference – I suppose most of it was shot outside. The only thing I didn't like so much was the music. And the ending was a bit violent – especially in close-up.

Woman: Yes, that was a bit too much, I thought. But generally, yes, it was excellent.

3

Interviewer: You were very young when you started acting, weren't you.

Woman: Yes. Looking back, I'm not sure that was the right thing, but no one advised me to wait. I thought I knew what I wanted and it just felt like the right thing to do at the time. You're so sure of yourself at that age. Now I wish I'd waited a bit and carried on with my education, maybe gone to stage school and got some proper training, but I was just impatient to get on with my life, I suppose.

4

Man: I've got all the papers somewhere. They're all in a file together somewhere. I can soon find them.

Woman: I hope so. If they're lost, it'll be a lot of work. It'll mean starting again on the whole project. And there could be other problems …

Man: I know. But I've got them … I had them all in a blue folder. I was checking them just yesterday in preparation for this meeting.

Woman: Mm. I have to say, there is a security element involved. Some of those papers were highly confidential. They mustn't be seen by our competitors.

Man: It's definitely not been out of the building. I might have left it on Tom's desk – I'll go and look there.

5

Woman: Well, I woke up one day and there were workmen digging a big hole right in front of my house. So I went out to ask them what they were doing and they said they were putting up a mast for the mobile phone company. And I said, 'But nobody told me.' Anyway, I rang up this gentleman in the town council and he said, 'There's nothing we can do about it because the company's allowed to put masts where they like, as long as they're not higher than 15m.' Well, that's not right, is it?

6

Woman: How did it go?

Man: Terrible. I dropped out in the first round.

Woman: Oh, bad luck.

Man: Well, it doesn't really matter I suppose. I knew the answers to a lot of the questions, but I just couldn't think of them. It seemed such an artificial situation, sitting in front of a microphone talking to people you couldn't see. It made me really nervous. It is a bit of a disappointment – not just not getting the prize, but the whole thing.

Woman: I'm not surprised you were nervous – I would have been too.

UNIT 1

page 15, Exam focus Paper 5 Speaking: introduction (Part 1), Exercise 2

1

Examiner: Where are you from, Joanna?

Joanna: I come from Krakow.

2

Examiner: Where are you from, Karl?

Karl: I'm sorry, I didn't understand the question.

Examiner: Where are you from?

Karl: Oh – I come from Heidelberg. It's a very old city, with a university. It's very beautiful. We get lots of tourists.

3

Examiner: Where are you from, Katerina?

Katerina: I come from Athens and I have one sister and one brother. My father is businessman and my mother is housewife, and I like going to the cinema very much.

4

Examiner: Where are you from, Jorge?

Jorge: I am come from Buenos Aires in Argentina, is very very big, nice, with many peoples living there.

UNIT 2

page 19, Listening: true or false? (Part 4), Exercises 2 and 3

Interviewer: You join us now as we welcome Tanya Streeter, who recently broke the world record in free diving, diving 160 metres without using any kind of breathing apparatus or air supply. Tanya, tell us how you came to take up free diving in the first place.

Tanya: Well, I was born in the Cayman Islands, near the Bahamas. My parents ran a water sports shop there, and they first took me swimming when I was only six weeks old. So being in the water was always a natural feeling for me.

I: So were you very young when you started free diving?

T: No, I only discovered it much later, after university in fact, when I was invited to join a group of people in a free diving class. When I turned up, I was the only woman there. The rest were all big guys, who wanted to learn how go deeper and shoot bigger fish when they went spear fishing. But actually I took to it immediately – I was the one who could hold my breath the longest and go the deepest.

I: But at first it was just a hobby?

T: I suppose so, but quite soon my teacher started encouraging me to take it up seriously and try to set records – I didn't know if I was capable of it but I wanted to try.

I: So what do you think was behind that?

T: I don't know … I suppose I was rather insecure as a child and so when I was older I wanted to make people proud of me, especially my mother and father. It seemed the natural way to prove myself … And it was through free diving that I started to understand that if you work hard you get results.

I: For your world record you went down to 160 metres … how do you actually get down so far? Presumably you don't swim down all that way.

T: No, no one could do that, they'd use up far too much energy. I stand on a special platform that's gradually lowered down bit by bit, then when I get as far down as I can, I release myself and shoot up to the surface again. I don't have to come up slowly, stage by stage, like a diver with a tank.

I: And all the time you're holding your breath?

T: Yes – I can hold my breath for just under three and a half minutes.

I: So what effect does all this have on you physically, when you're actually down there?

T: Well, the water pressure at these depths is enormous so my whole body's really compressed – my wet suit just hangs off me. And the rate at which my heart beats is very much lower than normal, because my heart's not getting much oxygen, and because of this it's hard to think clearly about what I'm doing, I can easily get confused and there's always the danger of losing consciousness completely. But there are regular divers watching me all the way down …

I: But in the end, you're on your own down there?

T: Well, yes and no … I mean, the most important thing is that I believe in my dive team. They're there to support me and they know exactly what to do if something happens … if there's a problem. There's no way I could take on something like this on my own.

I: Tell us about how you felt when you broke the world record …

T: Oh, it was an incredible feeling – not only for the record itself, although of course I'm pleased about that and it was a great achievement, but it's more than that. I think … it's amazing to be the person who shows what's possible, to be part of something which changes the perceptions of what people can do. People who think that free diving is life threatening misunderstand the sport. It's just the opposite – you're learning about the possibilities of the human species. After all, if I managed to dive to 160 metres, imagine what we can all do as human beings.

I: Tanya Streeter, thank you.

UNIT 3

page 34, Listening 1: multiple matching (Part 3), Exercise 2

I read quite a lot but I can't really say I prefer one sort of thing to another. I like to flick through the celebrity magazines, like *Hello*, to see how people who are rich and famous actually live and see the sort of clothes they wear. I feel a bit guilty because it's useless stuff really, you don't actually get anything out of it. I do read fiction as well but if it's a bit difficult, I have this bad habit of looking at the last chapter to find out what happens, then it doesn't seem worth reading to the end … and I have a look at the newspapers most days, though it might be just the headlines or to find out what's on TV.

UNIT 3

page 34, Listening 1: multiple matching (Part 3), Exercise 3

1

as Exercise 2 above

2

Well, I read a lot but I don't really go for fiction, I tend to prefer non-fiction like real-life crime … gangland stuff and so on. In the future, I'd like to become a criminal psychologist, trying to find out what makes people commit crimes – so I guess that's how I got interested in reading about that kind of thing. And for the last few months I've been really into biographies. At present I'm halfway through a book called *Raging Bull* by Jake La Motta. It's about a crazy boxer – they made a film of it with the same name starring Robert De Niro in the lead role. It's a great film.

3

A lot of my friends won't read anything if it was written more than five or ten years ago. They say old books aren't worth reading really, but I don't agree. I mean, if people have kept on buying them and reading them for 50 or a 100 years, they can't be that bad. Of course, it depends on the book; some of them can be a bit complicated and hard to read, but it's worth carrying on to the end. I read *Jane Eyre*, that was written over a 100 years ago and it's wonderful. And of course *Lord of the Rings* was written over 50 years ago and that's a masterpiece, even better than the film.

4

I really started getting into reading with the *Harry Potter* books ... actually I still enjoy them, but nowadays I mostly read science fiction, writers like Terry Pratchett; I like his books because they're all connected, they're all set in the same universe called Discworld, so you can get to know it better and better as you read more books. The last book I read was called *Solaris* – I can't remember the author's name – about a planet which is completely covered by water and it turns out to be ... Well, I won't tell you the end. It's actually a great book although it was really depressing. It's been made into a film but I don't think I'll be going to see it.

5

When I was small my parents used to read to me a lot, especially at bedtime. I used to like reading comics, and books with lots of pictures like the *Asterix* series. Nowadays I actually prefer reading to watching movies. You've got more time to think, you can get into the ideas more deeply. I work in the music business, which is great but it can be stressful and I find a good novel just helps me to escape from everything for a while. I suppose I'm a reading addict ... I usually have several books on the go at any one time. And as well as that I like reading music magazines to keep up with what's going on in the music world.

UNIT 3

page 34, Speaking: asking for and reacting to opinions (Parts 3 and 4), Exercise 2

A: Well, in this picture there's a man trying to cook a meal. And he's following a recipe in a cookery book.

B: That's right. It'll explain all the steps he has to follow. But he looks a bit confused. What do you think?

A: Yes, I agree. Some people just don't like reading instructions, do they? They'd rather work things out for themselves. I'm like that. I never read instructions!

B: But on the other hand, you can make a lot of mistakes without them.

A: Mmm, I suppose so.

B: Not everything you read nowadays comes from a book, does it? Look at the next picture for example. She's surfing the Internet.

A: Right. The Internet is really useful. You can find lots of information quickly, and you don't need to go to the library or buy books.

B: Well, yes, but you have to learn to read fast to see if a web page is relevant. Don't you think so?

A: OK, but the language is usually written in a simple way.

B: Yes, that's true. And another advantage is that you can do it in your own time at home ...

UNIT 3

page 37, Listening 2: multiple-choice questions (Part 4), Exercises 2 and 3

Anna: It's funny the way things can happen. My Auntie Carrie, you know, my American aunt, she has an amazing story about something that happened when she went to Paris – actually it was for her honeymoon, my uncle wanted her to see a bit of Europe and ... you know those stalls they have in Paris along the banks of the river?

Brendon: The ones that sell second-hand books?

A: That's right. So Aunt Carrie was there, looking through them ... I don't know what my uncle was doing, he's like you, Brendan, he'd run a mile from anything resembling a shop

B: Absolutely. Wise man.

A: Anyway, to get back to the story, she came across a book that had been one of her absolute favourites when she was a little girl, I think it was called *The Tale of a Bad Rabbit* or something like that, and she picked it up and on the inside cover she saw in her own writing: *Carrie Simons, 360 Greever Street, Illinois, USA.*

B: So it was her very own book?

A: Right. Well, obviously she wondered just how it had got there – she asked the stallholder, but he had no idea. Anyway, she bought it, and she used to read it to me when I was little.

B: That reminds me of something that happened to me a couple of years ago. I'd gone in for a music competition and I'd decided to play this piece of trumpet music that was really unusual – I had to order the music specially – it was really hard to get, you couldn't buy it in any of the shops. It was by a composer hardly anyone had heard of.

A: Typical of you to go for something obscure.

B: Yes, but it was great music, Anna, fantastic stuff. Anyway, when the day came for the competition I got to the place – it was about three hours' journey – and when I arrived, I was feeling really hot and bothered ... the train was late and I'd thought I wouldn't make it. Everyone else was already there at the concert hall, all the other competitors, in this sort of waiting room place waiting for their turn Anyway, I opened my bag and I found I'd left the music at home.

A: Oh, Brendon ... how awful!

B: Yes ... I was absolutely furious with myself, because this concert mattered a lot to me and I'd practised incredibly hard, and I just ... I just kicked my bag into a corner, and it hit the door of an old cupboard that was there in the corner, and the door flew open and out dropped all this paper ... it just looked like a load of waste paper that someone had meant to throw away. And I went over to put it all back and there on the top ... you'll never guess.

A: No ... not the music?

B: It was the exact music I needed right at the top of the pile.

A: And what happened about the competition?

B: I'd been so lucky, I just knew I was going to win – and I did.

A: Mm. There's another story I heard, I don't know, maybe I read it somewhere, and it's about this man called Joseph Figlock and he was walking down the street one day when a baby fell out of a high window and landed on him

B: What? But that's awful.

A: No – actually the baby was completely unhurt, and so was he ...

B: So he saw it coming and managed to catch it?

A: Yes, I don't know exactly what he did, but anyway the main thing was that the baby was safe. But actually that's not the end of the story, because a year later Joseph Figlock was walking down the very same street ...

B: Yes?

A: And the very same baby fell from the very same window, and they both survived again.

B: Mmm. He was obviously a fortunate sort of guy. The baby must have been quite a bit bigger by then – it must have been quite a weight to come falling on top of him – he could've been badly injured. And presumably he wasn't expecting it – it's not the sort of thing you go round expecting, is it. I wonder if it actually happened ...

A: Well, it could be true I suppose.

B: Mmm.

UNIT 4

page 42, Listening: sentence completion (Part 2), Exercise 3

Radio presenter: In this week's edition of *Celebrity Watch* we're looking at the career of someone who has become a household name at a remarkably young age. With his series of cookery programmes called *The Naked Chef*, he's made his name as one of the people responsible for the growing popularity of food programmes on British television. And he's not content with changing the face of cookery in Britain – his programmes are now being shown all over the world. Yes, we're talking about a young man called Jamie Oliver.

So who is he and where did he come from? In fact cooking's in Jamie's blood. He grew up in a restaurant in the countryside, which was owned and run by his parents. Jamie didn't like school much but he showed an early interest in cooking. He was working with the staff of the restaurant peeling potatoes, shelling peas and so on by the time he was eight, and at the age of 11 he cooked his first full meal – roast chicken. His parents said it was delicious – and Jamie knew this was what he wanted to do. So at the age of 16 he left school and went to London to train as a chef. Here he got to know a girl of his own age called Jools, who was a model and they started going out together. In spite of their youth this was the beginning of a lasting relationship – they eventually married. He then went on to work at The River Café, one of London's top restaurants. Then he had a stroke of luck. While he was working in The River Café, a TV crew came to make a programme about the restaurant. Jamie only appeared on it for a minute or two, but he was obviously impressive because the morning after it was shown, Jamie had phone calls from *five* top producers asking him if he'd be interested in making a television series of his own.

And that was when his career really took off. Jamie appeared in his own series on TV, cooking recipes that were simple and depended for their success on high quality ingredients rather than complicated techniques. The series was an overnight success, and attracted the kind of young, trendy audience that wouldn't normally watch food programmes. People especially liked Jamie's food because it was inspired by Italian cooking and seemed to reflect a modern casual lifestyle. Jamie was filmed zipping about London on a scooter and hosting parties for his friends, all to a rock and roll soundtrack. Then following his TV series, Jamie had another great success. He wrote a cookery book which went straight to the top of the best-seller lists and remained there at number one for more than 12 weeks.

In 2000, Jamie married his girlfriend, Jools, back in the country village where his parents still live. He was awake at 5 a.m. on the day of his wedding cooking the food for the guests himself with his father and a bunch of his friends.

Although he and Jools live in London, Jamie is still close to his parents and he has now followed family tradition by opening his own restaurant. This is a very special project for him. He took on a group of teenagers to staff it – they were all unemployed, and none of them had any experience in the restaurant business. Jamie taught them how to produce food which has had praise from even the most severe food critics.

But life isn't all work. He still finds time to play in a band called Scarlet Division, made up of Jamie and his high school friends. According to Jamie, who's on the drums, they sound like a mixture of 'Catatonia and Texas with a harder edge'. And although he's now a family man with two small children, he still travels around London on his scooter.

UNIT 5

page 57, Listening 1: radio adverts, Exercises 1,2 and 4

1
Whoever you are, wherever you are, whatever you're doing, you'll find a use for one of our penknives. They're light, they're compact and they fit easily in your pocket. You'll never again be without something to open bottles, or cut tomatoes on picnics, or open letters – in fact, you'll wonder how you ever managed without it. Pop in to see our wide selection today and take advantage of our special 10% discount. But hurry – this offer won't last long!

2
Does your hair make you want to pull it out in frustration? Is your bathroom full of hair care products that you've tried but just don't work for you? Girls, why not try 'Frizz-away', a whole new hair care system that will leave your hair looking shiny, soft and smooth. And for you guys, there's 'Iron Control for men' – it gives you total control over unruly hair at all times. We're giving away free samples of these revolutionary products in the town centre this afternoon. Why not come along? You won't regret it.

3
Are you fed up with listening to that irritating crackle and buzz on your radio? Then you're ready to move into the digital age! We can offer you a digital radio at the amazing price of only £50 – post and packaging free – that's right, free! And with its classy wooden case, it's right up-to-date and will look great in your living room. So why not take this opportunity to have crystal-clear sound and easy-to-tune stations at a price that suits your pocket? It's the future of entertainment in your home now, so don't be left behind. And if you can beat this price anywhere locally then we guarantee you your money back – so – call now, on 0800 43 06 75. What have you got to lose?

UNIT 5

page 60, Listening 2: multiple matching (Part 3), Exercise 2

Speaker 1: I come into town most Saturdays … I meet up with my friends, and we go round the shops. We don't actually buy much, there's not a lot for people our age, but I might get a CD or some make-up or something like that. Then we go and have coffee. We always go to the same place, it's called The Lemon Tree and it has really delicious cakes. They're a bit expensive though, so sometimes we just have to have coffee. But they're really nice there and they don't mind how long you stay.

Speaker 2: I'm a student here. I'm studying English and I'm staying with a family. I think it's a nice town, and the people are very friendly. I usually come here on Saturdays to go shopping, then I meet my friends in the café. But I was surprised at the prices when I came here first – they're much higher than in the shops in my country. Er … I'm looking for presents for my family. There are lots of gift shops but I haven't found anything yet. It's really hard buying presents, especially for my father. I want to get him something really special, because he paid for me to come here.

Speaker 3: Well, actually I can't stand shopping just for the sake of it, I can't think of anything I'd rather do less, and anyway I'm a university student and I've got no money. It's a nice town though, we get lots of tourists so there are plenty of gift shops and cafés and fast food places. I do sometimes have a coffee or something quick to eat when I come in to meet my friends – there's quite a lot of different places you can go to; they've just opened a new one in the High Street but I haven't been there yet.

Speaker 4: Well, I don't actually live here – I'm over from Australia on holiday, and I'm staying at the Youth Hostel here. I've spent most of the morning just wandering round the streets and looking at the shops. We don't have anything like that back home, some of them must have been built 500 years ago, and they haven't been modernised too much, so they've still got lots of character. I've taken lots of photos to send home. There's some really nice stuff in the shops – china and jewellery and so on – but I don't have much money left so I'm having to be careful.

Speaker 5: It's a lovely place to live, everyone knows one another and it's very friendly … I mean, we have some really first-class shops … there's one which sells artists materials – paints and canvas for oil paints and so on, and one selling old clocks … that's run by Mr Steele, he's a real enthusiast, I mean, that's not the sort of thing you'd find in the average shopping street, is it? The only problem is that it can be really difficult to park, especially on Saturday when all the locals come in to shop, but we live near the town centre so we can just walk everywhere. It's very convenient.

UNIT 5

page 63, Speaking 3: expressing uncertainty (Part 2), Exercise 3

Well, both the photos show people shopping. In the first photo there are two men and they're in a supermarket, while in the second photo there are three women and … I'm not sure, but they might be in a department store. The supermarket's very big and there are lots of shelves in the background. It's not very clear what's on them but probably food and drink and so on. There are two children with the men … perhaps they belong to the man in the blue shirt. There's a trolley full of bags in the front, and you can tell they've been doing a lot of shopping. It looks as if they've paid the cashier and are just going to leave. In the other photo the three girls are looking at the clothes hanging on rails and trying to decide which ones they want to buy. They seem to be looking for bargains, but I don't think they've bought anything yet.

UNIT 6

page 68, Listening 1: multiple matching (Part 3), Exercise 2

Speaker 1: Oh, the paparazzi – they'd kill or be killed to get a good picture. Like when we're filming on location the photographers are everywhere, and off set as well … even on my honeymoon. We were staying in a village in Italy, a tiny place, nowhere remotely well known, the last place you'd expect to find paparazzi, and the next thing we knew, we had photographs of these private moments in papers all over the world. That hurt. They're like hunters, the paparazzi, they just stalk us and hunt us down, and the pictures are their trophies.

Speaker 2: I think the whole face of news reporting has changed in the last few years. When I retired I got a digital camera and now it's always with me. Just walking around the city, you never know who or what you'll see. If I see a breaking news story, I might just be first in there. I can take photographs and then just email them off straightaway from my mobile phone to the television company or the newspaper. They don't care who I am, as long as it's a good picture, they'll pay. These days we're all paparazzi.

Speaker 3: Well, yes, people do get angry sometimes. Like once I snapped a couple of big stars while they were shopping in London. I won't tell you who they are, but you'd know them. Well, the guy came up to my car and was pounding on my window shouting at me. But they were in full view out in the streets, so I think we were within our rights. If we'd been outside their house looking through their windows and taking pictures then you could have understood them being so angry. Anyway, photographers are just another part in the celebrity promotion machine. The celebrities need us as much as we need them. When they want to publicise something, they'll do the rounds of the clubs and restaurants – just to be seen.

Speaker 4: I hate seeing myself in photographs. I always think I look awful in family snaps but I'd love to have my photograph taken professionally. Like the pictures of celebrities you see in the magazines – they've all been touched up so the people look thinner or more beautiful or whatever, Still, I do like having family photos around. We keep a lot on the computer but I'm not sure about that. It's very convenient, but if something goes wrong you could lose everything. I want to know my family photos will still be there for my grandchildren to look at.

Speaker 5: OK, you can't say we never follow anyone, that would be unrealistic – but a lot of celebrities actually encourage this sort of media interest, you know. And people complain about the use of telephoto lenses – but we need to use them. You get a more interesting photo that way because people aren't self-conscious, they're just being themselves. Basically, I just want to observe what they do and catch them in that moment. And most of the time people are really happy with what they see … the celebrities I mean, they live for the camera, whether they can actually see it or not.

UNIT 6

page 77, Exam focus Paper 5 Speaking: long turn (Part 2), Exercise 2.1

Examiner: Now, I'd like each of you to talk on your own for about a minute. I'm going to give each of you two different photographs and I'd like you to talk about them. Agna, here are your two photographs. They show people talking to one another in different situations. Please let Martin see them. Martin, I'll give you your photographs in a minute. Agna, I'd like you to compare and contrast these photographs, and say how you think these people are feeling. Remember you only have about a minute for this, so don't worry if I interrupt you. All right?

UNIT 6

page 77, Exam focus Paper 5 Speaking: long turn (Part 2), Exercise 2.2

Agna: The two photographs both show people talking and listening, but they're in different situations. In the first photo there's a young woman and a man who's older than her – he could be her grandfather or maybe it's her father. Anyway, I think it must be someone in her family. They're sitting outside in the garden. However, in the second picture I don't think the people know one another so well. There are three girls with a man who could be teaching them something – it must be some sort of sport because they are wearing sports clothes – it might be some sort of martial arts. They're indoors, it may be some sort of sports hall, I'm not sure. In the first photo I think the girl's talking to the man, or maybe they're talking together quietly. They look quite comfortable together whereas in the second photo the girls are listening to the instructor. He looks as if he is explaining something to them. They don't look so happy – they look as if they're concentrating, they take what he says very seriously, whereas the man and the girl in the first picture both look as if they are feeling happy and glad to be together.

Examiner: Thank you. Martin, do you often talk to people who are a lot older than you?

Martin: Well, sometimes, but my grandparents are quite hard to talk to because my grandfather can't hear very well, so I have to remember to talk clearly.

UNIT 7
page 80, Listening 1: multiple-choice questions (Part 4), Exercise 3

Interviewer: For a popular television series, a group of ordinary people were filmed taking part in a unique experiment in living history, a project called *Living in the Iron Age*. Here to tell us what it was like, we have two of the participants – Janet Smith …

Janet: Hello.

I: … and her ten-year-old son Daniel.

Daniel: Hi.

I: So what did the project actually involve, Janet?

J: Well, we all lived in Iron Age conditions in a really remote area in the west of Britain for seven weeks. We didn't have any modern facilities at all, no electricity or anything. We had to survive in mud huts. And we were basically investigating whether people who are used to a modern way of life could manage to live in the same way as Iron Age people did two and a half thousand years ago. It wasn't easy – 17 people started the project but five dropped out before the end.

D: We managed to stay to the end though!

I: What was the hardest part of the whole experience?

J: The first two weeks. I didn't expect the differences between the 21st century and the Iron Age would be so great. I thought I'd miss the luxuries, like cakes and chocolate, but actually it was just simple things like orange juice, and a cup of tea. One thing I found really hard to cope with was the lack of light. In modern life you're used to having light whenever you want it. It's something which you take for granted. You'd think you'd get used to not having it after a while, but I never did.

I: Daniel – how about you?

D: I didn't miss too much really, but I actually missed snacks 'cos, I just got a bit hungry in between the meals sometimes. I think that Iron Age people probably would have had larger meals than we did and as well as that they probably would have been able to have snacks, they would have had the things left over from the meals, and nuts and fruit and things like that between the meals as well.

I: So was there plenty to do during the daytime or did you get bored?

J: There were a lot of routine jobs, looking after the animals, milking, making bread, cheese, keeping fires going, getting water from the river. All those basic sort of things. Plus lots of other jobs, like making baskets, making candles, processing everything … there was always lots to fill the time. And I liked the fact that it didn't matter what you looked like, the way you dressed, because everybody was doing the same sort of jobs.

I: But you did have some free time, presumably?

D: Yeah …when it got dark we'd all get together round a fire. We did lots of story telling and singing. You know nowadays the radio's on all the time, there's television all the time, but we had to do it all for ourselves, make the instruments and everything, and you really appreciated it because it wasn't easy. But it was good fun.

J: And colour … I really noticed that – you see, there wasn't much of … not many of those modern colours like bright yellows and reds, it was all just gentle colours like brown and green – and so you noticed the variety in things like all the different shades of green in the leaves in the woods and the different shades of brown in the earth – not in the things people wore.

I: So what was the first thing you did at the end of the project when you came back to the 21st century?

D: Easy – ate chocolate and played my CDs.

J: When we left the camp, we went to a hotel, and the first thing I did was to … I had a warm bath full of bubbles – my first hot bath since the project began. It was such an important moment for me – it meant that seven weeks of living as a real Iron Age person were finally at an end. I enjoyed that bath so much – and I'll never forget what it was like living without soap and hot water! But looking back on it after all these months the whole thing was a wonderful experience, and I think, the best thing was the fact that we were all living together and sharing so much …

D: … and you just got to know each other much better and become really close friends.

I: Janet and Daniel, thank you …

UNIT 7
page 88, Exam focus Paper 4 Listening: extracts (Part 1)

1

One thing we noticed in New Zealand was that every little town seemed to have its own museum … usually just one room, but it was nice to go in there and there was usually someone who could explain the things… I remember in one there was a set of old school textbooks and exercise books from the early 20th century, obviously someone couldn't bear to throw them away, and it really made an impression on me – it was really moving to see them and to wonder about who might have used them all those years ago … I suppose, being a teacher, that struck me particularly.

2

Over in the United States, builders in Miami recently pulled down an old building to allow the construction of a new 40-storey skyscraper. As the workers were preparing the site, they noticed something strange in the ground. They stopped and had a closer look. They'd uncovered a perfectly preserved circle of large holes, almost 13 metres across. They called in the experts, who were able to date it as 2,000 years old, but no one knew who'd had the technology to build such a structure. It was the beginning of a long and controversial argument.

3

Man: I'd no idea they had so much here. It's quite overwhelming actually.

Woman: Yes … I just wish we had more time to do it justice.

M: We've only seen the stuff on the ground floor – the older artefacts – and there's a special exhibition of 20th century art on the top floor. I'm quite keen to see that. They had someone doing a two-hour guided tour…

W: What, of the whole gallery?

M: Well, just the main exhibits, but we're too late for it. This place really needs more than one day … I wish we'd come earlier in the holiday … the guidebook doesn't give any idea of what it's really like.

W: Well, let's go up and see that exhibition.

4

Well, I did a degree in archaeology and I did it because I wanted to, not because it would lead to any particular career. I mean, the obvious thing would be to get a job in a museum or something, but actually I really wanted to see the actual places, to find out what different places look like and how people live there, and what their history was. There are so many places where the art and culture and whole way of living is completely different. I want to tell people about it – to make a living through books and articles about them. I've already had a bit of stuff published. It's not going to make me rich but that doesn't matter. I'm really excited about it, actually.

5

M: They started off really well. When they scored that first goal I thought they really might have a chance.

W: Yes. It started to go wrong when Mills got sent off, didn't it? At least, that's what the commentator said. But I thought they deserved to win. At least from the way they were playing in the first half. I didn't see the second half though – some friends came round so I switched it off.

M: I saw the whole thing and they really went to pieces in the second half … and that's what's happened in every match recently. So I wasn't surprised they lost in fact.

6

Clare: Simon – how are you? Haven't seen you for ages. Are you still working at the bank?

Simon: No, I'm working for myself now.

C: What, as a consultant?

S: That's right. I'm really enjoying it even though it involves being away from home rather a lot because of the travelling. But I was expecting that. And I'd expected to take a cut in salary at first, but it hasn't worked out that way at all.

C: So do you find you're working harder?

S: No, in fact I'd say I'm doing shorter hours, which is great. And it's good to be my own boss ... I wish I'd made the decision sooner.

7

It's a sunny day over most of the country with just a bit of cloud in some areas but that should clear by late afternoon. And the settled weather is going to continue through the night with clear skies and a touch of ground frost. The outlook isn't so good I'm afraid, as we are going to get some quite strong winds coming down from the north later tomorrow so it looks as if we could be looking at some quite wintry weather for the next few days.

8

Man: I'll see you in a minute – you go on. I want to get a newspaper and something to drink.

Woman: Do you have time? It's almost ten o'clock.

M: Plenty of time. You always fuss.

W: Well, remember last year when we went on holiday. You said we had time then, and we ended up missing the plane.

M: It's not even due in for five minutes. There's plenty of time. It's platform six, just across the bridge. The first class carriages will be at the front, but I'll be there before it gets in anyway.

W: Just make sure you are.

UNIT 8

page 98, Exam focus Paper 4 Listening: note completion (Part 2), Exercise 1

Presenter: Well, the summer is approaching, and that means the wedding season is upon us. Here's Pete with some practical advice for all of those thinking of tying the knot in the near future. Pete, what advice have you got to pass on?

Pete: Well, getting married is of course a wonderful thing, but organising the event can be harder than you expect. And these days it's often the engaged couple who make most of the arrangements. You really need to start thinking about it and making your plans one year ahead.

The first thing of course is to decide what date you want to have the wedding on. You'll also need to choose your best man and bridesmaids, and check that they are free then. Then when you've done that, you need to make up your mind where you want the ceremony to be – for example it might be a church or register office, or another approved place – and book it. At the same time, choose the place where you want to have the reception, and book that too.

As soon as you have decided all this and made the bookings, the two of you need to sit down together with your address books and draw up your guest list. If you send out the invitations in good time, you'll have a clear idea of how many people to expect at the reception, and how much the whole thing's going to cost.

But that's just the beginning. Once you've done that you need to start thinking about all the details – and again this needs doing well ahead, at least six months. Of course what most brides think about above all is the dress ... but there's also the bridesmaids' dresses, and then you need to think about the flowers that will be in season in the month you are getting married so you can make up your mind which ones you want. Then another thing you have to do is contact the people who are doing the catering for the reception to decide on a meal that is inside your budget. You also need to think about where your guests are going to stay if they are travelling from a distance. If they can't get back home after the reception and need to stay overnight then you should book accommodation for them

well ahead – if you leave it to the last minute, you may not be able to find anything. You really do need to do it all in a systematic way otherwise the stress is enormous. And of course you'll need to think about what happens after the wedding too – make sure you've completed all your bookings for the honeymoon at least six months ahead.

Oh, and if you're planning to go abroad then remember three months before, find your passport and make sure that it's OK – you'd be amazed at the number of people who discover a week before their wedding that it's out of date. And also around this time you need to make arrangements for photographs – so that you'll have something to look back on in the years to come. And of course those people who are going to make speeches need to start planning them – usually it's the bridegroom, but these days it could be the bride as well, it really depends on you.

Presenter: And that's it?

Pete: Almost ... but don't lose sight of the fact that this should be a happy day – people can get so caught up in organising the day that they forget to enjoy it – and after all, isn't that the point?

Presenter: Pete – thank you. And we wish anyone out there getting married this summer good luck. And now on to ...

UNIT 8

page 100, Listening 2: Song, Exercises 2 and 3

Drowning by Backstreet Boys

Don't pretend you're sorry
I know you're not
You know you got the power
To make me weak inside
Girl you leave me breathless
But it's okay 'cause
You are my survival
Now hear me say
I can't imagine life
Without your love
Even forever don't seem
Like long enough

Chorus

'Cause every time I breathe
I take you in
And my heart beats again
Baby I can't help it
You keep me
Drowning in your love
Everytime I try to rise above
I'm swept away by love
Baby I can't help it
You keep me
Drowning in your love

Maybe I'm a drifter
Late at night
'Cause I long for the safety
Of flowing freely
In your arms
I don't need another lover
It's not for me
'Cause only you can save me

Oh can't you see
I can't imagine life
Without your love
And even forever don't seem
Like long enough

Repeat chorus

Go on and pull me under

Cover me with dreams, yeah
Love me mouth to mouth now
You know I can't resist
'Cause you're the air
That I breathe

Every time I breathe
I take you in
And my heart beats again
Baby I can't help it
You keep me
Drowning in your love
Every time I try to rise above
I'm swept away by love
And baby I can't help it
You keep me
Drowning your love

Baby I can't help it
Keep me drowning
In your love
I keep drowning
In your love
Baby I can't help it
Can't help it no, no

Repeat chorus

UNIT 8

page 101, Speaking 2: how to keep talking/adding ideas (Parts 3 and 4), Exercise 3

A: And the last picture … the gym. What do you think about that?
B: I don't like using exercise machines, so that's no good for me.
A: Mmm. And there wouldn't be much chance for people to talk to one another actually, because they'd be working out on their own. OK … so I think the best activity for young people to meet one another would be going to dancing classes.
B: For older people, it might be the theatre … if they actually produce the plays and act in them, it would be a good way to meet people.
A: Mm.
B: Er … and I think another reason why the theatre would be good is that when they actually perform the play, that's a big social occasion, and their other friends can come and watch.
A: Yes, and with the dancing classes as well, it's the same, it's not just the people learning to dance, they can perform for other people to come and watch, and they can talk about it afterwards.
B: And another good thing about both of them is…

UNIT 8

page 101, Speaking 2: how to keep talking/adding ideas (Parts 3 and 4), Exercise 4

Examiner: So can you tell me who you rely on more, friends or family?
Student A: Well, I think I rely on my family a lot. Especially my sister – we're very close. I think your family is really important because whatever happens, they're going to help you.
Student B: Yes, and about the family, another thing is that they really know you. They're known you since you were a baby, it's not like friends who maybe have known you for just two or three years.
Student A: But some of my friends have known me since I was a baby too. And there are some things I can say to them that I can't say to my family. We've had similar experiences all our lives, and also I suppose you make friends with the people you know you can rely on.
Examiner: And who do you think you confide in more, friends or family?

UNIT 9

page 109, Exam focus Paper 4 Listening: selecting from answers (Part 4), Exercise 1

Susie: TV programmes on decorating and home improvements have been getting lots of airtime recently. As part of one series, Phil Bradshaw was offered a complete makeover of any room in his flat – for nothing. It sounded like a great idea, but in fact, it wasn't all plain sailing. So, Phil, tell us what happened.
Phil: Well, I have a friend who works in television and she asked me if I wanted to be on the programme and for some bizarre reason I agreed … I suppose I was quite attracted by the idea of being on TV, if you want to know the truth. Though even then I knew that in fact you're not on TV much, because you're not allowed to be in the house when they do the actual work – the whole point is that you don't know what they'll do. You just appear at the beginning and the end – you have to leave the makeover completely up to them.
S: And did you make any special preparations?
P: Well, I chose my bedroom to be made over and I went into the whole thing in a kind of jolly way. I decided to treat it like a game, and I put little stickers on the furniture and stuff saying, *Leave me alone* for things like my desk lamp, that was really old, and my grandmother had given it to me so I didn't want them to … to …
S: … do anything to it?
P: Right, and I had *Do what you want with me* for things like … oh, the curtains, they'd definitely seen better days. So I thought with any luck they might get me some new ones.
S: Did the designers consult you about what sort of thing … what sort of image you wanted?
P: Yeah, we had a quick chat just a few days before they started filming. I said I'd like some decent storage space for all my stuff, the books and computer and so on. As far as the general image of the whole room was concerned, I said I wanted a look that wasn't too different from what I had already – I've always liked things that are quite modern, not too fussy or anything, but nothing too extreme, you know.
S: And then you had to move out of the flat while they were doing it?
P: That's right. So I didn't know what was going on … then at the end, they took me into the room, I had to have my eyes shut, then they told me to open them and … well … all I could see was white. Everything was white. And I mean everything. It's not exactly my favourite colour in the first place, and it was all over. It was like being in a tent … they'd gone for this sort of tent image with white cotton hanging all over the ceiling and a white floor and everything.
S: So what was your first reaction?
P: Well, they were filming me, so I tried to pretend that it wasn't too bad. I think I just said something like, 'Wow, I don't believe it!'
S: And what about later on?
P: Well, after the cameras were switched off they let me look around properly. The first thing I noticed was that they'd broken my grandmother's lamp. Then there were all sorts of little things … the curtains were too short, and they didn't close properly. Then, on camera the presenter had said, 'There are plenty of cupboards for all your books and your computer,' and it looked as if there were lots, OK, but when I opened the doors there was nothing inside – no shelves, nowhere to put anything. And the rest of the flat was a complete mess – they'd had the television crew in there for three days, and it's just a small flat. It was just awful.
S: So what did you do?
P: Well, after they'd all gone, and I'd had a chance to have proper look at all this, I have to confess that I sat in the middle of this utter chaos and I just burst into tears. I'm glad the film crew weren't there then because I'm sure they'd have been quite prepared to show that on film. It's the sort of reaction they're looking for but I didn't give them the chance. And that's the only good thing that came out of it really.
S: Phil, thank you very much for talking to us today.

UNIT 10

page 116, Listening: sentence completion (Part 2), Exercise 4

Presenter: Hello and welcome to this week's programme in our series, 'Use your Brain'. This week we're looking at the question, 'Can you train yourself to be a genius?' Well, Dominic O'Brien thinks you can. The holder of eight world titles in memory skills, Dominic has amazed people by his incredible ability to memorise huge amounts of information.

But Dominic wasn't always so successful. When he was at school he actually had quite severe learning difficulties. He had reading problems – when he tried to look at words, he couldn't see them clearly, they seemed to jump around in front of his eyes, and he actually developed a fear of reading. As well as this, Dominic found it hard to concentrate in class and his teachers regarded him as difficult because he always wanted to be moving around, he couldn't just keep still.

After he had finished school, Dominic carried on with his education because he didn't know what else to do. He started a course at college, but he dropped out before finishing the course. He had no qualifications and no idea what he wanted to do, and his future looked uncertain. Then one day by chance he saw a man on television who could memorise all the cards in a pack of playing cards … mixed up in any order. Dominic was very impressed by this, and he decided that this was something he wanted to be able to do. He began to work out his own system for training his memory. He started practising several hours a day, and soon he could memorise all the cards in not just one pack of playing cards, that's 52 cards, but over fifty packs – almost 3,000 individual cards.

So how does he do it? Dominic says he uses his imagination to help him, and he connects the cards with other things in his mind. Basically, he remembers what the cards are by thinking of them in connection with people – by thinking of each card as a famous face. For example, he might imagine the queen of hearts as the model Claudia Schiffer, and the ace of clubs as Nick Faldo, the golf player. Then, to remember the order of the cards, he imagines a story based on a journey, say from home to work, and he imagines the different people he has connected with the cards are part of that journey. So for instance he might imagine waking up beside Claudia Schiffer, getting out of bed and tripping over Nick Faldo … and so on. He only needs to look at each card once – but he's got to go over the story several times in his mind to remember it.

Dominic's skill has brought him worldwide fame. His ability to remember cards meant he won so much money when gambling in casinos that nowadays the owners will no longer allow him through the door. He appeared on the Oprah Winfrey show, and amazed everyone there by memorising the names of everyone in the audience.

But he doesn't just use the technique for entertainment. He's developed his own training courses for athletes and others involved in sport to help them get better results by focusing their minds on winning.

Dominic thinks that his memory training system is improving his mental capacity by 20% every year. He says his memory just keeps getting better with age – and he's convinced he can still be a champion when he is 95.

UNIT 10

page 126, Exam focus Paper 5 Speaking: collaborative task/discussion (Parts 3 and 4), Exercise 1.1

Examiner: Now, Agna and Martin, I'd like you to talk about something together for about three minutes. I'm just going to listen. Here are some pictures which show some things that can help people to study effectively.
First, talk to each other about how useful each of these things is in helping people to study. Then say which three you think are the most effective. You only have about three minutes for this, so once again, don't worry if I stop you. Please speak so that we can hear you. All right?

UNIT 10

page 126, Exam focus Paper 5 Speaking: collaborative task/discussion (Parts 3 and 4), Exercise 1.2

Martin: OK, the computer … studying with the computer is very useful, but the problem is not everyone has … not everyone has got a computer, so it's a problem for some people. What do you think Agna about the computer?

Agna: Well, it's very useful because students can surf the Internet and find a lot of useful facts about things like geography and history and what's happening in the world, and they can listen at the same time if their computer … if they can have sound, so it's really I think the best way of studying, especially if there are computers in schools.

M: But maybe not for everyone, I think …

A: And of course a computer is useful as well for writing, for writing essays, and you can check if your language is correct and in addition to that, you can check the grammar is alright. Then there are also special things … special programmes to put in to help students with special subjects …

M: Yes, although again these can cost a lot of money, don't you think that's a problem, Agna?

A: Well, maybe, but they're not all expensive.

UNIT 11

page 131, Exam focus Paper 4 Listening: multiple matching (Part 3), Exercise 1

Speaker 1: I'm a Public Relations manager for a fashion company in Milan. I work eight hours a day, Monday to Friday, and twice a year during the fashion shows I'll work evenings and weekends as well. I love being part of the fashion world and being surrounded by beautiful clothes and elegant people. My flat's close to the city centre so there are lots of restaurants and shops nearby and I'm only five minutes' walk from the office, which is great. I often have lunch with clients – no one in Milan eats at their desk – and a lot of my salary goes on paying bills – mostly on my mobile phone!

Speaker 2: I live in London and I work in TV advertising; I've been doing the job for five years and I still get a real buzz out of it. Working for television, I get the chance to meet lots of famous people and another perk is the travel – recently I've been to Sydney and Prague. In this business, you can go out almost every evening for nothing, to film premieres and parties, but I don't bother now – the novelty's worn off. I don't actually live in London so I have to commute to work every day – that's the worst thing about the job. The journey takes just over an hour each way and the trains are always crowded.

Speaker 3: I work in New York and I love the energy of the city. My job involves looking after celebrities and organising music events. I work nine hours a day and I'm under a lot of pressure at work – sometimes I just have to switch my phone off – but I meet people from all walks of life. I spend my entire salary every month on rent and socialising. New York girls care about keeping their bodies in good shape and I go to the gym several times a week. I eat out most evenings with my friends and at weekends I go to the beach in summer, or skiing in winter, and I'm never bored.

Speaker 4: I'm a lecturer at the University of Hong Kong. It's a very international environment – there are students and teachers from all over the world there. Hong Kong's busy and crowded – it's exciting, but in the summer it's quite hot and humid. Accommodation's not cheap because of the lack of space and everyone lives in small flats – my flat's right on the edge of the city, but there's an excellent bus and underground system in Hong Kong. It's good to get out of the city sometimes, just to get a bit of a break from the bustle, so I usually try to go out to one of the islands at weekends.

Speaker 5: I live in Tokyo and although it's crowded and busy, I love it. I live in a one-roomed apartment and I work as promotions manager for a music company. It's rewarding, but it's hard – I work 12 hours a day. In the evenings I have work-related dinners or meetings and I often don't manage to get to bed before 3 o'clock in the morning. But Tokyo's a 24-hour-a-day city, and I'm not worried about being out in the early hours, even if I'm on my own, there's no real risk. I spend quite a lot on my rent, and on clothes – young Japanese women are very fashion conscious – but I have a good salary every month and I never spend it all.

UNIT 11

page 136, Vocabulary 2: numbers and money, Exercise 1.4

Example: There's a special offer at the butcher's – if you buy ten kilos of meat you get a discount.
1 He was driving at ninety kilometres an hour.
2 You can call me on my mobile – the number's 0777 843 1905.
3 We hope to have finished by a quarter past five this afternoon, but it could be a bit later.
4 Temperatures tomorrow are expected to fall to eight degrees centigrade.
5 The total cost could be as high as one hundred and twenty thousand euros – perhaps even more.
6 We had expected the work to be finished by the 15th of February 2004 but in fact it had hardly been started by then.

UNIT 11

page 138, Listening 2: multiple choice (Part 4), Exercise 2

Interviewer: Today we're talking about happiness – what it is, how we get it, and which people are happiest. I have with me Ed Stevens, a psychologist who's making a special study of this area. So, Ed, first of all I suppose most of us think we'd be happier if we had more money – how true is that in your opinion?
Ed: Well, it *is* true up to a point, but the problem is that to get the maximum benefit you have to be poor to start with. If you're already rich, more money's not going to make a big difference to you. Millionaires, for example, are only slightly happier than people with a lot less money.
I: Really? I don't know if that makes me feel better or not …
E: No, a lot of people find that surprising, but in fact it's been the subject of quite a lot of research. But leaving money aside, the sort of culture you come from also seems to have an awful lot to do with it. Some of the happiest people appear to be those in hot countries, where people ask 'What can I do that's fun. What can I do that's interesting?' They don't spend time worrying about the bad things, like people seem to in colder countries. They think more about the *good* things that might happen.
I: But presumably everyone *wants* to achieve happiness?
E: Well, actually that's not the case.
I: Really?

E: Well, feeling good and enjoying yourself aren't the only things in life for people in a lot of cultures. They might have different priorities, or be searching for satisfaction of a different kind. They could be willing to give up a lot of fun to achieve goals that are really important to them … buying a car, for instance.
I: Or passing an exam … getting qualifications?
E: Exactly. And another thing, you have to remember that positive emotions aren't always the best ones. We do need negative feelings too … if you're swimming in the sea and you meet a shark, giving it a happy smile isn't going to help you much. It all depends on the situation.
I: If you're looking at different cultures, how do you know that people all mean the same thing when they talk about happiness, anyway?
E: Mmm. It can be a real problem – you'd probably say 'happy' was an easy word, but quite often there isn't an exact equivalent in other languages so you can't translate it directly. So in the research we do, I use lots of different words to do with ways of feeling, with emotions, to try to get round it.
I: So going back to the beginning of this discussion. What's the secret of happiness?
E: Well, it's often said that having children is one of the keys, but that doesn't seem to be completely true … In fact for many young married couples, there seems to be some evidence that their level of happiness falls slightly after the birth of children, and then it gradually rises again later on. There are certain things that Eastern Philosophers say about just approaching life in a way that's generally optimistic, that make a lot of sense to me.
I: Mmm. And finally – do you think it's possible for everyone to be happy?
E: I think it's possible for most of the people to be happy most of the time – but not all of it. And so maybe we shouldn't try. People seem to think they should live on the edge of happiness all the time. They're actually happy, but they think they should be happier. But in fact we're built to be positive, not joyful. We should live in that state so that when something good happens we can go up – feel better, you know?
I: Ed, Thanks very much. And now we …

UNIT 11

page 139, Exam focus Paper 5 Speaking: a complete test, Exercise 2

Part 1
Examiner: Good morning. Could I have your mark sheets, please? Thank you. My name is Susan, and this is my colleague Tom. He is just going to be listening to us. So you are Athene and Stefan?
Athene/Stefan: Yes.
Examiner: First of all we'd like to know something about you, so I'm going to ask you some questions about yourselves. Let's begin with your home town or village. Athene, where are you from?
A: I'm from Corinth, in Greece.
E: Can you tell me something about it?
A: It's very famous because we have a canal there, for the big boats, and also … and also we have Mycenae near by, many tourists go there and it is very very old, more than 3,000 years, and very beautiful.
E: And what about your family? Can you tell me something about them?
A: Yes, I have a brother who is older than me, he has 25 years and he will get married this summer. And my father is businessman, and my mother is working in a school, but not like a teacher, she is secretariat.
E: Thank you. And what about you, Stefan? Do you work or are you a student?
S: I am student. I just finish my school, and now I will go to study engineering at the university.
E: How important is English for this?
S: Oh it's very important for my work I think in the future because I would travel to many places and for this you need good English.

E: Now let's move on to what you do in your spare time. What kind of sports are you and your friends interested in?

S: Oh … I like very much football, and also I like to walk in the mountains with my friends, and to go in the small boat … the canoe? When it is the summer, it is very fine.

E: Thank you.

Part 2

E: Now I'd like each of you to talk on your own for about a minute. I'm going to give each of you two different photographs and I'd like you to talk about them.

Here are your photographs. They show people who are working hard. Please let Stefan see them. Stefan, I'll give you your photographs in a minute.

I'd like you to compare and contrast these photographs, saying which person you think is working harder. Remember, you have only a minute for this, so don't worry if I interrupt you. All right?

A: Well, in this first photo is someone studying. He seems to be studying quite hard because he is in his room – I think in his bedroom – and the papers are all over the room – many many papers over the desk and everywhere. In contrast in the other photo there are many people working but they are not study – I mean they are working in fast food restaurant and there are many customers and they look as if they are busy. The boy is … maybe he is taking an examination very soon but in the fast food they are working in part-time job for earning money. I think that they are both working hard but maybe the boy is working harder because he is thinking very much although it is true that the others look a bit stressed. But I think the boy is working harder, it is more difficult for him and is hard working on your own.

E: Stefan, do you often work late at night?

S: Excuse me? Can you repeat the question?

E: Do you often work late at night?

S: Sometimes I do, but I don't like it. I prefer to get up early in the morning if it's necessary to work.

E: Thank you. Now Stefan, here are your two photographs. They show people making money in different situations. Please let Athene have a look at them. I'd like you to compare and contrast these photographs, and say what you think might be good and bad about each way of making money. Remember, Stefan, you only have about a minute for this, so don't worry if I interrupt you. All right?

S: In both the photos there are people who make money but in the first photo the man is standing outside and in the second photo he is inside. In the first photo he sells things in the street – he looks not so happy and I think he don't make a lot of money – but maybe he is not bored and maybe he can meet interesting people. He can have time to talk! But he is not having customers in the photo. In the second photo he makes money by working in an office – maybe he buys and sells in a bank – or something. He is investing, or maybe stocks and shares. This is good because he can make much money – but maybe it is boring and not so much fun. He can lose a lot of money if he is not careful.

E: Thank you. Athene, how do you think the person in the second photo is feeling?

A: Oh, I think maybe very stressed because there is a lot of technology and it is … he must to decide everything very quick, and maybe it's a lot of money.

E: Thank you.

Part 3

E: Now, I'd like you to talk about something together for about three minutes. I'm just going to listen. Here are some pictures of things we can do to avoid getting stressed. First, talk to each other about how useful each one is. Then choose two that you think are the most important for students. You only have about three minutes for this so, once again, don't worry if I stop you. Please speak so that we can hear you. All right?

A: OK. Well, in the first picture, it's about the sport. Me, I like the sport but I'm not doing a lot of sports, is not enough time now, but I would like, and how about you Stefan?

S: For me, this is very good. If I am stressed, I do some sport and I will be better. I think this is very good because I am … I am active, so if I study very hard, then I go for football and I will feel very good.

A: Yes. Maybe you are right, this is very good for the stress, to do some sport but how about on the television? Do you think that's good, to watch sport on the television?

S: For me no but I know many people … for example, my father, he watches sport on the television always for relax. Then the music, this is good also if you have stress, because it makes you feel more calm.

A: I think for me is very very important the friends, so if people have some problem they can talk to their friend and then it is less stressful. But if there is no one then …

S: Yes, but it is important the right person …

A: Maybe. And then you must sleep enough, maybe eight hours. But for me is impossible! Eight hours! What about you Stefan?

S: No, it's not possible except sometimes at the weekend, then I am sleep a lot. Then the food … for me it is not so important to prevent the stress. I can eat what I want.

A: Yes, but it's important to be healthy, not to get tired or to have some allergies. And no always drinking coffee, coffee, coffee, especially in my country, is very strong, the coffee. But the next picture is good I think, if you are dancing and good music, you will be very happy and forget your problems. For me this is very good. Yes?

S: I'm not so sure. Maybe it's noisy, and a lot of smoke in these places. But I like to relax with playing computer games, that's quite good. But I used to do that more when I was young. Now it's not so interesting for me.

A: For me that's not so good. So for me to prevent the stress I think I choose the talking … to talk to someone who they know you very well, that's very good and you will solve all of your problems maybe. And the dancing. What about you Stefan? I think it's not the same.

S: No it's not the same. For me I think a good way for many people, is to do sport. Because it's good for the health, and you will to meet people, and to think about something that is … that is not about your problems. And then I don't know. Maybe music, because for everyone there is some music that they like and it can make you relaxed anywhere, you can always have music with you and choose what you would the most like to hear.

A: So we don't agree! But Stefan, I think for anyone, to prevent the stress, they must have the chance to share their problems, don't you think?

S: Well, maybe. But for me is not so important. If you are playing a game together, you can share something, and you forget about the problem. It's not so important.

E: Thank you.

Part 4

E: So what kind of job do you think is most stressful?

A: Well, for me, if the job is … like in the bank where you have too much responsibility and you can easily to lose many … a lot of money, that's very stressful. And I don't like the mathematics so is hard.

S: Yes, and all day long inside looking at the computer – very difficult. But also I think it's very hard to be a dentist. I would not like to do that job – my uncle is dentist, the pay is very good but it's very stressful.

E: So what do you think is more important, a high salary or job satisfaction?

A: Job satisfaction?

E: To have a job you enjoy.

S: Oh, I think of course you must have job satisfaction, because you are there so … so many hours every day and if you are not happy in your job maybe you will have problems. So it's important that you choose your job carefully. And if you are lucky also the people in your job will be help you and you will enjoy it.

A: But as well, it's important the money. If you are always worry about the money that's not good, so to have enough money, not too much but a nice house, a nice car, you can go for holidays ….

S: Sure. But if I would have to choose, I would have the good job, even if the salary is a little bit less, as long as it's possible to live.

E: So if you had enough money to live on without working, would you still want to work?

A: Oh … me! No, there are so many things you can do, if there is enough money, to travel, to have a nice time. Don't you think, Stefan?

S: I'm not so sure. Maybe if …

UNIT 12

page 145, Listening 1: sentence completion (Part 2), Exercise 2

Sally: And now it's time for Adrian Baker in News from America. And this month he's talking about the Stella Awards. Adrian, what exactly are the Stella awards?

Adrian: Well, the Stella awards are actually named after an 81-year-old woman called Stella Liebeck who got a coffee from a McDonalds take-away. When she'd bought it, she took it out to her car – it was in one of those insulated plastic cups, and when she was sitting in her car drinking the coffee, she spilled it on her leg and burned it. She thought someone ought to have warned her that the coffee was hot, so she took McDonald's to court. The court supported her claim, and said that McDonald's was responsible for her injury, and she was awarded compensation of an incredible $2.9 million. Well, the case got a lot of publicity, and it also inspired the competition that's now held every year in the United States, to find the most amazing stories about people who've made claims for compensation for injuries that seem totally their fault.

One of this year's stories is about a burglar called Terrence Dickson who got into a house by breaking a window. He collected up various valuables, then decided to leave the house a different way and go through the garage, he got in alright through the door which connected it with the kitchen, but then when he tried to open the automatic doors to the outside, he found the mechanism which operated them had broken. And he couldn't get back out of the garage into the house through the kitchen door because it had locked when he pulled it shut. So there he was, stuck. Terrence ended up staying there for eight days until the family got back from holiday. There was a case of Pepsi so he had something to drink and there was some canned food stored in the garage but of course he didn't have a can opener so all he had to eat was some dog biscuits he found there. Anyway, when he was finally released, the burglar took the owners of the house to court claiming he'd been caused mental suffering and he was awarded $500 000 compensation. Sounds incredible, but it's absolutely true.

Then there's the case of Kathleen Robinson, who was awarded an even bigger amount of compensation by a jury after she broke her ankle when she was inside a furniture shop. It happened when she tripped over a small child who was running around completely out of control inside the shop. The furniture shop had to pay her $780,000, which doesn't sound too unfair until you learn that it was actually her own child that she fell over.

Then in Delaware, Kara Walton fell from the window of a ladies room and knocked out her two front teeth. But what was she doing at the window in the first place? Well, she was trying to sneak out of a nightclub to avoid paying the bill for the drinks she'd had. She sued the owner, and she was awarded $12,000 and dental expenses.

Then finally there's the story of Mr Merv Grazinski. Mr Grazinski decided to go out and buy himself what's known as a camper van – the sort of thing where you have a driver's seat at the front and space at the back for sleeping and eating and so on. Now, the vehicle he bought had a device known as a cruise control, which allows it to automatically continue going at a particular speed, even if the driver takes his foot off the accelerator. So anyway, Mr Grazinski set off on his first trip. He was driving all on his own, and

as soon as he got to a straight stretch of motorway, he set the cruise control at 70 miles per hour. Then he calmly got up out of his seat and went into the back part of the van to make himself a cup of tea. So, not surprisingly, the camper van swerved off the motorway and crashed. Fortunately Mr. Grazinski wasn't badly hurt, but his van was completely destroyed. He sued the makers of the campervan on the basis that the driver's instruction manual hadn't warned him he had to stay in the driver's seat when he was driving. The jury awarded him $1,750,000 and the company actually changed their manuals afterwards to include an instruction saying that drivers should stay in their seats at all times.

Presenter: Thank you Adrian. How incredible!

UNIT 13

page 158, Listening: sentence completion (Part 2), Exercise 3

Interviewer: With us today in the studio is the television wildlife expert Charlotte Uhlenbroek. Charlotte, you've spent much of your life travelling round the world – where would you say is home?

Charlotte: It's hard to say. I was born in England and my mother comes from there but my father works for the United Nations and he's Dutch. When I was five we went to Nepal; I lived there for ten years and I suppose I still think of Nepal as home in a way, as that's where I grew up and went to school.

I: To an English school?

C: Well, American actually, but it was good because it had such a mixture of students, they came from all over the world.

I: And where does your interest in animals come from?

C: I've always loved them – when we were living in Nepal I used to wander the streets trying to rescue stray dogs. Anyway, I did zoology and psychology at university, then when I left, I got a job at the BBC.

I: So is that how you became a TV presenter?

C: No, at that stage I was working as a researcher. Then one evening a friend asked if I'd heard that volunteers were wanted to work on a project in Africa, and I phoned up straightaway.

I: So then you returned to Africa?

C: Yes, I spent four years there studying chimpanzees, and at the same time I was working for my PhD…. it was on the subject of animal communication. And then the BBC invited me to take part in a programme about the project.

I: Did you find TV presenting was a big challenge?

C: Well, not really. Because it was my subject it was quite easy, like telling a friend what was going on. I didn't feel as if I was talking to millions of people. And I enjoyed it because it was so different from academic research, where you always have to communicate everything in a very formal way. I don't think that science always needs to be like that. You don't become inaccurate just by using normal language.

I: Charlotte, you've spent years out in the wild with dangerous animals. You must have had some alarming experiences. Did you ever really feel you were in danger?

C: Well, I think probably my worst experience was when I was pursued by killer bees through the jungle, and I fell 30 metres down onto a narrow ledge, with another 50-metre drop below me. But in general, if you learn about the way animals communicate and their social structure, you're generally safe enough. I was watching a pair of young gorillas once and they decided to show off. The younger one walked up, kicked me, and looked at his brother as if to say, 'what did you think of that?' The other one started beating his chest and then just knocked me down and sat on me.

I: Weren't you terrified?

C: No, not really, because I could see that they wouldn't hurt me. They were just teenage gorillas showing off.

I: Mmm. So is there anything you've learned from animal communication that you've been able to apply to human relationships?

C: Well, when we're communicating with other people we tend just to take notice of the words we hear, but in fact we're also unconsciously picking up clues on body language all the time and I think studying animals has made me more aware of this.

I: And finally what about the future of primates such as chimpanzees?

C: It doesn't look good. Hunters are killing the females for their meat and selling the babies to traders nowadays. They're adorable, but they should never be bought as pets. There's a tendency to think of them as amusing caricatures of humans. But they are sophisticated animals in their own right. In the wild, they can live until they are 50 years old and they can become four times stronger than man – if only they're allowed to.

I: Charlotte, thank you.

UNIT 13
page 159, Speaking 2: quiz, Exercise 2

Mike: It's amazing how little we know about the world.

Win: What do you mean?

M: Well, I was listening to a programme the other day about the Moon – did you know it has a huge influence on weather patterns on the Earth? And that if it disappeared then the weather would change – and animals and birds could be in danger?

W: Yes, I think I've heard that before – but I'm sure you don't know where the English word Earth actually came from.

M: No – was it Latin? Greek?

W: No, it's Germanic.

M: Oh, OK. But do you know … do you think that lightning can strike more than once in the same place?

W: Yes, I know a lot of people think that it can't, but some tall buildings are struck by lightning quite often – the Empire State Building, for example.

M: Right, and there are even cases of people who've been struck more than once and still survived.

W: But there are other things that people believe are true that aren't, like I think I read somewhere that barbecues are bad for the environment, but it's not actually true.

M: No?

W: No, the fuel for barbecues comes from replaceable resources and so they're actually kinder to the environment than other forms of fuels.

M: Talking of fuels, do you know when the supply of oil will run out?

W: Quite soon?

M: No, actually it may be never. There are lots of reserves of oil, and the idea that they'll run out may be totally false.

W: Really? Well, I suppose that's good news if it's true. But thinking of dramatic things – I bet you can't tell me what's the most violent natural event that ever happened on Earth.

M: Well, I know that there was a big earthquake in Ecuador in 1906 – and a huge volcano in Indonesia – was it either of those?

W: No, it was a meteor hitting the Earth about 65 million years ago – the one that people think caused the extinction of the dinosaurs.

M: A meteor – I wouldn't have guessed that.

W: And a last one – do you know what a *tsunami* is?

M: What?

W: A *tsunami*

M: Oh… Is it when all the snow comes down off the mountain…?

W: No. It's a giant wave that comes from the sea … a tidal wave. I think it was originally a Japanese word.

M: Oh well, I can see that we'd both better brush up on our general knowledge!

UNIT 14
page 169, Listening 1: multiple matching (Part 3), Exercise 1

1

My uncle's in the Royal Air Force. He's a base commander, and when I was about 15 he showed me all round the base and let me see all the planes there and explained all about them. It was a real inspiration to me. I've always loved planes, ever since my mum and dad gave me a radio-controlled model aircraft when I was about eight years old. And I was always building model planes and that taught me how aircraft are … how they're structured and just how complicated they are. So anyway, now I want to do a course in aerospace engineering at university and I hope eventually to work in aircraft design.

2

When I was young, people always used to ask me what I wanted to do, and I didn't really know … I'd have quite liked to be a vet, but you need really good qualifications. And I wondered about joining the police but I thought it might be a bit dangerous. At present I'm doing office work – it's OK but I'm still waiting to find something I'm really good at, then hopefully I can make my fortune. If by some miracle that ever happened, I'd buy myself a tiny cottage on an island miles from anywhere with a huge, wild, wooded garden and live there all on my own.

3

I had a good job and a happy marriage and everything, but I never thought much about it. I was OK, just carrying on doing what I was doing and living from day to day, and then one day, the day my first child was born, all that changed out of the blue and I was standing there in the hospital holding her for the first time and I thought 'I really want the best for you, I want you to have everything' and I didn't know it was in me to feel like that about anything. But she's six months old now and I still feel the same.

4

I started skiing when I was very young. When I was 16 I went to America to train full time, but I came home after I fell out with my coach. Looking back I think I was too young to go off and live in a different country. The best thing so far has been winning the British Championships, and now I want to qualify for the next winter Olympics. My parents have been amazing. If it wasn't for them I wouldn't be where I am now. But my university work's important too – I want to do as well as possible in both my skiing **and** my degree.

5

When I was a child I used to spend ages looking at maps of the world, and dreaming about where I could go. I've always been fascinated by the idea of seeing the limits people can go to, and what I'd like to do is go round the world and take in the hottest place, the coldest place and so on. There's a place in Siberia so cold that people say your eyeballs can freeze – but people do live there. I dream of seeing all these places before I die but I'll have to start soon or I'll never make it.

Unit 1 test

1 Complete these sentences with one of the words from the box. (10 points)

| ago already before ever for when yet |

1 I've never been to Spain ....
2 I've known her .... ten years.
3 I first went to China two years ....
4 This is the first time I've .... eaten Japanese food.
5 I last went to the cinema three months ....
6 I ran to the phone .... I heard it ringing.
7 I've hated flying .... as long as I can remember.
8 I don't want anything to eat. I've .... had lunch.
9 I can't remember .... I last had a holiday.
10 I haven't finished my homework ....

2 Correct the mistakes in the following sentences. (10 points)

1 I've been to India two years ago.

....

2 I don't want to go to Oxford. I've been already there.

....

3 This is the best meal I ate for ages.

....

4 He eats so much. I haven't understood how he can do it.

....

5 When I was a child, I've wanted to be a professional actor.

....

6 I took my driving test twice so far.

....

7 Have ever you met anyone famous?

....

8 How many times have seen you Mary this week?

....

9 I've been knowing him all my life.

....

10 This book is really long. I've read it for almost six weeks.

....

3 Chose the correct alternative to complete the following text.   (10 points)

What kind of films do I like? Well, I'm particularly keen on (1) *active / action* films, and I love
(2) *science / scientific* fiction. I'm also quite fond of (3) *thrillings / thrillers*. What I really hate are
(4) *musicians / musicals*, which I think are really (5) *bored / boring*, and (6) *horror / horrific* films – I
don't like being (7) *frightened / frightening*!

Whatever the film is, it must have a good (8) *plot / scene*, excellent (9) *acts / acting*, and of course an
exotic (10) *setting / set*, plus lots of special (11) *affects / effects* and an (12) *exciting / excited*
(13) *climax / final*. My favourite (14) *director / conductor* is Quentin Tarantino, who I think has made
some (15) *outstood / outstanding* films, like *Pulp Fiction* and *Kill Bill*. My favourite (16) *act / actor* is
probably Jim Carrey. He's so (17) *amused / amusing*.

I must admit that I really love going to the cinema. The whole experience is great, from queueing up
to buy your tickets at the (18) *box / case* office, to taking your seat, although I try to avoid sitting in
the front (19) *line / row* if possible, because it hurts your neck looking up at the (20) *stage / screen*.

4 Complete the following sentences, using the correct form of the word in bold.   (10 points)

1 Although he was very tall, he was .... known as 'Shorty'. **CONFUSE**

2 The next .... of *Romeo and Juliet* begins at 7.30. **PERFORM**

3 Nobody believe the .... he gave us. **EXPLAIN**

4 He tried to threaten me, but when that didn't work, he tried using .... instead.
   FLATTER

5 I like their songs, but they aren't very .... They sound just like The Beatles. **ORIGIN**

6 The staff at the hotel gave us lots of .... about the city. **INFORM**

7 The film wasn't very .... , so we left early. **ENJOY**

8 Everybody expected an exciting game, but only three .... showed up, so it was
   cancelled. **CONTEST**

9 I've never been particularly .... , and was always bad at games at school. **COMPLETE**

10 I call my mother .... , usually at the weekend. **REGULAR**

5 In each of the following sentences, there is an extra word which should not be there.
Cross it out.   (10 points)

1 When did you at last go to the cinema?

2 How many times have you ever been to the theatre this year?

3 It's almost three o'clock! Haven't you already finished lunch yet?

4 The show was a really enjoyable and we had lots of fun.

5 Who does usually presents the evening news in your country?

6 I've been known him for as long as I can remember.

7 I bought this computer since when I started college.

8 This is the best film what I've seen for a long time.

9 Have you seen *Susanna*? It's a romance film set in the 1920s.

10 I've not never eaten Mexican food before.

Unit 2 test

1   Complete the following text, using the correct form of a word from the list.   (5 points)

ENCOURAGE   FLATTER   DEPRESS   EXCITE   FRUSTRATE

When I was asked to represent my town in a national photography competition, I was both
(1) .... about the prospect, and (2) .... that somebody thought my pictures were good
enough. My friends were very (3) .... about my chances of winning. 'Go on,' they said. 'You're
bound to win.'

Anyway, I spent a few days out and about with my camera, but was unable to find anything that
inspired me. It was extremely (4) .... , it always is when you are trying to do something that just
won't work, and I was beginning to feel a bit (5) .... about the whole thing.

2   Complete the following sentences, using the correct form of a word from the list.   (5 points)

CONFUSE   FRIGHTEN   INTEREST   THRILL   IRRITATE

1   I was absolutely .... when my team won the match.

2   He asked me if I would be .... in joining the club.

3   I got a bit .... when he kept tapping his teeth with the end of his pencil.

4   It was the most .... moment of my life. I've never felt so scared!

5   Your explanation is a bit .... , could you repeat it?

3   Correct the mistakes in the following sentences.   (10 points)

1   Learning English is not difficult as learning Chinese. ....

2   My new computer was quite not as expensive as my old one. ....

3   The north of the country has a more cold climate than the south. ....

4   My History teacher is less strict than my Maths teacher. ....

5   Timothy is one of the least friendliest people I've ever met. ....

6   Would you rather to go to the cinema or the theatre? ....

7   This is the more delicious meal I've ever eaten! ....

8   I prefer watching football to playing it. ....

9   In my opinion, it's far difficult to work after lunch than it is before lunch. ....

10   Jo is far more good than me at playing golf. ....

4   Complete the words in bold with a suitable negative prefix.   (10 points)

1   He was ......**capable** of explaining anything clearly, and so all his students ......**understood**
    his instructions.

2   I'm afraid you have ......**sufficient** funds to pay for your course, so ......**fortunately** we'll
    have to ask you to leave.

3   He's a very ......**active** person, and because he smokes he's rather ......**healthy** as well.

4   It's ......**possible** for you to enter the competition. You're far too ......**experienced**.

5   I would ......**trust** anyone who says they can invest your money and double it in six months. It's
    just too ......**credible** to be true.

5 Complete the gaps in the following sentences with a definite article (*the*) or (-) when no article is needed. (10 points)

1 He was .... first person to row across .... Atlantic.

2 We spent a week in .... Rome, and .... sun didn't shine once!

3 British food has a bad reputation abroad, but actually .... British are .... very creative and imaginative cooks.

4 .... Internet and .... mobile phone have revolutionised the way we work.

5 We went for a sailing holiday on .... Lake Geneva, and by .... chance

met some old friends.

6 Complete the second sentence so that it has a similar meaning to the first sentence, using no more than five words, including the word given. (10 points)

1 I've never met such a boring person!

the

He's .... I've ever met.

2 I prefer watching videos to going to the cinema.

would

I .... go to the cinema.

3 I really didn't believe how stupidly he behaved.

was

It .... stupidly he behaved.

4 She's very clever. However, she's also very lazy.

on

She's very clever, but .... she's also very lazy.

5 The food in this restaurant is much better than the food in the other restaurant.

nearly

The food in the other restaurant .... as the food in this restaurant.

Unit 3 test

1   Match the sentences 1–10 to sentences a)–j) below.   (10 points)

1   I fully expected to pass my driving test, but failed because of a couple of small mistakes.

2   My classmates and I were all very confident about the exam.

3   Everywhere I looked, all I could see was miles of desert in every direction.

4   I lead a healthy lifestyle, and like to keep fit.

5   I spend a lot of time in the school library.

6   I have a useful technique for remembering new words I learn.

7   Tom is very industrious and works extremely hard.

8   Half of the class were asleep.

9   Some of my exam results were a bit disappointing.

10   On the whole, the children enjoyed the film.

☐ a)   There was nothing else as far as the eye could see.

☐ b)   The others were looking out of the window or daydreaming.

☐ c)   It is here that I can concentrate and get my work done.

☐ d)   This is one reason why I never smoke.

☐ e)   Some of them, however, found it a bit boring.

☐ f)   Unlike him, I prefer to take things easy.

☐ g)   None of us expected to fail.

☐ h)   It was one of the most frustrating experiences of my life.

☐ i)   However, most of them were excellent.

☐ j)   I write them down on small cards and look at them when I have a quiet moment.

2   Choose the correct alternative in each of these sentences.   (5 points)

1   I look *as / like* my mother, but in other respects I take after my father.

2   She started work at the company *as / like* a cleaner, and over the next fifteen years rose to become the manager.

3   My brother isn't as tall *as / like* me, but we look very similar.

4   I've always thought of English *as / like* a very colourful language.

5   You look as *like / though* you could do with a holiday.

3 Complete the following dialogues using a word from the box. There are five words that you do not need. (5 points)

| advantage   agree   foot   hand   know   position   realise   suppose   sure   true |

1 'What's the capital of Albania?'
'I'm not .... Is it Tirana?'

2 'I love the weather in the spring. It's so pleasant.'
'Yes, but on the other .... , it can be a bit changeable.'

3 'There's no excuse for people being rude, is there?'
'That's ....'

4 'Do you think that learning English is difficult?'
'I .... so.'

5 'I've always thought that eating less meat is good for you.'
'Yes, and another .... is that you don't spend so much money.'

4 Correct the mistakes in the following sentences. (10 points)

1 She tried hardly, but she kept missing. ....

2 The tickets should have cost us £10 each, but we got in freely. ....

3 She's usually quite a cheerful person, but late she seems a bit depressed. ....

4 He's not here. He's perhaps overslept. ....

5 They didn't certainly work very hard for the exam. ....

6 I had hoped our team would do good in the match, but they lost by three goals. ....

7 He spoke to us unfriendly, and made us feel very unwelcome. ....

8 He near didn't catch his train. Another two minutes and he would have missed it. ....

9 After the show, you must come home straight. ....

10 I won't be able to finish this report by the weekend. It would be very impossible. ....

5 Complete the following text, using the correct past form of the verbs in bold. (20 points)

I want to tell you about something that (1) **happen** to me a few years ago. It (2) **be** a cold November day, and I just (3) **arrive** in London for a job interview. I (4) **be** a bit early, so I (5) **go** to a nearby café. I 6) **enjoy** a coffee and a slice of cake when suddenly somebody (7) **come** up behind me and (8) **grab** my mobile phone, which (9) **lie** on the table next to me. They then ran out of the café. I was absolutely furious, because I (10) **only / buy** the phone the previous week, and it (11) **cost** me a lot of money. Well, I (12) **run** after the thief, but while I (13) **chase** him, I (14) **slip** on the icy pavement. By the time I (15) **get** back on my feet, the thief (16) **disappear**.

Anyway, I went to the job interview. While the manager of the company (17) **interview** me, there (18) **be** a knock on the door.

'Ah, this will be our coffee,' the manager said.

I (19) **turn** round as the person with the coffee came in. To my utter amazement, it was the same person who (20) **stole** my phone only half an hour before.

Unit 4 test

1 Complete the following sentences with the correct form of the verb in bold. In some cases, more than one form is possible. (10 points)

1 Look at those black clouds. I'm sure it **rain**. ....

2 Are you hungry? I **make** you a sandwich. ....

3 My driving test **be** a week on Thursday. ....

4 John's flight **arrive** at Heathrow airport at 7 o'clock tomorrow morning. ....

5 I want to go out tonight, but I don't think I **finish** my homework by then. ....

6 This time next week, I **lie** on a beach in the Bahamas. ....

7 Thanks a lot for lending me your umbrella. I **return** it tomorrow, if that's OK. ....

8 What you **do** tomorrow afternoon? ....

9 I arrived here on 28 October last year, so tomorrow I **be** here for exactly one year. ....

10 We need to leave at 6 o'clock. You **be** ready to go then? ....

2 Complete the following sentences with a suitable preposition. (10 points)

1 Are you responsible .... making all this mess?

2 I don't get on with my brother, but I'm quite close .... my sister.

3 I've never been particularly interested .... football.

4 Going to Australia has always appealed .... me.

5 He's rather unfriendly, and I must admit I'm a little afraid .... him.

6 She's always wanted to train .... a classical dancer.

7 He had a great talent .... singing, and decided to become an opera singer.

8 I don't know if we'll go for a picnic. It depends .... the weather.

9 I'm so busy, I just don't have time .... a holiday.

10 I hadn't seen her for years, until one day she suddenly appeared .... television.

3 Complete the following sentences by rearranging the jumbled letters in bold to make words connected with food. (10 points)

1 Cheese and eggs are examples of **yaird** products. ....

2 You should try to eat lots of **hefsr** fruit. ....

3 Too much **olochlreste** is bad for your heart. ....

4 **rvengeaiats** are people who don't eat meat or fish. ....

5 It's very important to eat a **danbleac** diet. ....

6 You should avoid foods with a high **oportiropn** of fat. ....

7 Eggs, nuts and beans are a good source of **niptroe**. ....

8 Root **bevegtlsae** are cheap, and they're also good for you. ....

9 Some people think that insects are a **tinsourtui** form of food. ....

10 Rice, potatoes and bread are rich in **eboyhratcards**. ....

4   Choose the best alternative to complete the following sentences.   (5 points)

1 He woke up, got out of bed and .... his arms.

   a) nodded   **b)** clenched   **c)** stretched

2 She .... her head in agreement.

   a) nodded   **b)** shrugged   **c)** bent

3 The doctor took my .... and told me to stay in bed for a few days.

   a) heat   **b)** temperature   **c)** fever

4 I'm not surprised you've got such a .... throat. You haven't stopped talking all day.

   a) rough   **b)** hurt   **c)** sore

5 That box looks very heavy. Don't .... yourself carrying it up the stairs.

   a) damage   **b)** hurt   **c)** wound

5   Correct the mistakes in the following sentences.   (5 points)

1 Good morning. I'd like some informations about English courses, please. ....

2 She's very pretty, and she's got a lovely hair. ....

3 We can't go out tonight because we've got a little money left. ....

4 If you want to know what's going on in the world, watch the news or buy newspaper. ....

5 I eat very few meat because too much can be unhealthy. ....

6   In each of the following sentences, there is an extra word which should not be there.
Cross it out.   (10 points)

1 Fresh fruit and vegetables are good for you because they are rich in the vitamin C.

2 Nuts and dried beans are an excellent source of some protein for vegetarians and vegans.

3 Being succesful it depends on a combination of intelligence, luck and hard work.

4 My girlfriend is tall, slim and has a wonderful hair which goes all the way down to her waist.

5 She knew a very few people in the room and consequently felt rather uncomfortable and out of place.

6 I've really hardly seen any of my friends this week, as most of them are away on holiday.

7 This time next week I'll have be sitting on a beach in the Bahamas!

8 I'm not sure what I'm doing this weekend, but I'll probably to meet my friends in town.

9 I've got a roughly sore throat. I'd better make an appointment to see my doctor as soon as possible.

10 I didn't do much of work at the weekend because the weather was so good.

Progress test 1 (Units 1–5)

1   Complete the following sentences by putting the verbs in bold into the correct tense.   (15 points)

1   I **meet** Eric at the pub last night.
   ....

2   All my life I **love** travelling.
   ....

3   He works up to twelve hours a day. I **not/understand** how he does it.
   ....

4   Why are my eyes red? I **peel** onions, that's why!
   ....

5   We **watch** television when suddenly there was a knock on the door.
   ....

6   I was surprised when he greeted me like an old friend, because I **never meet** him before.
   ....

7   Be careful, or you **drop** that glass.
   ....

8   Apparently the place we're going to for our holiday is very expensive, so by the time we return, we **spend** all our money.
   ....

9   My new job is going to pay much more than this one, so this time next month I **earn** a small fortune!
   ....

10 Here's your class timetable. As you can see, your first lesson **begin** at 9 o'clock tomorrow.
   ....

11 I went abroad for the first time last month. Before that, I **never leave** the country before.
   ....

12 Do you know who **direct** the *Matrix* films?
   ....

13 Do you realise it **not rain** for almost four weeks?
   ....

14 He told me that he **work** for the same company for almost thirty years, and had no plans to leave.
   ....

15 She asked me how much my new car **cost**.
   ....

2   Correct the mistakes in the following sentences.   (15 points)

1   He suggested them to go to Barcelona for their holiday.
   ....

2   I've been knowing Val ever since we went to school together.
   ....

3   I don't like living here because I've got a few friends, so my social life is extremely boring.
   ....

4   When have you started work here, last year or the year before?
   ....

5   Who was break my computer?
   ....

6   She smokes too much. She's already been smoking two packets this morning.
   ....

7   I rather go to the beach than the cinema.
   ....

8   In my opinion, no other country is exciting or interesting as Cuba.
   ....

9   Environmentalists tell us that animal species such as tiger will be extinct within thirty years.
   ....

10 One advantage of living in a city like the New York is the huge choice of things to do.
   ....

11 Has anyone told you that you look exactly as your sister?
   ....

12 No matter how hardly he ran, he couldn't keep up with her.
   ....

13 He couldn't tell his teacher why had he missed most of his lessons.
   ....

14 We asked to our teacher if we could leave the lesson early.
   ....

15 We haven't got many money left, so we'll have to economise until the end of the month.

....

3 Complete the following texts using a word from the box.   (20 points)

acting   advertisements   applauded   audience cholesterol   commercials   confusing   consumer encouraging   frightened   frustrated   marketing outstanding   plays   plot   protein   reviews   setting vegetarian   vitamin

The film was (1) .... ; there was a really clever (2) .... with a surprising twist at the end, the (3) .... (central Africa) was interesting and exotic, and the (4) .... was excellent (James Brandon was particularly good as the doctor).

The theatre was packed, and it was definitely one of the best (5) .... I had seen for ages. At the end, the (6) .... got to their feet and (7) .... appreciatively. However, the newspaper (8) .... weren't quite as enthusiastic.

I must admit felt rather (9) .... when I failed my driving test, especially as my instructor had been so (10) .... One of my problems is that I find the road system in the town so (11) .... , and I'm (12) .... by other drivers on the road.

I try to avoid foods that are high in (13) .... , because it's so bad for the heart. Instead, I eat lots of foods which are rich in (14) .... C, like fruit and vegetables. I've often considered giving up meat altogether and becoming a (15) .... I mean, you get just as much (16) .... in cheese and eggs as you do in meat, don't you?

We all live in a (17) .... society these days: our newspapers are full of (18) .... , and there are endless (19) .... on television telling us to 'buy, buy, buy!' Some (20) .... departments will go to any lengths to make us buy their company's products.

4 Complete the second sentence with a reporting verb so that it has a similar meaning to the first sentence.(5 points)

1 'Why don't we go to Paris for the weekend?'
   She .... going to Paris for the weekend.

2 'Would you like to come to my place for dinner tonight?'
   She .... me to her place for dinner.

3 'I'm sorry I hurt your feelings.'
   He .... for hurting my feelings.

4 'Don't forget to do your homework.'
   He .... me to do my homework.

5 'If you don't help me, I'll never talk to you again.'
   She .... never to talk to me again if I didn't help her.

5 Chose the correct alternative to complete the following sentences.   (15 points)

1 My parents got divorced *when / since / for* I was very young.

2 He always wanted to be *finance / financial / financially* independent.

3 There was a great deal of *confuse / confusion / confusing* when we arrived at the hotel.

4 I think you must have *misunderstood / disunderstood / ununderstood* my explanation.

5 She was rather *unexperienced / disexperienced / inexperienced*, which is probably why she didn't do so well.

6 In England, summers are often cool and wet, *whereas / therefore / in* addition in Italy they are usually warm and dry.

7 We had a/an *fairly / absolutely / completely* fantastic holiday.

8 Are you responsible *to / for / of* making all this mess?

9 I'm fond of my brother, but much closer *with / for / to* my sister.

10 There were very *little / few / any* students at school today.

11 Several people were *damaged / wounded / injured* in the accident.

12 The new Skowdy Sunset is the perfect car *to / with / for* old people.

13 Make sure you ask the shop for a *recipe / receipt / reduction* in case you need to return your purchases.

14 How do you want to pay for that, in cash or *by / in / with* credit card?

15 I always buy things in bulk because it's more *economical / economic / economising*.

6   Complete the second sentence so that it has a similar meaning to the first sentence, using no more than five words, including the word given.   (20 points)

1   'You broke my camera!' John said to me.

   blamed

   John .... camera.

2   'Did you post my letter?' James said to Alice.

   if

   James asked .... his letter.

3   My flight arrives in London this time tomorrow.

   be

   This time tomorrow, my flight
   .... in London.

4   The doctor prescribed me some painkillers.

   gave

   The doctor .... for some painkillers.

5   He only recognised two or three people in the crowded room.

   very

   There .... he recognised in the crowded room.

6   I have to look after the office in the afternoon.

   responsible

   I .... after the office in the afternoon.

7   The train left at 7 o'clock. We arrived at the station at quarter past seven.

   had

   The train .... time we arrived at the station.

8   She tried really hard, but couldn't persuade us to go with her.

   how

   No matter .... she couldn't persuade us to go with her.

9   I think it's going to rain.

   as

   It .... it's going to rain.

10   I prefer watching football to playing it.

   than

   I'd .... play it.

7   Answer the following questions about the FCE exam:
                                                            (10 points)

1   Which of the following things should you *not* do in the FCE Speaking test:

   a) Speak clearly.

   b) Make your answers interesting.

   c) Ask the examiner to repeat something if you don't understand the question properly.

   d) Behave very formally, and only speak when you are asked a question.

2   True or false: In the Writing paper, it's a good idea to write a first draft of each essay, then write it again neatly.

3   True or false: When you write a letter in the FCE Writing paper, you must include your address and the address of the person to whom you are writing.

4   When you do the tasks in the Reading paper, what is the *first* thing you should do for each text?

   a) Read the questions and highlight the key words.

   b) Read the text carefully so that you understand everything about it.

   c) Read the title of the text and any headings, then skim the text for its general meaning.

   d) Look at each paragraph of the text, and highlight the key words.

5   True or false: In the Paper 3 (Use of English) error correction task, there is an extra unnecessary word in **every** line of the text.

6   If you write a story in the FCE Writing paper, what elements should you include in your story? Complete this test with appropriate words from the box.

ending   events   linking   plot   tenses

A good story should have a good (1) ...., with a dramatic, funny or unexpected (2) .... You should use (3) .... words and time markers to show the order of (4) .... It is also important to make correct use of narrative (5) ....

Unit 6 test

1   Choose the correct alternative in each of these sentences.   (10 points)

1   You *can't be / can't have been* at home last night; I tried phoning you six times.

2   I don't know where Jackie is. She had a late night last night, so she *must have / can't have* overslept.

3   I suppose he *might / must* have got lost, but I doubt it.

4   You turned down a free trip to Mexico? You *could / must* be mad!

5   To get such a brilliant exam result, he *couldn't / must* have worked really hard.

6   She can't *has / have* been there because I didn't see her.

7   I didn't do my homework because I couldn't *to be / be* bothered.

8   I don't know if they heard us. They might *be / have been* listening at the door.

9   She can't still *working / be working* at the British Council, can she?

10   He may *have want / want* to leave early tomorrow.

2   Rewrite these sentences in the passive.   (10 points)

1   We are going to employ a new secretary next week.

   ....

2   Students must pay their fees by the end of the week.

   ....

3   Everybody must turn off their mobile phones in class.

   ....

4   I suddenly noticed that somebody was watching me.

   ....

5   People grow coffee in Brazil.

   ....

6   Overwork causes stress.

   ....

7   Nobody told me about the timetable changes.

   ....

8   Oh no! Somebody has stolen my wallet.

   ....

9   The police are interviewing a man about the robbery.

   ....

10   The voters have elected a new Prime Minister.

   ....

3   The words in bold have been used in the wrong sentences. Decide which sentences they belong in.   (10 points)

1   The advantage of a digital camera is that you don't need to buy **batteries**. ....

2   This computer **keypad** is really well designed; it's very easy on the wrists. ....

3   My new computer **ring tone** is awful; it really hurts your eyes if you look at it for too long. ....

4   The **keyboard** on this camera lets you get in really close on your subject. ....

5   Your mobile phone has a really annoying **film**. Why don't you change it, or better still, turn it off? ....

6   It's time you got a new **zoom lens** for your computer. You move this one, and nothing happens. ....

7   Your mobile phone just beeped. You must have received a **mouse**. ....

8   I've tried calling him, but I keep getting a/an **screen**. ....

9   Oh no! The **engaged tone** on my mobile phone have run out again. ....

10   The **text message** on your mobile phone has to be unlocked before you can use it. ....

4   Complete the following sentences, using only one word, in each space.   (10 points)

1   I don't think it's a good thing to always tell the .... Sometimes you have to lie to get what you want.

2   Eddie's really good at .... jokes. Unfortunately, most of them are really bad.

3   I can't .... French, but I can understand it when I hear it.

4   Goodbye, take care and keep in ....

5   If you've got problems at work, why not have a .... with your boss?

6   Thanks for the information. Could you put it in .... and send it to me?

7   The cheque is in the .... I sent it this morning, so you should get it tomorrow.

8   There were no advertisements for the concert. I found out about it by word of ....

9   If you want to find out more about Longman books, visit their .... at www.longman.com.

10   He didn't .... anything to me about the party.

5   Complete the second sentence so that it has a similar meaning to the first sentence, using no more than five words, including the word given.   (10 points)

1   I don't believe you saw her, otherwise she would have mentioned it.

   have

   You .... her, otherwise she would have mentioned it.

2   I'm sure he was delighted with the result.

   been

   He .... delighted with the result.

3   You can't use the computers after 7 o'clock.

   be

   The computers .... after 7 o'clock.

4   I didn't see the story in the paper, but people told me what happened.

   word

   I didn't see the story in the paper, but I found out about it .... mouth.

5   I'd like to talk with you later today.

   have

   I'd like to .... you later today.

Unit 7 test

1 Complete the following text using relative pronouns. (10 points)

At midday, (1) .... Lorraine eventually finished the letter, she turned to her boss. '(2) .... should I address it to, Mr Lyons or Ms Harrison?' she asked. Mr Jenkins glared at her irritably over his paper.

'Don't ask stupid questions!' he snapped. 'Just write "To (3) .... it may concern" at the top'. He then went back to the crossword, (4) .... he had been struggling with for the past half hour.

Lorraine didn't ask her boss (5) .... he wasn't working like everybody else. She decided she'd had enough. Clutching the letter (6) .... had taken her almost all morning to write, she walked over to the desk (7) .... he was sitting, rolled the letter into a ball and stuffed it into his half-full coffee cup.

For once, Mr Jenkins, (8) .... short temper was well known, was speechless. As Mary stared down at him, his lower lip trembled slightly, and for the first time since she had joined the company, Lorraine saw what could have been fear in his eyes.

'I'm leaving now,' she said simply. 'And you are the reason (9) .... I'm leaving. You are, without a doubt, the most unpleasant, incompetent person I've ever met.' Then she turned her back on the man (10) .... had not said a kind word to her in the six months she had worked there, and walked out of the office triumphantly.

2 Choose the correct alternative in each of these sentences. You will need to choose both parts correctly to make the sentence work. (10 points)

1 Nowadays, if you *had wanted / would want to / want to* travel to exotic countries, you *just phone / have just phoned / will just phone* a travel agency.

2 If we *had spent / spent / spend* less on going out and other luxuries during the week, we *will save / won't save / wouldn't have saved* enough money to go on holiday.

3 If prices *are continuing / had continued / continue* to rise, we *would have / won't have / would have had* enough to pay the rent any more.

4 If you *spent / are spending / spend* a little time with your children, they *would have behaved / wouldn't behave / will behave* so badly.

5 If they *worked harder / work harder / had worked harder* at school, their teachers *won't treat / would treat / treat* them with more respect.

6 If you *hadn't arrived / arrive / had arrived* on time, we *wouldn't have missed / will miss / will have missed* the film.

7 If she *didn't make / hadn't made / doesn't make* so much noise, she *would have woken / will wake / wouldn't have woken* all the neighbours.

8 Look at this fantastic offer. If you *will buy / buy / had bought* a new Comsario computer, the company *would give / could give / gives* you a free printer and scanner!

9 I *would have called / will call / would call* you last night if only I *am knowing / had known / do know* you were at home.

10 I *will resign / would resign / resigned* if I *had / had had / could have* a boss like yours.

3   Complete the following sentences, using the correct form of *make* or *do*.   (10 points)

1   Not enough research is being .... in the field of alternative power sources.

2   I've .... all the housework, so now I want to relax.

3   You're not .... enough effort. You must try harder.

4   He shouldn't .... fun of people who are less fortunate than him.

5   If you want to .... business in another country, it's a good idea to learn the language.

6   Very few people have managed to .... a successful living from acting.

7   She asked the interviewer a lot of questions, and .... a really good impression.

8   If you want to arrive on time, ... sure you leave early.

9   Instead of .... a complaint to the manager, we wrote directly to the chairman at their head office.

10 Don't worry about your exams. Just .... your best.

4   Complete the following sentences by rearranging the jumbled letters in bold.   (10 points)

1   My favourite **busjtesc** at school are History and Geography. ....

2   A lot of companies making **seosccmti** such as lipstick and face cream are criticised by animal rights activists. ....

3   What **exlusriu** would I miss most if I lived on a desert island? Well chocolate and hot running water for a start! ....

4   Cotton and silk have largely replaced wool and leather as clothing **estmriala**. ....

5   What's the most important **onitnvine** ever? The mobile phone of course! ....

6   I lost my car keys last Friday. Luckily, I had a **prsea** key with me. ....

7   You've made **tstaisfycora** progress, but I'm sure you could do better. ....

8   Working as a teaching assistant for six months was a really **baluvlea** experience. ....

9   I saw an interesting **ahrstoicli** film about the French Revolution. ....

10 They measured the temperature changes using very precise **ticiscenif** instruments. ....

5   In each of the following sentences, there is an extra word which should not be there. Cross it out.   (10 points)

1   Leonardo da Vinci, whose his inventions prepared the way for modern science, is most well-known for his painting of the Mona Lisa.

2   Over there you can see the church where my parents got married in almost 25 years ago.

3   The one thing I miss it the most about living abroad is my mother's cooking.

4   New York, where my father works there, is one of the most exciting cities in the world.

5   Our school library has a multi-media equipment which is designed to maximise our learning potential.

6   You can borrow my camera if you would promise to be very careful with it.

7   If I didn't have so much work to do, I would have go away this weekend.

8   We shouldn't be spending so much money on spare expensive luxuries – we just can't afford them at the moment.

9   Despite of the fact that it was below freezing outside, we went for a walk.

10 She got an excellent grade in the exam, even all though she had done hardly any work.

Unit 8 test

1 Complete the following sentences, using the correct form (gerund or infinitive) of the verbs in bold.

(10 points)

1 Did you remember **get** me some shampoo from the chemist? ....

2 She tried **paint** the room a bright white, but it still looked dark. ....

3 Although I was in a hurry, I stopped **talk** to Samantha when we met on the high
    street. ....

4 I'd really like **take** a holiday. ....

5 He seems **be** happy, but it's difficult to tell. ....

6 I really regret **tell** him that he was ugly and stupid. ....

7 The teacher wasn't happy with our homework, and so we were made **do** it again.
    ....

8 I've often considered **leave** my job. ....

9 You should stop **smoke**. It's not good for you. ....

10 I remember **meet** her at the party, but I can't remember what she looks
    like. ....

2 Match the sentences 1–10 to sentences a)–j) below.   (10 points)

1 You've been on the computer all evening.

2 I found out that Jenny had borrowed my mobile phone without my permission.

3 Every time I open my mouth, I say something really stupid.

4 I don't mind your music, but it is a bit too loud.

5 Your exams are next month.

6 Everyone likes Martin. He gets invited out all the time.

7 Thanks for asking me to come camping with you, but unfortunately I've got a holiday job.

8 You seem to be having some problems with your homework.

9 I know that you're not particularly keen on Mexican food.

10 I wasn't consulted about the plans for the weekend.

☐ a) If only I was as popular.

☐ b) I wish you'd talked about it with me before making a decision.

☐ c) If only I wasn't so bad at expressing myself.

☐ d) I wish she'd asked me first.

☐ e) Suppose I helped you. How does that sound?

☐ f) Would you rather I made something less spicy?

☐ g) It's high time you started doing some serious work.

☐ h) I'd rather you turned it down.

☐ i) I really wish I didn't have to work all summer.

☐ j) It's time you turned it off.

3 Complete the following sentences, using the correct form of a word from the box.   (10 points)

CREATE   CULTURE   DEPEND   DISGUST   FAME   HARM   NATURE   NERVE   SUPPORT   WASH

1   You can't put this jumper in the washing machine. It says 'Not machine ……….' on the label.

2   I thought David Beckham was ………. all over the world, but my American friends have never heard of him.

3   Yuck! Who made this coffee. It's absolutely ………. !

4   She's very ………. ; she never helps me or encourages me in anything I do.

5   There's something a bit ………. about somebody who spends all their time alone in a dark room.

6   Sally's extremely ………. . She's always making things with her hands.

7   Naturally I was a bit ………. on my first date. Who isn't?

8   He's totally ………. . I know that if I ask him to do something, he'll do it.

9   The dog looked quite vicious, but actually he was quite ………. and wouldn't hurt a fly.

10   My home town has a large ………. centre, which includes a cinema, a theatre and an art gallery.

4 Decide if the words in bold are the correct words for that sentence. If not, complete the sentence with a suitable word.   (10 points)

1   Helen, I'd like to introduce you to my **nephew**. She's my sister's eldest daughter. ……………………….

2   This is a picture of my **brother-in-law**. He married my eldest daughter last summer. ……………………….

3   She's very **sympathetic**, always donating money to charity and giving people expensive presents.
    ……………………….

4   He's so **talkative**. Just for once I wish he'd be quiet. ……………………….

5   He says he'll be Prime Minister one day. I don't think I've ever met such a **modest** man. ……………………….

6   You've lost your job, you can't pay your mortgage and your girlfriend has left you. I'm amazed you can still remain so **optimistic** about the future! ……………………….

7   She's quite **sociable**, and is a great person to invite to a party. ……………………….

8   The **bridegroom** looked lovely in a white dress and with flowers in her hair. ……………………….

9   At the **honeymoon** after the wedding ceremony, everybody congratulated the happy couple, and they ate, drank and danced until midnight. ……………………….

10   When Charles and Alice got **married**, they immediately started looking for somewhere suitable to hold the wedding. ……………………….

5 Complete the second sentence so that it has a similar meaning to the first sentence, using no more than five words, including the word given.   (10 points)

1 My father made me wash his car at the weekend.

   made

   I ……………………………………….. my father's car at the weekend.

2 I wish you wouldn't interrupt me all the time.

   on

   I wish you wouldn't ……………………………………. me all the time.

3 Smoking so much is very bad for your health.

   unhealthy

   It's …………………………………….. so much.

4 It's getting late, so we should go home.

   went

   It's getting late, so ……………………………………. home.

5 I regret losing my temper with him.

   have

   I ……………………………………. my temper with him.

Unit 9 test

1 Complete the text using the expressions from the box. (10 points)

| made sure used to be given would get used to treat got used to never let |
| used to live didn't have would walk get used to being |

When I was young, I (1) .... in a big city. Our house was in a rather rough area, and my parents (2) .... me stay out after dark. We didn't have much money, so of course we (3) .... all the luxuries that so many children take for granted these days. My parents didn't own a car either, so if we wanted to go out we (4) .... everywhere, or take the bus. Both my parents worked hard, so I (5) .... special jobs around the house to help out. For example, when my parents came home from work, I (6) .... things ready for dinner, and sometimes even cooked it myself.

In the last year, however, things have changed. I'm now a successful writer and I have a large house in the country. It's so different from my old home. I still haven't (7) .... the peace and quiet, and I still can't (8) .... so far away from my parents. And there's much less crime here. When I first moved here, I (9) .... that all the windows and doors were securely locked, but I don't bother any more. And I (10) .... every visitor as a potential criminal. All that has changed now, of course.

2 Complete sentences 1–10 using expressions a)–j) from the box. (10 points)

a) set in Kenya in the 1940's
b) competing to attract audiences
c) treated as a rubbish tip for years
d) considered to be one of the most beautiful towns in the country
e) originally opened in 1465
f) originally thought to have belonged to the emperor Vespasian
g) situated on the edge of the village
h) taken when she was a girl
i) looking for a good night out
j) once respected by all his patients

1 My house,.. , has a lovely view over the countryside.

2 A photograph of my mother, ... , hangs on the wall near the door.

3 An old pub in my town centre, ... , has just been closed down.

4 My home town, ... , is fighting a government decision to build a main road through its centre.

5 Hundreds of young people, ... , arrive in the town every evening.

6 Five cinemas in the area, ... , have cut their ticket prices by 50%.

7 An ancient Roman helmet, ... , has just been identified as a child's toy made in the 1960s.

8 Her last film, ... , was considered to be a cinematic masterpiece.

9 The village doctor, ... , has just been arrested for unprofessional behaviour.

10 The local park, ... , is finally going to be cleaned up by the council.

3 Correct the mistakes with spelling in the following sentences.   (10 points)

1 I don't really mind what I wear, as long as it's fashionble and made of a good-quality materiel, like silk. ....

2 I don't like the dessign of this suite, and I don't think I would look right in it. ....

3 Tarquin is wearing a pail blue shirt and dark coton trousers by Moronio of Milan. ....

4 He was wearing a waterprof leathar jacket and black lace-up work boots. ....

5 The dress code for the reception was smart-cashual, but he turned up wearing jeans and an orange v-nekked sweater. ....

6 This jacket is not only practacal, but it also maches my trousers. ....

7 That shirt really siuts you, although I'm not so sure about the stripped purple and yellow tie. ....

8 My bedroom is very basic: apart from a bed, some bookshelfs and a wardobe, there's very little else. ....

9 There's a photocoppier in the corner of the office, and a hot-drinks vending mashine by the door. ....

10 Opposite the door, there's a cubboard where we keep all our old records, and a filling cabinet containing details of current customers. ....

4 Complete the following sentences with an appropriate verb to make a phrasal verb with *up*. You have been given the first letter of each word.   (10 points)

1 Happy birthday! Here's your present. Sorry I w............. it up so badly.

2 I can't lift this suitcase. Could you help me p............. it up?

3 I'm trying to s............. up enough money to buy a new car.

4 It was a busy day, and we didn't manage to c............. up the shop until almost 8 o'clock.

5 This room is in a terrible mess. I think we should t............. it up.

6 There are still a few cakes left. Ask the children if they want to f............. them up.

7 Where's Ted? He's upstairs s............. up the holes in his trousers.

8 Come on, it's time to go. G............. up your things and then we can leave.

9 You're going to be late. D............. up your coffee and get going.

10 I've already w............. up the dirty dishes, but I haven't cleaned the kitchen yet.

5 In each of the following sentences, there is an extra word which should not be there. Cross it out.   (10 points)

1 I'm sure that I'll soon be get used to getting up so early every morning.

2 When I was a child, I would to spend hours watching television every weekend.

3 At the end of the meeting, we gathered up to all our things and went home.

4 In my bedroom, there's a picture of my home town, which painted by my uncle when he was at art school.

5 At the back of the school you will find a flight of stairs is leading to the library and computer room.

6 In all my view, the best way of making the common room more comfortable is by adding some easy chairs and some pot plants.

7 It seems so to me that the best place for the common room would be on the south side of the building.

8 This report is because to recommend a few solutions to the problems of students using mobile phones at school.

9 These days, adults they are always complaining about the attitude of young people, but I suppose that has always been the case.

10 I like wearing jeans because they are comfortable, and of course they are a practical, because you can wear them in so many situations.

Progress test 2 (Units 6–10)

1   Chose the best alternative to complete the following sentences.   (20 points)

1   Students at my school *don't need to / are supposed to / are not allowed to* smoke anywhere in the school building.

2   You *don't have to / mustn't / aren't supposed to* attend afternoon classes; they are optional.

3   You *shouldn't have handed / didn't have to hand / were supposed to hand* in your homework yesterday. It's too late now.

4   'Sarah, *this / there / it* is my best friend, Maureen'. 'Hello, Maureen. Nice to meet you.'

5   Don't worry about your exam. *There's / It's / He's* not worth worrying about.

6   Since I was 15 *I wanted / I've wanted / I want* a sports car.

7   This is the first time I've *already / ever / never* been out of the country.

8   This is such a great film. *I'm seeing / I've been seeing / I've seen* it more than 10 times!

9   Mr Miggins is the *least / less / lowest* popular teacher in our school.

10   She looks as *like / if / whether* she's going to cry.

11   Have you heard from Ian *later / late / lately*?

12   When he shook my hand, I realised we *met / were meeting / had met* somewhere before.

13   By the time I take my FCE exam, I *will learn / will have learnt / will be learning* English for almost four years.

14   She *apologised / excused / denied* breaking my camera, and blamed Eddie instead.

15   When I met him in London, he explained that he *had just returned / just returned / was just returning* from a 6-month holiday in Australia a few days earlier.

16   She had just won first prize in a writing contest. She *will have been / must have been / can't have been* absolutely delighted.

17   Several people *have fired / were fired / have been fired* since the new manager took over the running of the company.

18   The manager is currently *been interviewed / interviewing / being interviewed* by a local newspaper.

19   Brian, *whose / who / who's* father is chairman of the company, has just started work in the Sales department.

20   If we *work / worked / had worked* harder, we would have passed the exam.

2   Correct the mistakes in the following sentences.   (15 points)

1   You'll do well in the exam if you will work hard enough. ....

2   I am not let to go out after 10 o'clock. ....

3   Although I had lots of work to do, I stopped having a coffee and a bit of fresh air. ....

4   She's often considered to give up her job to travel around the world. ....

5   I'm so fed up. If only I have a good job and decent career prospects. ....

6   You are so annoying. I really wish you will go away and leave me alone. ....

7   It's almost midnight. It's time I am going to bed. Goodnight, everyone. ....

8   I recognise you. Did you used to be lead singer with the Purple Nasties? ....

9   'Man with Duck on Head', painting in 1934, is one of Van Gruber's most famous pictures. ....

10   In the attic there's an old box contains my grandfather's old army uniform. ....

11   We needn't have arrive so early. We've got ages before our flight leaves. ....

12   You don't must come late tomorrow, or you'll be in serious trouble. ....

13   There's a pity you missed the film. It was brilliant. ....

14   I suddenly had the strangest feeling that I was been watched from one of the top-floor windows. ....

15   I'm sure he can't intended to offend you when you met him. He's really a very nice person. ....

3 Complete the following sentences by putting the words in bold into the correct form. (10 points)

1 I've never really understood the .... of computer games.
popular

2 She has an extremely active and colourful ....
imagine

3 His accusations were .... It was obvious you were innocent.
ground

4 He's a .... good-natured young man who is always willing to help out.
please

5 He stood up .... and shook my hand.
enthusiast

6 You behaved in a very .... manner, running away like that.
coward

7 I've never been so .... in my life.
fury

8 I'm afraid you have .... experience to join this company.
sufficient

9 After he was hit on the head, he was .... for almost ten minutes.
conscious

10 I was very .... by the progress I made in my English.
encourage

4 Complete the following sentences with an appropriate preposition or particle. (10 points)

1 It's time we got .... to some serious work.

2 They didn't take .... what I said, so I had to repeat everything.

3 I didn't go to Italian lessons, but I managed to pick .... some of the language when I travelled around Italy.

4 She's very intelligent. .... the other hand, she's rather lazy.

5 The police are looking .... the cause of the accident.

6 Fresh fruit and vegetables are rich .... vitamin C.

7 I'm quite industrious and have never been afraid ....
hard work.

8 I'd like you to tidy .... the mess you've made.

9 'What does *imbroglio* mean?' 'I don't know. Try looking it .... in a dictionary.'

10 She's always looked .... on people who are less fortunate or successful than her.

5 Chose the best alternative to complete the following sentences. (15 points)

1 She knows everything about me. I'm sure she can read my *head / brain / mind*.

2 I'm not looking forward to *making / taking / going* my exams.

3 Did you get good *points / scores / marks* in your English test?

4 Guess what? I've *succeeded / won / passed* all my exams!

5 My desk is really *cramped / organised / cluttered*; it's always piled high with paper and other bits and pieces.

6 My company *does / makes / goes* a lot of business in the USA.

7 I would like to *give / do / make* a serious complaint.

8 My school has some excellent *features / subjects / facilities*, including an indoor swimming pool.

9 Don't be shy. *Tell / Say / Speak* your mind!

10 I need to return these trousers to the shop, but I don't have the *receipt / bill / addition*.

11 At the moment, we're living on a/an *economy / budget / fee* of about £70 a week.

12 There's a great *publicity / spot / commercial* on television for British Airways.

13 I had a bad dose of flu, but I *healed / cured / recovered* quickly.

14 This book is *absolutely / extremely / fairly* fantastic – you really must read it!

15 At the end of the play, the *spectators / audience / viewers* got to their feet and applauded.

6 Complete the second sentence so that it has a similar meaning to the first sentence, using no more than five words, including the word given. (20 points)

1 I found it difficult to explain my ideas to her
across
I found it difficult to ....
to her.

2 Please understand that it's no good getting angry with me.
in
Please understand that ....
.... angry with me

3 I can't decide what to do when I leave school.
mind
I can't .... what to do
when I leave school.

4 You should have arrived two hours ago.

supposed

You .... two hours ago.

5 When I was younger, I would often get into trouble with my teachers.

to

When I was younger, I .... into trouble with my teachers.

6 I really regret upsetting her so much.

I

I .... her so much.

7 I don't like it when you shout at me all the time.

keep

I wish .... at me all the time.

8 I didn't see him because he didn't come.

have

If he .... seen him.

9 See that man over there? He stole my wallet.

stole

That's .... my wallet.

10 I suddenly realised that somebody was watching me from across the street.

was

I suddenly realised that I .... from across the street.

7 Answer these questions about the FCE exam.

(10 points)

1 True or false: In the key word transformations task in Paper 3 (Use of English), contracted words (e.g., *can't, won't, I'll*) count as *two* words.

2 Look at this extract from a letter of complaint. What is wrong with it?

a) It is rude.

b) It uses language which is not appropriate.

c) The spelling is bad.

d) It is disorganised.

e) There are some grammar mistakes.

Dear Sir / Madam
I am writing to complain about the service I received recently in your restaurant. I would be grateful if you would refund my money. First of all, although we had made a reservation, we had to wait almost half an hour for a table. When the food arrived, it was cold. We had to wait for almost an hour for the food to come, and the music was much too loud …

3 In the FCE Speaking test, how long should you try to speak for when you are asked to compare and contrast the photographs?

a) 1 minute   b) 2 minutes   c) 3 minutes
d) 4 minutes

4 True or false: When your partner is describing his / her photographs in the FCE Speaking test, you cannot interrupt them.

5 True or false: If you write a *report* in the FCE Writing test, you should begin 'Dear Sir/Madam' and end 'Yours faithfully'.

6 In the Listening Test of the FCE, how many times do you hear each listening passage:

a) Once   b) Twice   c) Three times   d) You hear some parts *once*, and some parts *twice*.

7 In the Writing test, how long should each of your compositions be?

a) Between 80 and 110 words   b) Between 110 and 140 words   c) Between 120 and 180 words
d) Between 160 and 220 words

8 In Part 2 of the FCE Listening test, you have to listen to a passage and complete some notes. Do you need to complete these notes using *complete sentences*?

9 In Part 5 of the FCE Use of English Test, you have to put words into their correct form in a text (e.g., *complain – complaint, possible – possibility,* etc.). True or false: In some cases, you do *not* need to change the word.

10 In Part 3 of the FCE Speaking test, you have to discuss a situation or complete a task with your partner. Decide which of the following things you *should* do during this task (choose two answers):

a) Listen to your partner and respond to what he/she says.

b) Try to talk more than your partner.

c) Talk to the examiner, and not your partner.

d) Use short answers (e.g. *Yes/No*) if your partner asks you a question.

e) Agree with all the suggestions your partner makes.

f) Only speak when you are asked a question by the examiner.

g) Encourage your partner to speak if he/she is quiet, nervous, etc.

Unit 11 test

1 Decide what the missing word is in each of the following sentences and write it in the correct place. (10 points)

1 I don't know how speak French, but I can understand a bit.

2 If you don't book a ticket soon, you won't able to get a seat.

3 I was amazed when I succeeded getting a place on the course.

4 We're sorry we weren't to meet you on Saturday.

5 I could gone to university, but I took a job in my father's company instead.

6 She to pass her exam, even though she hadn't done any work.

7 When he was younger, Tim could quite violent and aggressive.

8 I knew to play the piano when I was only five.

9 In my opinion, young people be able to leave school at 14 if they really want to.

10 I ride a bike, although my brother keeps trying to teach me.

2 Complete sentences 1–5 using a word or phrase from the box. (5 points)

| am going to pass   are going to catch   get   had spent   promise to return |
| should get down to   should leave   will gladly lend   would still have buy |

1 If you .... a packet of 'Sparkle' detergent, you .... another one absolutely free.

2 If I .... less last week, I .... enough money to go out tonight.

3 If you .... it before Saturday, I .... you the money.

4 If you .... the early train, you .... as soon as possible.

5 If I .... my exams, I .... some serious studying immediately.

Complete sentences 6–10 using a word or phrase from the box. (5 points)

| are going to be   cook   eat   hadn't been   let   might be able to go |
| pass   promise to work   will wash up   wouldn't be |

6 If you .... us leave early today, we .... late tomorrow.

7 If you .... all those chocolates, you .... sick.

8 If you .... me dinner, I .... the dishes afterwards.

9 If you .... so stupid, we .... in this ridiculous situation.

10 If they .... their exams, they .... to university.

3 Complete the sentences using a word from the box. (5 points)

| case condition even provided unless |

1 I'll lend you my car .... that you pay for the petrol.

2 I wouldn't help him .... if he gave me a million pounds.

3 You won't pass the exam .... you work really hard.

4 Take an umbrella with you in .... it rains.

5 He'll give me a pay rise on .... that I agree to work overtime.

4 Complete the following sentences by rearranging the jumbled letters in bold. The first letter of each word is correct. (10 points)

1 There are several good jobs being **asvridedet** in the newspaper. ....

2 I've got a job **iwtrieenv** at half past eleven today.

3 I didn't get the job because I didn't have enough **eeeecnprix**. ....

4 He had excellent exam results, but he didn't have any professional **qslitfiauionac**. ....

5 She filled in the **alincaptiop** form and sent it to the company. ....

6 The company I want to work for has asked for the names of two **rreeeesf**. ....

7 He's lost his job. It must be very difficult being **udeylonmep**. ....

8 My job is OK, but there aren't many opportunities for **potmorino**. ....

9 The post offers a **slyaar** of £30,000 a year. ....

10 What I like most about my job are the **feblilex** working hours. ....

5 Choose the correct word in the following sentences. (5 points)

1 Ask the waiter for the *bill / tip / receipt*, then we can pay and leave.

2 I've just received my bank *commission / statement / deposit*. I've got an overdraft of almost £700!

3 If you want to *extract / withdraw / dismiss* money from your account, you'll need some kind of identification.

4 I'd like to *change / convert / transform* these US dollars for euros, please.

5 He wasted a lot of his money *for / with / on* unnecessary luxuries.

6 Complete the second sentence so that it has a similar meaning to the first sentence, using no more than five words, including the word given. (10 points)

1 My boss fired me last week.
   got
   I .... last week.

2 I can't solve this problem.
   know
   I .... solve this problem.

3 When I was younger, I had the chance of moving to Australia, but decided not to.
   have
   When I was younger, I
   .... Australia, but decided not to.

4 Unfortunately I failed the test.
   manage
   Unfortunately, I .... the test.

5 The bank will lend you the money if you can guarantee to pay it back within two years.
   as
   The bank will lend you the money
   .... can guarantee to pay it back within two years.

Unit 12 test

1 Complete the second sentence to make a passive form of the first sentence. (10 points)

1 He showed me the way to the post office.

   I .... the way to the post office.

2 My dog loves it when I take her for a walk.

   My dog .... taken for a walk.

3 I'm fed up of people taking advantage of me.

   I'm fed up .... advantage of.

4 Nobody knows where he lives.

   It .... where he lives.

5 Many people believe he came from South Africa.

   He .... from South Africa.

6 Some people thought the Earth was flat.

   The Earth .... flat.

7 I can't remember my teachers ever shouting at me.

   I can't remember .... my teachers.

8 People say that chocolate is bad for you.

   Chocolate .... bad for you.

9 They made me feel really stupid.

   I .... really stupid.

10 A team of experts are examining the damage.

   The damage .... a team of experts.

2 Put the words in the right order to make sentences. (5 points)

1 your serviced did last have When you car?

   ....

2 removed you had a Have ever tooth?

   ....

3 cut really You to hair your need get.

   ....

4 decorated house to have the We're whole going.

   ....

5 plastic ever surgery consider Would having you?

   ....

3 Decide if the words in bold are the correct words for that sentence. If not, complete the sentence with a suitable word. (10 points)

1 I arrived home extremely late, and **strolled** quietly up the stairs so as not to wake anyone up.

   ....

2 Could you ever **wonder** being penniless and living on the streets? ....

3 The room is so hot and airless, I feel like I'm **suffocating**. ....

4 He **peered** at me so angrily that I thought he was going to hit me. ....

5 I'm sorry, but I don't **believe** a single word you've told me. ....

6 He was **swallowing** his lip and looking very nervous. ....

7 She **hammered** quietly on the door. 'Come in,' a voice said from inside. ....

8 I opened the door and **panted** in surprise when I saw him standing there with a knife in his hand. ....

9 Rob **paced** nervously up and down the corridor, occasionally checking his watch. ....

10 He **stared** quickly out of the window for a second or two, then went back to his paper. ....

4 Complete the text with a word from the box. There are some words that you do not need.

(15 points)

> acquit burglary convicted conviction defence did evidence forgery
> innocent judge jury made pleaded prison prosecution robbed
> sentenced stole suspended trial witnesses

One night, Laurence Bailey (1) .... his local bank and (2) .... almost £100,000. It wasn't his first crime: a year before he had been charged with (3) .... after breaking into several houses in the neighbourhood, and had received a (4) .... sentence. When he went to court, the (5) .... had warned him that if he broke the law again, he wouldn't be so generous; the next time it happened, Laurence would receive a (6) .... sentence.

The morning after his latest crime, he was arrested. Several (7) .... who saw him do it (8) .... a statement to the police. A date was sent for his (9) ....

He (10) .... not guilty, but the (11) .... had all the (12) .... they needed and, despite the best efforts of his (13) .... lawyer, he was found guilty by the (14) .... He was (15) .... of the crime and locked away for five years.

5 In each of the following sentences, there is an extra word which should not be there. Cross it out.   (10 points)

1 A mugger who attacks people in the street and steals their money and other valuables.

2 In a court of law, the lawyer for the defence tries to prove it that the defendant is innocent.

3 I'm really fed up of people are telling me how to how to behave all the time.

4 The jury learned that the robber was been seen to break into the bank through an upstairs window.

5 He is believed that to be living somewhere in the south of France, in a large villa somewhere near the sea.

6 Before I'm tempted to spend it on something that I don't need, I need to get away this money into my bank account.

7 I'm going to visit Sam in hospital. Do you think I should take him a bunch of the grapes?

8 Oh no! I've had my wallet was stolen from my jacket pocket!

9 I really can't imagine be living on my own and away from my family. Can you?

10 Would you ever consider about getting a tattoo or having your nose pierced?

Unit 13 test

1   Match the sentences 1-5 to sentences a)–e) on the right. Complete the second sentences using an expression from the box.   (5 points)

awful drizzle   a new job   a play   historical novels   a good book

1 I don't mind the cold.
2 It's not a holiday I want.
3 I don't want to go to the cinema again on Saturday.
4 I'm not particularly keen on thrillers.
5 I don't want to go to Jim's party.

a) What I really want tonight is to sit at home on my own with ....
b) What I really can't stand is this ....
c) What I really enjoy reading are ....
d) What I'd really like to do for a change is go and see ....
e) What I need to do is to find ....

2   Correct the mistakes in the following sentences.   (10 points)

1 I've spent very much money this week that I can't afford to go out tonight. ....

2 I've been studying in Oxford for such long time that I feel like it's my second home. ....

3 I really don't think I'm enough strong to deal with the problem. ....

4 I'm far so tired to go out tonight. ....

5 She was such happy she couldn't stop smiling. ....

6 She's so angry so she can hardly speak. ....

7 I'm sorry, but I haven't got enough of time to help you. ....

8 I can't continue, I'm feeling such exhausted. ....

9 So few students arrived on time this morning. ....

10 Everyone likes him because he's too friendly and helpful. ....

3   Complete the following sentences using the correct form of a word from the box. There are some words that you don't need.

bark   cat   cloud   crow   dog   flood   fog   parrot rain   rat   rivers   snarl   snow   sun   wing

1 I felt ill this morning, but now I feel as right as ....

2 As far as I'm concerned, the only .... on the horizon is my forthcoming exam.

3 She's really upset. She's in .... of tears.

4 He's a wonderful person, with a warm .... smile.

5 He's too busy to see you. He's absolutely .... under with work.

6 I'm fed up working for the .... race. I want to be my own boss and work when I want, where I want.

7 My father often loses his temper, but really his .... is worse than his bite.

8 The party was supposed to be a surprise. Who let the .... out of the bag?

9 How far is it from London to Brighton? About 60 miles, as the .... flies.

10 When you arrive, Mrs Jenkins will take you under her .... and show you around.

4 Complete the following sentences by rearranging the letters in bold. (10 points)

1 We couldn't go outside because of the **rltonartie** rain. ....

2 There was a very violent **nthstumdeorr**, with lightning which lit up the night sky for miles around. ....

3 The **mcietal** in Singapore is very hot and humid for most of the year. ....

4 With **pratseemrute** in excess of 40 degrees for most of the year, the desert in Ethiopia is one of the hottest places in the world. ....

5 The **hrguodt** was the result of a long, hot summer with virtually no rain. ....

6 During the **inchaurer**, winds speeds exceeded 100 miles per hour, and hundreds of buildings were destroyed or damaged. ....

7 **havslnceaa** are a big problem in some mountain areas, especially when it becomes warmer and the snow begins to melt. ....

8 The river is continuing to rise, and the Thames Water Authority have issued a warning about the possibility of **golfdino** in the area. ....

9 The rain wasn't heavy. It was just a light **wsroeh**. ....

10 The police are warning drivers about **hpyatc** areas of fog along the M40. ....

5 Complete the following sentences with a suitable preposition or particle. (5 points)

1 Could you look .... the children while I'm out?

2 I hardly ever take time .... work because I'm always too busy.

3 I don't like having to deal .... other people's mistakes.

4 He grew .... in Korea, but he actually has Japanese nationality.

5 I'm very attached .... my pet poodle, 'Rambo'.

6 Complete the second sentence so that it has a similar meaning to the first sentence, using no more than five words, including the word given. (10 points)

1 I didn't feel well enough to go to work.

   too

   I felt .... to work.

2 This is the best film I've ever seen.

   such

   I've .... film.

3 I'd love a Ferrari, but they cost far too much money for me.

   rich

   I'm .... a Ferrari.

4 I don't like spicy food, but I hate bland food even more.

   what

   I don't like spicy food, but .... bland food.

5 Tell me about the weather in your country.

   is

   What .... in your country?

Progress test 3 (Units 11–14)

1 Complete the second sentence so that it has a similar meaning to the first sentence, using no more than five words, including the word given. (20 points)

1 It was wrong of you to borrow his car without asking.

   have

   You .... car without asking.

2 'I wouldn't go out alone, if I were you,' he said to me.

   advised

   He .... out alone.

3 FCE candidates should remember to bring a pen, pencil and eraser to the exam.

   reminded

   FCE candidates .... will need a pen, pencil and eraser.

4 I was too tired to do any more work.

   that

   I was .... not do any more work.

5 He's a really unhelpful person.

   an

   He's .... person.

6 I don't like it when people tell me what to do.

   told

   I don't .... to do.

7 Do you think you'll manage to come on time tomorrow?

   be

   Do you think .... come on time tomorrow?

8 She thought she would win the competition, but she didn't.

   succeed

   She didn't .... the competition.

9 I'll let you leave early providing you work late tomorrow.

   on

   I'll let you leave early .... work late tomorrow.

10 You can't smoke in here.

   not

   You .... smoke in here.

2 Complete these sentences using the correct form of the verb in brackets. (10 points)

1 What I really enjoy is .... on a beach watching the sun set. (sit)

2 He is .... to have disappeared while on a mountain-climbing expedition. (believe)

3 He can't give you a lift because he's getting his car .... (repair)

4 I could have .... successful if only I had tried hard enough. (be)

5 I .... hard since 8 o'clock, and I really need a break. (work)

6 When we got to the airport, I realised I .... my passport at home. (leave)

7 The time next week, I .... here for exactly six months. (be)

8 As a child, he would refuse .... fresh fruit or vegetables. (eat)

9 He tried .... a couple of tablets, but they didn't help his headache. (take)

10 We .... the television when we suddenly became aware of a strange noise upstairs. (watch)

3 Complete these sentences with one word only. (10 points)

1 Passengers are reminded .... smoking is strictly forbidden during the flight.

2 It's advisable .... keep your money in an inside jacket pocket at all times.

3 I'm afraid I'm not rich .... to buy you a Ferarri.

4 We had .... fun at the party that we didn't want to leave.

5 Isn't it time you .... your car repaired?

6 Have you just .... a hair cut?

7 When you get to the top of the hill, you'll be .... to see my house.

8 I'm so angry with myself! If .... I hadn't been so stupid!

9 I love .... told ghost stories.

10 Travellers are warned about the dangers of crime, but .... few are actually victims of crime.

4 In each of the following sentences, there is an extra word which should not be there. Cross it out. (10 points)

1 He was very talented, and could to play the violin when he was only six.

2 She managed to be pass all her exams with top marks.

3 Even if it's a nice day, we can go to the beach for a barbecue.

4 Take an umbrella with you in case of it rains.

5 At one time, she was said that to be the richest woman in the country.

6 He is thought to have live somewhere in the foothills of the Pyrenees.

7 I had got my car stolen last week.

8 It was such a hard work that most of the students simply gave up.

9 I don't like cold weather, but what then I really dislike is when it snows.

10 You ought not to leave early if you want to catch the early train.

5 Complete these sentences using the correct form of the verbs in the box. One verb can be used more than once. There are some verbs that you do not need. (10 points)

| break deal do face give go leave let look |
| make pay resign take turn |

1 After five years together, their marriage finally .... down.

2 He asked me to .... after his cats while he was away.

3 You'll have to .... with your problems yourself.

4 He .... to me for help, but I told him to leave me alone.

5 It's time you .... up to your responsibilities as an adult.

6 After three years he .... from the job and moved on.

7 I needed money, so decided to .... out a bank loan.

8 I was unable to .... off the money I had borrowed.

9 The jury decided he was innocent, but the judge .... him off with a warning.

10 I want to .... some time off work.

6 Replace the words in bold with a more appropriate word. (20 points)

1 My job pays me an annual **wage** of £25,000. ....

2 There are no good jobs being **publicised** in the paper this week. ....

3 I **won** a lot of useful experience when I did voluntary work in India. ....

4 Most British shops refuse to **receive** euros as payment, but there are some exceptions. ....

5 You've got a good job. How much do you **gain** every month? ....

6 I **imagine** where Jane is? I haven't seen her all day. ....

7 He heard somebody behind him, but when he **stared** over his shoulder, there was nobody there. ....

8 While we were out at the theatre, somebody **stole** our house. ....

9 'How do you **admit**, guilty or not guilty?' the judge asked. ....

10 Because he had seen the crime, he had to **do** a statement to the police. ....

11 The company managed to **score** their goal of opening offices in several European capitals. ....

12 I **fulfil** a dream that one day I'll be able to get out of the rat race. ....

13 One of the advantages of a **backpacking** holiday is that your flights, transfers and accommodation are all arranged for you by one company. ....

14 Last year we went on a luxury **expedition** around the Caribbean on the world's largest passenger ship. ....

15 A **panel** of thieves broke into the bank and removed over £2 million from the safe. ....

16 When I arrived, there was already a long **pile** of people waiting to get into the building. ....

17 Remember that it's a secret; don't let the **dog** out of the bag. ....

18 The south of China has a hot and humid **weather** in the summer. ....

19 My favourite **month** is spring, when it begins to get warmer again. ....

20 She's **rained** under with work, and can't come out this weekend. ....

7 Decide which of the following sentences are *True* and which are *False*.   (20 points)

1   You can use a dictionary in the Reading paper. ....

2   There are five parts in the Reading paper. ....

3   The Reading paper lasts for one hour and fifteen minutes. ....

4   You will have marks removed if you get an answer wrong in the Reading paper. ....

5   You should use a *pencil* to fill in your answers on the Reading paper answer sheet. ....

6   The Writing paper lasts for two hours. ....

7   You have to answer three questions in the Writing paper. ....

8   Part 1 of the Writing paper is always a formal letter. ....

9   Each of your answers in the Writing paper should be between 180 and 220 words long. ....

10 It is necessary to include addresses when you write a letter in the Writing paper. ....

11 There are five parts in the Use of English paper. ....

12 The Use of English paper lasts for one hour and fifteen minutes. ....

13 You will have an extra ten minutes at the end of the Use of English paper to transfer your answers to the answer sheet. ....

14 In the Listening paper, you will hear **one** of the listening passages **once only**. ....

15 You will have a few minutes at the end of the Listening paper to transfer your answers to the answer sheet. ....

16 The Speaking test lasts for about half an hour. ....

17 Including yourself, there will be three other people in the room when you do the Speaking test. ....

18 You should speak as quickly as possible during the Speaking test. ....

19 If you don't understand something in the Speaking test, you can ask the examiner to repeat it. ....

20 At the end of the Speaking test, the examiner will tell you if you have passed or failed. ....

Test keys

Unit 1 test

1 1 before   2 for   3 ago   4 ever   5 ago   6 when   7 for
8 already   9 when   10 yet

2 1 I *went to*   2 I've *already been there* / I've *been there already*
3 I've *eaten*   4 I *don't/can't* understand   5 I *wanted to*
6 I've *taken*   7 *Have you ever*   8 *have you seen*   9 I've *known*
10 I've *been reading*

3 1 action   2 science   3 thrillers   4 musicals   5 boring   6 horror
7 frightening   8 plot   9 acting   10 setting   11 effects
12 exciting   13 climax   14 director   15 outstanding   16 actor
17 amusing   18 box   19 row   20 screen

4 1 confusingly   2 performance   3 explanation   4 flattery
5 original   6 information   7 enjoyable   8 contestants
9 competitive   10 regularly

5 1 at   2 ever   3 already   4 a   5 does   6 been   7 since
8 what   9 film   10 not

Unit 2 test

1 1 excited   2 flattered   3 encouraging   4 frustrating/depressing
5 depressed/frustrated

2 1 thrilled   2 interested   3 irritated   4 frightening   5 confusing

3 1 not *as* difficult   2 *not quite* as   3 a *colder* climate   4 ✓
5 the *unfriendliest/least friendly* people   6 rather ~~to~~ go
7 the *most* delicious   8 ✓   9 far more difficult
10 far *better* than

4 1 incapable/misunderstood   2 insufficient/unfortunately
3 inactive/unhealthy   4 impossible/inexperienced
5 mistrust/incredible

5 1 the/the   2 -/the   3 the/-   4 The//the   5 -/-

6 1 the most (1 point) boring person (1 point)
2 would rather (1 point) watch videos than (1 point)
3 was (1 point) incredible how (1 point)
4 on the (1 point) other hand (1 point)
5 isn't nearly (1 point) as good (1 point)

Unit 3 test

1 1 h)   2 g)   3 a)   4 d)   5 c)   6 j)   7 f)   8 b)   9 i)   10 e)

2 1 like   2 as   3 as   4 as   5 though

3 1 sure   2 hand   3 true   4 suppose   5 advantage

4 1 tried *hard*   2 got in *free*   3 but *lately*   4 Perhaps *he's
overslept.*   5 They *certainly didn't* work   6 do *well*   7 spoke to
us *in an unfriendly way*   8 He *nearly* didn't   9 come home
straight *away/immediately*   10 *completely/absolutely* impossible

5 1 happened   2 was   3 had just arrived   4 was   5 went
6 was enjoying   7 came   8 grabbed   9 was lying
10 had only bought   11 had cost   12 ran   13 was chasing
14 slipped   15 got   16 had disappeared   17 was interviewing
18 was   19 turned   20 had stolen

Unit 4 test

1 1 is going to rain   2 will make   3 is   4 arrives   5 will finish/will
have finished   6 will be lying   7 will return   8 are you doing/are
you going to do   9 will have been here   10 Will you be

2 1 for   2 to   3 in   4 to   5 of   6 as   7 for   8 on   9 for
10 on

3 1 dairy   2 fresh   3 cholesterol   4 Vegetarians   5 balanced
6 proportion   7 protein   8 vegetables   9 nutritious
10 carbohydrates

4 1 c)   2 a)   3 b)   4 c)   5 b)

5 1 some *information*   2 got *lovely hair*   3 got *little money*
4 buy *a* newspaper   5 very *little* meat

6 1 the   2 some   3 it   4 a   5 a   6 really   7 have   8 to
9 roughly   10 of

Progress test 1 (Units 1–5)

1 1 met   2 have loved   3 don't/can't understand   4 have been
peeling   5 were watching   6 had never met   7 will drop
8 will have spent   9 will be earning   10 begins   11 had never
left   12 directed   13 hasn't rained   14 had worked   15 had
cost

2 1 suggested *going/that they go* to   2 I've *known* Val   3 I've *got
few* friends   4 When *did you start* work   5 Who *broke/has
broken*   6 already *smoked*   7 I'*d/I would* rather   8 is *as* exciting
9 such as *tigers/the tiger*   10 a city like *New York*   11 exactly *like*
your sister?   12 how *hard* he ran   13 why *he had*   14 asked
our teacher   15 got *much* money

3 1 outstanding   2 plot   3 setting   4 acting   5 plays
6 audience   7 applauded   8 reviews   9 frustrated
10 encouraging   11 confusing   12 frightened   13 cholesterol
14 vitamin   15 vegetarian   16 protein   17 consumer
18 advertisements   19 commercials   20 marketing

4 1 suggested   2 invited   3 apologised   4 reminded
5 threatened

5 1 when   2 financially   3 confusion   4 misunderstood
5 inexperienced   6 whereas   7 absolutely   8 for   9 to   10 few
11 injured   12 for   13 receipt   14 by   15 economical

6 1 blamed me (1 point) for breaking his (1 point)
2 Alice if she (1 point) had posted (1 point)
3 will be (1 point) arriving (1 point)
4 gave me (1 point) a prescription (1 point)
5 were a (1 point) few people (1 point)
6 am responsible (1 point) for looking (1 point)
7 had (already) left (1 point) by the (1 point)
8 how hard (1 point) she tried (1 point)
9 looks (1 point) as if / though (1 point)
10 rather watch (1 point) football than (1 point)

7 1 d)
2 False (you should make a plan, and use this plan to write your essay)
3 False
4 c)
5 False (there are usually between three and five lines which do not contain an extra word)

6 1 plot   2 ending   3 linking   4 events   5 tenses

Unit 6 test

1 1 can't have been   2 must have   3 might   4 must   5 must
6 have   7 be   8 have been   9 be working   10 want

2 1 A new secretary is going to be employed next week.
2 Fees must be paid by students by the end of the week.
3 Mobile phones must be turned off in class.
4 I suddenly noticed that I was being watched.
5 Coffee is grown in Brazil.
6 Stress is caused by overwork.
7 I wasn't told about the timetable changes.
8 Oh no! My wallet has been stolen.
9 A man is being interviewed (by the police) about the robbery.
10 A new Prime Minister has been elected.

3 batteries = 9   keypad = 10   ring tone = 5   keyboard = 2
film = 1   zoom lens = 4   mouse = 6   screen = 3
engaged tone = 8   text message = 7

4 1 truth   2 telling   3 speak   4 touch   5 word   6 writing
7 post   8 mouth   9 website   10 say

5 1 can't / couldn't (1 point) have seen (1 point)
2 must (1 point) have been (1 point)
3 can't be (1 point) used (1 point)
4 by word (1 point) of (1 point)
5 have a (1 point) word / chat with (1 point)

Unit 7 test

1 1 when   2 Who   3 whom   4 which   5 why   6 which/that
7 where   8 whose   9 why   10 who

2 1 want/just phone   2 spend/will save   3 continue/won't have
4 spent/wouldn't behave   5 worked/would treat
6 had arrived/wouldn't have missed   7 hadn't made/wouldn't have woken   8 buy/gives   9 would have called/had known
10 would resign/had

3 1 done   2 done   3 making   4 make   5 do   6 make   7 made
8 make   9 making   10 do

4 1 subjects   2 cosmetics   3 luxuries   4 materials   5 invention
6 spare   7 satisfactory   8 valuable   9 historical   10 scientific

5 1 his   2 in   3 it   4 there   5 a   6 would   7 have   8 spare
9 of   10 all

Unit 8 test

1 1 to get   2 painting   3 to talk   4 to take   5 to be   6 telling
7 to do   8 leaving   9 smoking   10 meeting

2 1 j)   2 d)   3 c)   4 h)   5 g)   6 a)   7 i)   8 e)   9 f)   10 b)

3 1 washable   2 famous   3 disgusting   4 unsupportive
5 unnatural   6 creative   7 nervous   8 dependable   9 harmless
10 cultural

4 1 niece   2 son-in-law   3 generous   4 ✓   5 ambitious   6 ✓
7 ✓   8 bride   9 reception   10 engaged

5 1 was made (1 point) to wash (1 point)
2 keep on (1 point) interrupting (1 point)
3 (very) unhealthy to (1 point) smoke (1 point)
4 it's time (1 point) we went (1 point)
5 shouldn't (1 point) have lost (1 point)

Unit 9 test

1 1 used to live   2 never let   3 didn't have   4 would walk
5 used to be given   6 would get   7 got used to
8 get used to being   9 made sure   10 used to treat

2 1 g)   2 h)   3 e)   4 d)   5 i)   6 b)   7 f)   8 a)   9 j)   10 c)

3 1 fashionable / material   2 design / suit   3 pale / cotton
4 waterproof / leather   5 casual / necked   6 practical / matches
7 suits / striped   8 bookshelves / wardrobe
9 photocopier / machine   10 cupboard / filing

4 1 wrapped   2 pick   3 save   4 close   5 tidy   6 finish
7 sewing   8 Gather   9 Drink   10 washed

5 1 be   2 to   3 to   4 which   5 is   6 all   7 so   8 because
9 they   10 a

Progress test 2 (Units 6–10)

1 1 are not allowed to   2 don't have to   3 were supposed to hand
4 this   5 It's   6 I've wanted   7 ever   8 I've seen   9 least
10 if   11 lately   12 had met   13 will have learnt   14 denied
15 had just returned   16 must have been   17 have been fired
18 being interviewed   19 whose   20 had worked

2 1 *you work* hard   2 not *allowed* to   3 stopped to *have*
4 considered *giving* up   5 I *had* a good job   6 you *would* go
7 I *went* to   8 Did you *use* to   9 *painted* in 1934
10 box *containing* my   11 have *arrived* so   12 You *mustn't* come
13 *It's* a pity   14 was *being* watched   15 he *can't have intended /didn't intend* to

3 1 popularity   2 imagination   3 groundless   4 pleasantly
5 enthusiastically   6 cowardly   7 furious   8 insufficient
9 unconscious   10 encouraged

4 1 down   2 in   3 up   4 On   5 into   6 in   7 of   8 up   9 up
10 down

5 1 mind   2 taking   3 marks   4 passed   5 cluttered   6 does
7 make   8 facilities   9 Speak   10 receipt   11 budget
12 commercial   13 recovered   14 absolutely   15 audience

6 1 get my (1 point) ideas across (1 point)
2 there's no point (1 point) in getting (1 point)
3 make up (1 point) my mind (1 point)
4 were supposed (1 point) to arrive (1 point)
5 used (1 point) to get (1 point)
6 wish I (1 point) hadn't upset (1 point)
7 you wouldn't / didn't (1 point) keep shouting (1 point)
8 had come, (1 point) I would have (1 point)
9 the man (1 point) who stole (1 point)
10 was being (1 point) watched (1 point)

7 1 True
2 d)
It is disorganised (e.g., the writer asks for his money back at the beginning of the letter, when it should be at the end).
3 a)
4 True. Your partner must be allowed to speak without interruption.
5 False.
6 b)
7 c)
8 No, one or two words answers are needed. You can only use numerals (e.g., 31 instead of thirty-one) and abbreviations (e.g. *a.m.* instead of *in the morning*)
9 False. All the words must be changed.
10 a), g)

Unit 11 test

1 1 how *to* speak   2 won't *be* able   3 succeeded *in* getting
4 weren't *able* to   5 could *have* gone   6 She *managed* to
7 could *be* quite   8 knew *how* to   9 people *should* be
10 I *cannot/can't* ride

2 1 buy/get   2 had spent/would still have   3 promise to return/will
gladly lend   4 are going to catch/should leave   5 am going to
pass/should get down to   6 let/promise to work   7 eat/are going
to be   8 cook/will wash up   9 hadn't been/wouldn't be
10 pass/might be able to go

3 1 provided   2 even   3 unless   4 case   5 condition

4 1 advertised   2 interview   3 experience   4 qualifications
5 application   6 referees   7 unemployed   8 promotion
9 salary   10 flexible

5 1 bill   2 statement   3 withdraw   4 change   5 on

6 1 got the (1 point) sack (1 point)
2 don't know (1 point) how to (1 point)
3 could have (1 point) moved to
4 didn't manage (1 point) to pass (1 point)
5 as long (1 point) as you (1 point)

Unit 12 test

1 1 was shown   2 loves being   3 of being taken   4 isn't known
5 is believed to come   6 was thought to be   7 ever being
shouted at by   8 is said to be   9 was made to feel   10 is being
examined by

2 1 When did you last have your car serviced?
2 Have you ever had a tooth removed?
3 You really need to get your hair cut.
4 We're going to have the whole house decorated.
5 Would you ever consider having plastic surgery?

3 1 ✗ crept/tiptoed   2 ✗ imagine   3 ✓   4 ✗ stared   5 ✓
6 ✗ biting/chewing   7 ✗ knocked   8 ✗ gasped   9 ✓
10 ✗ glanced

4 1 robbed   2 stole   3 burglary   4 suspended   5 judge
6 prison   7 witnesses   8 made   9 trial   10 pleaded
11 prosecution   12 evidence   13 defence   14 jury
15 convicted

5 1 who   2 it   3 are   4 been   5 that   6 away   7 the   8 was
9 be   10 about

Unit 13 test

1 1 b) awful drizzle.   2 e) a new job.   3 d) a play.
4 c) historical novels.   5 a) a good book.

2 1 spent *so* much   2 for *such a long time/so long* that
3 I'm *strong enough*   4 far *too* tired   5 was *so* happy   6 angry
(that) she   7 *enough time*   8 feeling *so* exhausted   9 *Very* few
10 he's *so* friendly

3 1 rain   2 cloud   3 floods   4 sunny   5 snowed   6 rat   7 bark
8 cat   9 crow   10 wing

4 1 torrential   2 thunderstorm   3 climate   4 temperatures
5 drought   6 hurricane   7 Avalanches   8 flooding   9 shower
10 patchy

5 1 after   2 off   3 with   4 up   5 to

6 1 too ill (1 point) to go (1 point)
2 never seen (1 point) such a good (1 point)
3 not rich enough (1 point) to buy (1 point)
4 what I really hate (1 point) is (1 point)
5 driving (1 point) conditions (1 point)

Progress test 3 (Units 11–14)

1 1 shouldn't (1 point) have borrowed (1 point)
2 advised me (1 point) not to go (1 point)
3 are reminded (1 point) (that) they (1 point)
4 so tired (1 point) that I could (1 point)
5 such (1 point) an unhelpful (1 point)
6 like being (1 point) told what (1 point)
7 you'll be (1 point) able to (1 point)
8 succeed in (1 point) winning (1 point)
9 on condition (1 point) that you (1 point)
10 aren't / are not (1 point) allowed to (1 point)

2 1 sitting   2 believed   3 repaired   4 been   5 've been working
6 had left   7 will have been   8 to eat   9 taking   10 were
watching

3 1 that   2 to   3 enough   4 such   5 had/got   6 had   7 able
8 only   9 being   10 very

4 1 to   2 be   3 Even   4 of   5 that   6 have   7 got   8 a
9 then   10 not

5 1 broke   2 look   3 deal   4 turned   5 faced   6 resigned
7 take   8 pay   9 let   10 take

6 1 salary   2 advertised   3 gained/got   4 accept   5 earn/make
6 wonder   7 glanced   8 burgled/robbed   9 plead   10 make
11 achieve   12 have   13 package   14 cruise   15 gang
16 queue/line   17 cat   18 climate   19 season   20 snowed

7 1 False
2 False (there are 4 parts)
3 True
4 False
5 True (you will also need an eraser to correct any mistakes)
6 False (it lasts for 1 hour and 30 minutes)
7 False (two questions)
8 False (it is sometimes an informal letter)
9 False (120–180 words)
10 False (although you wouldn't be penalised if you did)
11 True
12 True
13 False
14 False (you hear each part twice)
15 True
16 False (it lasts for about 14 minutes)
17 True (your partner, the interviewer and a marker)
18 False (you should speak at normal speed)
19 True
20 False (He/she will just say *Thank you. That is the end of
the test.*)

Teacher's notes for photocopiable activities

1A Missing words noughts and crosses p.161

Aim:

- to review adverbs and other expressions commonly used when talking about when something happened or happens

Exam link

Paper 3 (Use of English), Part 2

Time

15 minutes, or at teacher's discretion

Preparation

Make one copy of worksheet 1A for each pair of students.

Procedure

1 On the board, draw an ordinary 'noughts (0) and crosses (X)' (tic-tac-toe) grid. Number each square 1–9 and play a quick game with your students. They choose their squares and you try to stop them getting a row of three.

2 Divide the class into pairs, and give each pair a copy of worksheet 1A.

3 Explain that the aim of the game is for the students to compete against each other to try to get a row of three squares, horizontally, vertically or diagonally. In this case, they do this by choosing a square, looking at the sentence and then choosing a word from the grid at the top of the page to go in that square.

4 Each time they choose a word from the grid, they should delete it. That word cannot be used again in another sentence.

5 Working in their pairs, they play game 1. Once one of them has got a row of three squares, they move to game 2 and then to game 3.

6 Allow them about ten minutes for this, and then check the correct answers with the whole class.

7 The winner in each group is the student who has won the most games. If a student has won a row of three squares, but has chosen a wrong word for a sentence, the other student in that pair automatically becomes the winner of that game (regardless of his/her own mistakes).

Options and alternatives

Whole class activity: Divide your class into two groups, and give each group enough copies of the sheet for all of them to see. Put one copy up on the board (enlarged or copied onto an OHT). The students then play against each other in their

two teams. If one of the teams chooses an incorrect word to complete a sentence, that square is automatically awarded to the other team, who then take their turn.

ANSWERS

1 since 2 ever 3 already 4 ago 5 yet
6 when 7 usually 8 never 9 when 10 ago
11 already 12 for 13 already 14 for 15 ever
16 when 17 since 18 ever 19 since 20 ago
21 never 22 for 23 already 24 yet 25 never
26 for 27 since

© Pearson Education Limited 2004 **PHOTOCOPIABLE**

1B First to the top p.162

Aim

- to practise wordbuilding by adding suffixes to make words work in context

Exam link

Paper 3 (Use of English), Part 5

Time

15 minutes, or at teacher's discretion

Preparation

Make one copy of the playing grid 1B for each group of four students. Make one copy of team A's answers and one of team B's answers for each group of four students. For this activity, you will also need two counters (or two coins) for each group.

Procedure

1 Divide the class into groups of four students. Each group should divide themselves into pairs. These will be team A and team B.

2 Give each group a copy of the playing grid 1B. Give team A in each group a copy of team B's answers, and give team B a copy of team A's answers.

3 Explain that the aim of the game is to be the first team to get to the top of their sentence 'ladder'.

4 Team A begins by moving their counter (or coin) onto sentence 1 of their ladder and deciding on the correct form and spelling of the word in bold, which they then say to team B. Team B tells them if they are right or wrong. If they are wrong, team B should not tell them the correct answer.

5 If team A are correct, they move to sentence 2 and wait until their next turn before attempting the answer. If they are wrong, they stay where they are, and wait until their next turn before attempting the answer again.

6 Steps 4 and 5 are repeated by team B.

7 The winning team are the first team to reach the top of their ladder, or who are the closest to it after about 10–15 minutes of play.

Options and alternatives

Whole class activity: Divide the class into two teams and give each team enough copies of sheet 1B for all of them to see. Make an enlargement or OHT of 1B and put it on the board. Each team takes it in turn to answer their sentences, as in steps 4–5 above, with one student from each team writing their answer on the board. If they are correct, tick off that sentence on the displayed sheet. The winner is the first team to have all their sentences ticked off.

> **ANSWERS**
> *These are on sheet 1B in the answer boxes.*
> © Pearson Education Limited 2004 **PHOTOCOPIABLE**

2A Key words risk 1 p.163

Aim:

• to review and practise language used for contrasting and comparing

Exam link

Paper 2 (Writing), reports; Paper 5 (Speaking), Part 2; Paper 3 (Use of English), Part 3

Time

15–20 minutes

Preparation

Make one copy of activity 2A for each group of four students. Separate the answers from the bottom of the page and keep these aside.

Procedure

1 Divide your class into groups of two, three or four students.

2 Give each group a copy of sheet 2A.

3 Working in their teams, they should take it in turns to transform the sentences on the sentence sheet, and write their answers in the appropriate space on the answer sheet.

4 Each time they write their answers, they should decide how certain they are that their answers are correct, and 'risk' points (5 points if they are about 50% sure their answer is correct, 10 points if they are about 75% sure their answer is correct, or 15 points if they are 100% sure their answers are correct), which they tick in the box to the right of their answer.

5 When both teams have transformed all their sentences, give each group a copy of the answers.

6 They then mark each other's sentences. If the answer is correct, the team are awarded the number of points they risked. If the answer is wrong, they lose them.

7 The winning team is the team who have won the most points when all the sentences have been marked.

Options and alternatives

Whole class activity: Divide the class into two teams and give them the sentence sheet. They take it in turns to transform the sentences, which you write on the board. Points are won and lost in the same way as in step 6 above.

Following up

This activity can be adapted for any FCE Paper 3 Part 3 test, which can otherwise be a very dry task.

> **ANSWERS**
> *These are on the students' sheet.*
> © Pearson Education Limited 2004 **PHOTOCOPIABLE**

2B Get it right! p.164

Aims:

• to review use of articles (*a/an/the*)
• to review layout of semi-formal letter, especially paragraphs

Exam link

Paper 2 (Writing), all Parts

Time

15 minutes, or at teacher's discretion

Preparation

Make one copy of worksheet 2B for each pair of students.

Procedure

1 Tell your students to imagine that they have applied for a place on an English course, and have received a letter from the director of the school. They are going to write a reply to the director.

2 Give each pair of students a copy of worksheet 2B. Explain that this is the letter they have written. Ask them to skim the letter, and then ask them if they think there is anything wrong with it. (Answer: There are no paragraphs. The letter is missing definite and indefinite articles.)

3 In their pairs, they should identify where the articles are missing and complete the articles grid following the example for number 1. They should write the word preceding the article, the article itself, and the word or words that follow it in the grid.

4 When they have done this, they should identify where the paragraph breaks come, and write this in the Paragraph breaks grid, following the example for number 1.

5 The first pair to correctly complete both grids is the winner (or alternatively, the pair who has done the most after about 10–15 minutes of play).

Options and alternatives

This activity could be made more challenging by removing the answer grids and just giving the students the letter.

ANSWERS

Articles:

1 on the English course   **2** joining the course
3 are a few details   **4** attending the course
5 at a hotel   **6** in the morning   **7** In the afternoon   **8** join the FCE class   **9** taking the exam   **10** is a canteen   **11** from the college itself

Paragraph breaks:

1	… Ms Harcourt	*and*	Thank you …
2	… the course.	*and*	There are …
3	… hotel.	*and*	As far …
4	… December.	*and*	I would be …
5	… college itself?	*and*	I look forward …
6	… from you.	*and*	Yours sincerely …

Dear Ms Harcourt

Thank you very much for your letter confirming my place on the English course at the St Luke's in Cambridge. I am very much looking forward to joining the course.

There are a few details that I need to correct. First of all, I am attending the course for six weeks, not four. Secondly, I am arriving on June 23, not July 23. Furthermore, I am staying in college accommodation while I am there, and not at a hotel.

As far as my classes are concerned, I would like to concentrate on speaking and listening in the morning, as my job requires these skills. In the afternoon I would like to join the FCE class, as I will be taking the exam in December.

I would be grateful if you could tell me whether there is a canteen at the college. Could you also let me know how far the college accommodation is from the college itself?

I look forward to hearing from you.

Yours sincerely,

© Pearson Education Limited 2004 **PHOTOCOPIABLE**

---

3 Find the mystery word p.165

Aim:

- **to review and practise some common adverb collocations**

Exam link

Paper 1 (Reading), Part 3

Time

15–20 minutes

Preparation

Make one copy of worksheet 3 for each group of two or three students.

Procedure

1 Divide the class into pairs or groups of three, and give each pair or group a copy of worksheet 3.

2 Ask them to read through sentences 1–13, and to ask you about any vocabulary they are not sure of.

3 Explain that each sentence 1–13 has a follow-on sentence a)–m). They must match these sentences (for example, sentence 1 matches sentence m)). They should then look at the gap in the second sentence and decide what word is missing. The first letter has been given to them. Each word appears in Unit 3 of their coursebook.

4 When they have decided what that word is, they should write it in the grid at the bottom of the page. One letter for each square on the grid.

5 Explain that if they do this correctly, they will reveal another adverb in the shaded vertical strip.

6 The first pair or group to reveal this adverb is the winner.

ANSWERS

Sentence matches:	Missing word:
1 m)	unusually
2 l)	surprisingly
3 a)	securely
4 e)	absolutely
5 h)	extremely
6 j)	fairly
7 d)	totally
8 c)	powerfully
9 b)	completely
10 k)	rather
11 i)	incredibly
12 g)	poorly
13 f)	vividly

The 'mystery' word is *uncomfortably*.

© Pearson Education Limited 2004 **PHOTOCOPIABLE**

4 What do you think? p.166

Aim:

- **to practise talking on a food/health related subject for three minutes**

Exam link

Paper 5 (Speaking), Part 3

Time

About 20 minutes

Preparation

Make one copy of worksheet 4 for each group of four students.

Cut the sheets in half, one part for team A, one part for team B.

Procedure

1 Divide your class into two groups. These will be team A and team B

2 Give one group a copy of the team A paper, and give the other group a copy of the team B paper.

3 Explain that the two questions on their paper are typical of the kinds of question they might be asked in the FCE Speaking test. Below each question, they will see a grid with ten words or expressions that would be useful when answering that question.

4 Working in their groups, they should try to think of five more useful words or expressions that could be used to answer the question, and to write these on the grid. They should make sure that the other group does not hear them.

5 Students then get into groups of four, two students from team A and two students from team B. One student from team A in each group begins by asking team B question 1. The two members of team B should talk to each other for **three minutes** to answer the question.

6 Each time team A hears a word or expression that matches one of theirs on their grid, they should put a tick next to it.

7 Step 5 is then repeated by team B (who asks the question to team A).

8 Steps 6–7 are then repeated for question 2.

9 The winning team is the pair in each group who spoke the most words that appeared on the other team's grid.

Options and alternatives

Teacher-centred activity: Divide the class into two groups, and ask each group to nominate two or three speakers (remember that very occasionally students do the speaking test in groups of three). Ask the first group the first question on worksheet 4, and let the nominated speakers talk for three minutes. Tick off any words that they say on the grid. Ask the nominated speakers in the second group the second question.

Repeat this process for the other two questions on the worksheet, with different speakers nominated by each group.

The winning group is the group who matched the most words on the grids.

(NB: The empty spaces on the grids are not used in this version.)

Following up

Encourage students to keep a record of about 10 or 15 useful words and expressions for the different topics that come up in the exam (these topics are mostly covered in the Coursebook) and to review these from time to time.

5A Spend, spend, spend! p.167

Aims:

- **to review verbs commonly used for reported speech**
- **to identify what people are talking about**

Exam link

Paper 3 (Use of English), Part 3; Paper 4 (Listening), Part 3

Time

20–25 minutes

Preparation

Make one copy of worksheet 5A for each group of two or three students.

Procedure

1 Divide your class into pairs or groups of three.

2 Give each group a copy of worksheet 5A.

3 Explain that they must work in their groups to rearrange the letters in bold to form reporting verbs. They should read the first sentence in each group, and this gives them a clue as to what the reporting verb is. Allow them about 5–10 minutes for this.

4 Explain that you are going to read out a series of short monologues. They should listen carefully, and match each monologue with one of the sentences A–J. There are three sentences that do not have a corresponding monologue.

5 Read each monologue below twice, at normal speed. After each one, allow your students a few moments to choose the correct answer.

6 Feedback with answers. The group that matched the most monologues correctly is the winner.

Following on

There are three sentences (C, D, J) that do not have a matching monologue. Ask your students to write short monologues/excuses for these sentences.

ANSWERS AND TEACHER'S SCRIPT:

1 He must be made of money, the way he throws it about. Designer clothes, the latest fashion accessories, CD's: you name it, he'll buy it. I have to save for weeks if I want to buy even the smallest luxury! (Answer = B accused)

2 My father found a receipt for £260 for a Gucci bag and a pair of shoes I'd bought. He said I was wasting too much of my money. So I said 'All right dad, I'll go a bit easy from now on.' I gave him my word, so you'll have to go shopping on your own today! (Answer = E promised)

3 You go into a shop. It's full of the latest designer gear and hot fashion accessories. Straight away, you're in another world. You stop worrying about work, about school, about family problems and so on. Out comes the credit card, and you feel a big smile spreading across your face. (Answer = H described)

4 I wouldn't mind if you spent the money I gave you on useful things. I don't expect you to save every penny I give you. But you buy so much rubbish. I mean, did you really need an automatic banana peeler with a built-in radio? (Answer = I told)

5 We all love spending money on nice things. We call it retail therapy, don't we? You're no worse than anybody else. But if I were you, I'd try to put some aside for a rainy day. You must be able to pay for those important things in life when they come along. (Answer = F advised)

6 My father says I get through too much money every week, but it's really not true. Sure, I go out on Friday and Saturday nights, and once or twice during the week, but I try to save a bit when I can. (Answer = A denied)

7 My mother says I'm getting through too much money going out in the evening. She says she wouldn't mind so much if it was my own money I was spending and not hers. Of course I had to say sorry and promised her it wouldn't happen again. (Answer = G apologised)

5B Shopping race p.168

Aim:
- **to listen to key words related to shopping, and to follow directions**

Exam link

Paper 5 (Speaking), all Parts

Time

About 15–20 minutes, or at teacher's discretion

Preparation

Make one copy of the situations worksheet, and one copy of the map, for each group of three students.

Procedure

1 Divide your class into groups of three.

2 Give two students in each group a copy of the situations worksheet. They should not show this to the other student in the group.

3 Give the other student in each group a copy of the map.

4 Explain that the students with the situations sheet are going to read some short texts aloud One student reads the 'Student A' sentence, the other student reads the 'Student B' sentence (which is a short, functional sentence containing important key words and phrases). Each text gives a clue about a particular type of shop or other building that they would expect to find in a town centre.

5 The student with the map must listen carefully, follow their directions, and match the type of shop with one of the buildings A–R on the map. He/she has a list of the shops, etc., in the box above their map. He/she should listen carefully, as there are more buildings on the map than there are dialogues.

6 The students with the situations sheet read their texts aloud. They should read each one twice, at normal speed, and allow the student with the map a few moments to choose their answers.

7 Allow your students about 12–15 minutes for this, and then stop them. The group that identified the most shops on the map is the winner.

Options and alternatives

Make this a teacher-centred listening activity by dividing your class into pairs, and giving each pair a map, then reading the situations yourself.

ANSWERS

A chemist   **C** department store   **D** post office
F travel agent   **G** shoe shop   **I** bank   **K** cinema
L library   **M** garden centre   **O** book shop
Q café

6A Modal hit and miss p.170

Aims:
- **to review use and construction of modal verbs (past and present)**
- **to complete short paragraphs with missing sentences**

Exam link

Paper 1 (Reading), Part 3

Time

15–20 minutes

Preparation

Make one copy of worksheet 6A for each group of four students. Cut the sheet in two along the dotted line.

Procedure

1 Divide your class into teams of four. Divide each team into two groups, (group 1 and group 2).

2 Give group 1 a copy of the group 1 section of worksheet 6A. Give group 2 a copy of the group 2 section. The two groups in each team should not show their paper to each other.

3 Group 1 begins by looking at question 1 on their paper. There is a sentence missing from the middle of the short paragraph. Group 2 has that sentence somewhere on their grid.

4 Group 1 reads the two sentences from question 1 out aloud, and then asks group 2 for a grid reference (e.g. B3). Group 2 reads out the sentence in that space on the grid.

5 If the whole team think that the sentence fits into the middle of the paragraph in question 1, group 1 writes the number of the question in the appropriate space on their grid. If it doesn't fit, they ask for another grid reference, and so on until both groups think that the sentence fits into question 1.

Group 2 must not help group 1 locate the correct sentence. If any team is caught doing this, they are disqualified from the game.

6 Steps 3–5 are repeated for questions 2–7. As the game progresses, it becomes much faster, as group 1 becomes familiar with the sentences on group 2's grid.

7 The winning team is the first team to match all the sentences correctly.

Options and alternatives

'Bingo'-type game: Divide your students into pairs and give each pair a copy of the Group 1 paper. You keep the Group B paper. Tell your class to look at number 1. You should then start reading out the sentences on the Group B paper in random order. As soon as one of the pairs in the class thinks that the sentence you have read fits into number 1 on their paper, they shout *Bingo!* If they are correct, they win 1 point. If they are wrong, they are disqualified from that round. You should then repeat the process for numbers 2–6 on their paper.

ANSWERS

Group 1's finished grid should look like this

	1	2	3	4
A	6		5	
B		1		7
C				3
D	4		2	

6B Imperfect passive p.171

Aims:
- **to review form and function of the passive voice**
- **to identify unnecessary words in a text**

Exam link

Paper 3 (Use of English), Parts 2 and 4

Time

15–20 minutes, or at teacher's discretion

Preparation

Make one copy of worksheet 6B for each group of three students. Cut the sheets in half along the dotted line.

Procedure

1 Divide your class into teams of three.

2 Give each team a copy of part 1. Allow them five minutes to read the text. They should try to remember as much information as possible.

3 Ask them to return part 1 to you, and then give them part 2.

4 In their teams, they should try to do the following:
- Complete the gaps with appropriate passive forms of the active verbs they read in part 1.
- Identify and remove any words in the text which are unnecessary. There is one mistake in most (but not all) of the lines.

5 Allow them about 10–15 minutes for this, and then tell them to stop.

6 The winning team is the team who correctly completed most of the gaps *and* identified most of the unnecessary words at the end of the set time period.

Options and alternatives

Stage 5 can be shorter if you don't have enough time (e.g. you could allow them five minutes instead of ten), or longer if you want students to do as much of the task as they can.

ANSWERS

This is the correct version. The missing words are in *italics*, and the extra words are crossed through.

Jules Jordan was born in 1973. His parents died ~~off~~ when he was only a baby, so he *was brought up* by his aunt and ~~their~~ uncle, James and Janice Peabody. They didn't treat ~~with~~ him very well; he *was* rarely *given* enough food ~~which~~ to eat and *was* never *shown* any real affection by them. When he was only ~~before~~ 7 years old, he *was sent* to boarding school. He was very unhappy there, and often got into ~~a~~ trouble with the teachers. After only two terms, he *was expelled*, and *was sent* to live with his grandfather, ~~is~~ Joseph Jordan. He *was encouraged* to work hard by his grandfather. He became interested in information technology when he was 15, and he set up ~~for~~ his own website design company when he was ~~then~~ only 18 years old, a remarkable achievement considering that the Internet *was* still *being developed* and people ~~they~~ were unsure in which direction it was heading. Since then, thousands of websites around ~~about~~ the world *have been designed* by his company, Cranberry Technology, and he has ~~been~~ made in excess of £170 million. In 2001, he *was presented* with a Golden Crown award for his services to British industry. His name ~~it~~ *is known* to people all over the world, and his biography is currently *being written* by the author Max Jeffries.

© Pearson Education Limited 2004 **PHOTOCOPIABLE**

7A Relative matching p.172

Aims:
- to review use of relative pronouns in relative clauses
- to match text extracts with a suitable heading

Exam link
Paper 1 (Reading), Part 1; Paper 3 (Use of English), Part 2;

Time
15–20 minutes

Preparation
Make one copy of worksheet 7A for each group of two or three students. Cut the texts in part 2 into separate cards. Put both sets into different envelopes.

Procedure
1 Divide your class into pairs or groups of 3.
2 Give each group a set of part 1. Explain that these are headings for magazine articles or stories. In their

pairs/groups, they should spend five minutes talking about the headings. What do they think they are about? What key words and expressions would they expect to find, etc.

3 After five minutes, give each group a set of part 2 cards. Tell them that these are extracts from magazine articles, stories. They must do two things with this:
   A: They must match the extracts with a suitable heading. There is only one heading for each extract, and there are five headings that do not belong to any of the extracts. Tell them to beware of distracters.
   B: The relative pronouns have been removed from the extracts. They must decide what these are, and write them in.

4 The first group to successfully complete A and B in 3 above is the winner.

ANSWERS

1 This does not match any of the extracts   2 F (*who/which / that/whose*)   3 This does not fit any of the extracts   4 B (*when/which / that/which* or *that*)   5 This does not fit any of the extracts   6 E (*Who/whom/which / that*)   7 This does not match any of the extracts   8 D (*Whose/Who/which / that*)   9 G (*where/which / that/when*)   10 A (*which / that/where/which / that*)   11 C (*who/which / that/which*)   12 This does not match any of the extracts

© Pearson Education Limited 2004 **PHOTOCOPIABLE**

7B Collocations crossword p.174

Aim:
- to review collocations

Exam rationale
Paper 3 (Use of English), Part 1

Time
About 15 minutes

Preparation
Make one copy of worksheet 7B for each group of four students. Cut each sheet in half along the dotted line.

Procedure
1 Divide your class into groups of four. They should divide themselves into pairs.
2 Give each **group** a copy of the crossword grid on worksheet 7B. Give each **pair** a copy of the group A or group B clues. Explain that the grid does not have any numbers on it, but some of the letters for the answers are already there.
3 Explain that the clues each pair have are different, but will give the same answer. These answers all collocate with the words in bold in their sentences. They all appeared in Unit 7 of their coursebook.

4 Your students should work together to complete the crossword grid by discussing their clues and deciding on an appropriate word that fits both. During the activity, they should not show their clues to the other pair. In some cases, more than one answer is possible for the clues.

5 The first group in the class to complete the crossword correctly is the winner.

Options and alternatives

Whole class activity: This is a livelier version of the game, and can be played by smaller classes (up to ten students) Make three A3 enlargements of the crossword grid and attach these to the board. Divide the class into three teams. Each team is allocated their own grid. As they choose their answers to the sentences, one student in each team comes up to the board and writes them on their grid. The first team to complete the grid is the winner.

ANSWERS

These answers apply to both group A and group B's sentences:

A experience **B** luxuries **C** instruments
D advances/developments **E** conditions
F progress **G** spare **H** cookery **I** historical
J latest **K** swift **L** advances/developments

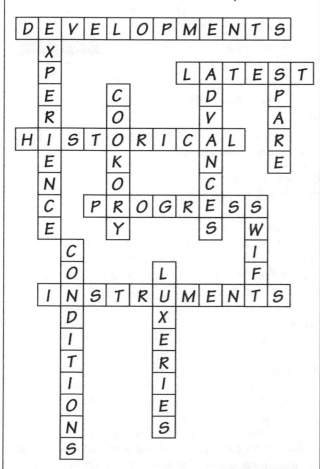

---

8 Get it together p.176

Aims:

- **to review verbs which can be followed by both a gerund and an infinitive form**
- **to review adjectives used to describe personality**

Exam link

Paper 1 (Reading), Parts 3 and 4

Time

15 minutes, or at teacher's discretion

Preparation

Make one copy of worksheet 8 for each pair of students.

Procedure

1 Divide your class into pairs.

2 Give each group a copy of worksheet 8.

3 Explain that columns A, B and C can be linked to form a complete sentence. Students must draw a line between the three parts of the sentence.

4 They must then decide whether to use the verbs in column B in their gerund (-ing) form, or as an infinitive (to + infinitive). In some cases, either may be possible. Some verbs can be used more than once. They can only decide which form of the verb to use by successfully matching columns A, B and C.

5 Column D contains an adjective of personality. Once they have matched columns A, B and C, they should decide which adjective best describes to personality of the person speaking.

6 The first pair to correctly match all four columns is the winner. Alternatively, set a time limit – the winning pair is the pair who have matched the most sentences, put the verbs into their correct form and chosen the most correct adjectives (award 1 point for matching each sentences, 1 point for using the correct verb form in each sentence, and 1 point for choosing the correct adjective for each sentence.

ANSWERS

Thanks for the invitation to your party. I really like **to meet/meeting** new people. Shall I bring something to eat, or a bottle of something? (Sociable)

I know your suggestion is the most sensible one. However, please understand that I prefer **to do/doing** things my way to any other. (Stubborn)

Of course I remembered **to post** your letter and buy you some milk when I went shopping.   (Reliable)

I don't have many memories of the meeting last month. However, I do remember everyone **telling** me to shut up and give everyone else a chance to speak!   (Talkative)

Of course I'd like **to make** a donation to your charity. Here's a cheque for £10,000.   (Generous)

I don't want to tell everyone how successful and powerful I am in my job. I would prefer **to tell** them that I'm just an ordinary office worker. (Modest)

I've stopped **worrying** about my job, my relationship problems and my financial difficulties. As far as I'm concerned, things can only get better from now on! (Optimistic)

I was in a terrible hurry, but I could see that Anne was upset. So I stopped **to have** a chat with her and cheer her up. (Thoughtful)

I don't try **to do** too many things at once. I believe in working at my own pace and taking regular breaks. (Sensible)

I tried **applying** for the post of managing director, and was successful! What's next? Maybe I'll start my own multinational company. (Ambitious)

© Pearson Education Limited 2004 **PHOTOCOPIABLE**

9 Find the differences p.177

Aims:
- to find the differences between two similar pictures, focusing on key items
- to promote student interaction

Exam link
Paper 5 (Speaking), Part 2

Time
10–15 minutes, or at teacher's discretion

Preparation
Make one copy of worksheet 9 for each group of 2. Cut this in half, Student A and Student B.

Procedure
1 Divide your class into pairs.
2 Give one student in each group a copy of the Student A picture, and one student a copy of the Student B picture. They should not show these to each other.
3 Explain that their pictures are the same, but there are 12 small differences. They must work together to find these differences without looking at each other's pictures. They should do this by describing their pictures to each other and by asking each other questions (e.g. *What does the man look like? Does she look happy?*, etc.).
4 The first group to find all 12 differences is the winner. Alternatively, set them a time limit of five or ten minutes – the winning team is the pair who identify the most differences in that time limit.

Options and alternatives
Teacher-centred activity: Divide your class into 4 teams, and give each team a copy of the Student A picture. You have a copy of the Student B picture, which you should not show them. Each team should take it in turns to ask you a question, to which you can only answer *Yes* or *No*. Whenever a team identifies a difference between your picture and theirs, award them 1 point.

ANSWERS
In student B's picture:
1 The man is looking slightly annoyed.
2 His computer is a laptop, not a desktop computer.
3 The in-tray is almost full.
4 There is a glass on the table next to him, not a mug.
5 To his right there is a two-drawer filing cabinet.
6 On the filing cabinet there is a vase of flowers, not a pot plant.
7 The book on his desk is open.
8 The window is closed.
9 The sign on the wall says 'Department B30', not 'Department V13'.
10 A woman is walking out of the room.
11 The clock on the wall says 8.45 not 9.15.
12 The man is very tidily dressed.

© Pearson Education Limited 2004 **PHOTOCOPIABLE**

10A Phrasal verbs bingo p.178
Aim:
- to review some common phrasal verbs introduced throughout the course

Exam link
Paper 3 (Use of English), all Parts

Preparation
Make one copy of the bingo cards on page 178, and cut them into individual team cards (team 1, team 2, etc.). Also copy and cut up the phrasal verbs on page 179 – one copy only – and put the cards into an envelope.

Time
10–15 minutes

Procedure
1 Divide your class into five teams, and give each team a bingo card. Allow them a few moments to read through the sentences.
2 Explain that you are going to read some phrasal verbs to them. After each phrasal verb, they should look at their cards and decide if it can be used in any of their sentences. They should then write the phrasal verb **in its correct form** in the relevant gap on the sentence. As

soon as they have completed all six sentences, they shout *Bingo* and win the game.

3 Take the calling cards at random from the envelope, and read each phrasal verb out aloud. Pause for a few moments after each phrasal verb to allow the student teams to discuss whether or not it can be used in one of their sentences.

4 Continue doing this until one of the teams calls *Bingo*.

5 Check their answers with those below.

Options and alternatives

If you have a very large class, divide them into groups of 6. Give one student in each group a copy of the phrasal verbs cards, and the others a bingo card. The student with the phrasal verbs cards reads them out as in steps 3 and 4 above. The other students play the game as normal.

ANSWERS

Police are *looking into* the disappearance of two children.

She started off as a family doctor, and *went on to* become a successful surgeon.

We've done nothing all day. It's time we *got down to* some serious studying.

Everybody said he should retire, but he *went on* working until he was 91.

I don't speak the language fluently, but I *picked up* a few words when I was there on holiday.

Are you listening? Have you *taken in* anything I've said to you?

My mother says she's *looking forward to* meeting you next week.

I needed a hobby, so I *took up* photography.

Has anyone tried to *find out* how much the tickets will cost?

What do you want to be when you *grow up*?

When I was young, children were *brought up* to respect the law.

I'll just *look up* the word in my dictionary.

We need to *work out* how much food we'll need for the party.

The Ferrari team want to *test out* their new car on the racetrack.

How long have you been *going out with* her?

Mrs Garcia *looks down on* anyone who hasn't had a college education.

Do you *eat out* a lot, or do you do a lot of cooking at home?

I've always *looked up to* Bill for his courage and determination.

He's *looking out for* a nice apartment in the city centre.

I'm always very busy, but I can usually *fit in* time to see my friends.

We must *get across* the simple fact that drugs are dangerous.

10B Which writing task? p.180

Aims:
• **to identify extracts from different FCE Paper 2 tasks**
• **to complete extracts with a word which has been removed**

Exam link

Paper 2 (Writing), all Parts; Paper 3 (Use of English), Part 2

Time

About 15 minutes

Preparation

Make one copy of worksheet 10B for each group of three students. This will be their 'playing board' (if you can, make an A3 enlargement – this will make it easier for the students to play on). Each group will also need three coloured counters (or coins) and a dice. Make one copy of the answers below for each group of three students.

Procedure

1 Write the following on the board:
   a Informal letter
   b Semi-formal letter
   c Story
   d Report
   e Article
   f Composition

2 Divide your class into groups of three, and give each group a copy of the playing board, a dice and three counters.

3 Explain that the sentences/sentence extracts on their board are all taken from the different FCE essay types on the board. Each sentence also contains a missing word.

4 To play the game, they must do the following:
   – Take it in turns to role their dice and move along the board moving from the Start space and following the numbers.
   – When they land on a space, they must decide what kind of essay the sentence/extract comes from, and write this on that space.
   – They must then decide what the missing word is (there is only one word missing from each sentence), and write this on the same space.
   – They should then write their initials on that space If they land on a space which another student has completed, they should role their dice again and move on until they come to an uncompleted space.
   – When they reach the Finish space, they must stop playing.

5 When each player has reached the Finish space, give each group a copy of the answers. They should award themselves points as follows:
   • For identifying the type of essay: 1 point
   • For correctly completing the gap: 1 point

6 The winner in each group is the student with the most points.

ANSWERS

Number	Essay type	Missing word
1	Informal letter	forward
2	Semi-formal letter	would
3	Story	what / who
4	Report	that
5	Informal letter	at
6	Article	about
7	Report	with
8	Semi-formal letter	like
9	Article	that
10	Composition	much
11	Composition	for
12	Semi-formal letter	the
13	Report	of
14	Story	made
15	Article	for
16	Composition	would
17	Informal letter	for
18	Composition	have
19	Story	While / As
20	Composition	hand
21	Article	they
22	Report	an / the
23	Story	when
24	Semi-formal letter	in
25	Article	like
26	Semi-formal letter	about
27	Informal letter	if
28	Story	woke
29	Report	to
30	Informal letter	from

© Pearson Education Limited 2004 **PHOTOCOPIABLE**

11A Conditional connections p.181

Aims:
- **to review different conditional constructions (including mixed conditionals) and their relevant conjunctions**
- **to practise referencing skills**
- **to identify unnecessary words**

Exam link
Paper 2 (Writing), all Parts; Paper 5 (Speaking), all Parts

Time
15 minutes

Preparation
Make one copy of worksheet 11A for each group of two, three or four students. Cut these into sets of cards along the dotted lines, and put each set into an envelope.

Procedure
1 Divide your class into teams of two, three or four, and give each team a set of cards.
2 Tell them to open their envelope and spread the cards out in front of them.
3 Explain that on the right-hand side of each card, they will see the first clause of a conditional sentence. On the left-hand side of each card, they will see the second clause of a conditional sentence.
4 The aim of the activity is to join the cards together (similar to dominoes) so that the sentence clauses are correctly linked. They should be careful, as there is more than one possibility for some of the clauses. However, there is only one possible sequence for the whole set. To help them, the first and last cards are marked START and FINISH.
5 When they have matched their sentences, they should look at them carefully, as each one contains an extra, unnecessary word that should not be there (note that the extra word is by sentence, **not** by clause).
6 The first team to match their sentences and identify the extra word in each one is the winner.

ANSWERS
The sentences are in their correct order on worksheet 11A

Special offer! If you ~~decide~~ buy a TZX phone card, you get another one absolutely free!

If you want to succeed in ~~the~~ life, work hard and don't forget to grovel!

If prices continue to rise as fast as they are now, we won't have enough to live on ~~for~~ anymore.

If you spend all your money on necessities, you will never be able to enjoy ~~by~~ yourself!

Take an umbrella with you in case ~~there~~ it rains later on.

We can go for a walk later ~~only~~ unless it rains.

If we spent more ~~of~~ time at home, we wouldn't spend so much of our money all the time.

If my boss ~~she~~ had paid me a bit more, I would probably have stayed on.

If I had been ~~like~~ more ambitious when I was younger, I wouldn't be stuck in the boring, dead-end job now.

If I ever needed extra money, the bank was always ~~being~~ happy to lend me some.

I'm going to buy a new computer even if I have to steal the money ~~away~~ from someone!

The bank was always willing to lend me money on condition that I paid it back ~~to~~ within 6 months.

Providing ~~as~~ you are prepared to work overtime, you can make a lot of money in this job.

I'll let you borrow my car provided that you cook ~~for~~ me a meal tomorrow.

You've very welcome to use my trainers if you ~~will~~ clean them properly after you've used them.

If you hadn't warned ~~with~~ me about it first, I would have been in considerable trouble.

Don't eat those apples unless they've been ~~quite~~ washed first.

In case of ~~the~~ fire, sound the alarm and run to the nearest exit.

If you didn't ~~do~~ work so hard all the time, you wouldn't feel so tired every day.

Even if I was a millionaire, I wouldn't give you any ~~thing~~ of my money.

© Pearson Education Limited 2004 **PHOTOCOPIABLE**

11B Useful expressions p.182

Aim:
• to review/practise some useful FCE Speaking test expressions

Exam rationale
Paper 5 (Speaking), Parts 3 and 4

Time
10 minutes

Preparation
Make one copy of worksheet 11B for each pair of students.

Procedure
1 Divide your class into pairs, and give each pair a copy of worksheet 11B.
2 Explain that this sheet contains expressions that would be useful for different functions in the FCE Speaking test. The functions are underlined in the left-hand column. Also, in the left-hand column, they will see the first part of each expression. The second part is in the right-hand column.
3 They must take it in turns to match the first part of an expression on the left with its appropriate second part on the right.
4 Allow them about 10 minutes for this, then tell them to stop. The student in each pair who has made the most correct matches is the winner.

ANSWERS
Agreeing with somebody
That's my **view exactly.**
I think you're **absolutely right.**
That's **right.**
I can't help **thinking the same.**

Disagreeing with somebody
I'm afraid I **don't agree.**
I'm not entirely **sure about that.**
I'm not so **sure about that.**
I see things **differently myself.**
Asking somebody to say something again
I'm **sorry?**
I'm afraid I didn't **catch that.**
Could you **repeat that please?**
Would you mind **repeating that.**
Giving yourself time to think
May I think about **that for a moment?**
Let **me see.**
I haven't really **thought about it before.**
Hm, that's an **interesting question.**
Asking somebody what they think
What's your **opinion?**
What are your **feelings about it?**
What are **your views on …**
How do you **feel about …**
Saying things in another way
What I **mean is …**
To put it **another way …**
In other **words …**
What I'm **trying to say is …**
Interrupting someone
Sorry to **interrupt, but …**
Could I just **say that …**
Could I just **come in here and say …**

© Pearson Education Limited 2004 **PHOTOCOPIABLE**

12A Crossword race p.183

Aim:
• to review and introduce verbs that describe physical action

Exam link
Paper 2 (Writing), story

Time
15–20 minutes, or at teacher's discretion

Preparation
Make one copy of worksheet 12A for each group of six students. Separate part 1, and the crossword grids parts 2(A) and 2(B).

Procedure
1 Divide your students into groups of six, and ask them to divide themselves into two teams of three players. Give each team a copy of the words in part 1, and ask them to work together for about five minutes to check that they understand what the words mean. They can use a dictionary for this if they want. They should then put the words somewhere they cannot see them.

2 Give one team in each group a copy of the crossword in part 2(A), and give one team in each group a copy of the crossword in part 2(B).

3 The two teams must try to complete their crossword as quickly as possible, using the words from part 1. They may need to change the form of some of the words. In some cases, more than one answer may be possible, but only one will fit if they are to complete their crossword, so some trial and error may be necessary.

4 Let your students do the activity for about 10 minutes, and then ask them to stop. The winning team in each group is the team that completed most clues on their crossword grid. Alternatively, the winning team is the team in each group that completes their crossword first.

Following on

Students should use their dictionaries to check the meanings of the words they are unfamiliar with, and develop a 'bank' of the words, together with sample sentences showing how they are used.

Each team has a different selection of words. The team members from team A can pair up with a team member from team B, and exchange information about their words (what they mean, when they are used, the past forms of the words, etc.).

ANSWERS

Crossword 2(A)

Across:
1 chew   4 whispering   7 crept   8 stared
9 strolling   12 wondered   13 screamed
Down:
2 hugged   3 slapped   5 suffocate   6 muttering
8 sipped   10 peered   11 smacking

Crossword 2B

Across:
1 wept   2 stammered   3 gasping   6 knock
7 believed   9 shout   10 gripped   11 glanced
Down:
1 wade   2 staggered   4 gazed   5 punched
8 imagine   11 gobble

© Pearson Education Limited 2004   **PHOTOCOPIABLE**

12B Key words risk 2 p. 185
See notes for 2A Key words risk 1 on page 147

13A First to 48 p.186

Aim:
• to review uses of *enough, so, such, too* and *very*

Exam link
Paper 3 (Use of English), Part 2

Time
20 minutes

Preparation
Make one copy of worksheet 13A for each group of three students.

Procedure

1 Divide your class into groups of three, and give each group a copy of worksheet 13A.

2 Explain that the jumbled words in 1–12 can be formed to make complete sentences. The first word of each sentence is in its correct place. Each sentence is also missing one of the words from the box at the top of the page.

3 The words in the box carry a point value. If used correctly in the appropriate sentences, the total point value of the combined words is 48.

4 Working together in their groups, students must rearrange the words to make sentences, and insert the correct word from the box. They should write this sentence in the box below each set of jumbled words.

5 While they are doing this, you must monitor the groups carefully. Each time one of the groups produces a correct sentence, write the number of points won in the small box to the right of their sentence.

6 As soon as one team gets 48 points (i.e. they get all their sentences correct), they win the game.

Options and alternatives
For a quicker game, you can lower the total number of points they need to win (e.g. you could reduce it to 36 or 24, etc.).

ANSWERS

  1 Unfortunately there were *very* few of his friends in the class.
  2 The film was *so* boring that we left the cinema.
  3 Everyone likes him because he's *such a* nice guy.
  4 Have we got *enough* time to have a coffee before our train leaves?
  5 It was *too* hot to work, so we went to the beach.
  6 Unfortunately I don't think there's *enough* pizza to go round.
  7 I'm afraid you're *too* unreliable to be trusted with this job.
  8 Luckily *very* few houses were damaged during the storm.
  9 We're having *such* hot weather at the moment.
  10 I love being with him because he's *such* good company.
  11 He was *such* a horrible boss that half his employees resigned.
  12 The homework was *so* difficult that I decided not to do it.

© Pearson Education Limited 2004   **PHOTOCOPIABLE**

13B The wrong words p.187

Aim:
• to focus on unnecessary words in sentences

Exam link
Paper 3 (Use of English), Part 4

Time
15–20 minutes

Preparation
Make one copy of worksheet 13B for each team of four students. Cut this in half, into Set A and Set B sections four.

Procedure
1 Divide your class into groups of four. These groups should then divide themselves into pairs.
2 Give one pair in each group the Set A sentences, and the other pair the Set B sentences. They should not show these to the other pair.
3 Explain that each sentence contains one extra, unnecessary word. In their pairs, they should identify these words in each sentence (they are all based on similar mistakes in Units 1–13 of their coursebook).
4 Also explain that although the Set A sentences sheet are different from those on Set B, the extra unnecessary words are all the same, but in a different order. Once both pairs have identified the words in their sentences, they should work together to match their sentences based on the extra unnecessary word that is not needed in both of them. They should read their sentences out to each other, without looking at each other's paper, and explain which word does not fit in each sentence.
5 The winning team is the first group in the class to match their sentences.

ANSWERS
1 J (the) 2 G (to) 3 H (be) 4 A (would)
5 B (being) 6 I (it) 7 C (like) 8 D (have)
9 F (a) 10 E (such)

© Pearson Education Limited 2004 **PHOTOCOPIABLE**

14 First to zero p.188

Aim:
• to review some of the main grammar and vocabulary points from the Coursebook

Exam link
Paper 3 (Use of English), all Parts

Time
20–30 minutes

Preparation
Make one copy of worksheet 14 for each group of four

students. Cut into cards along the dotted lines, and make sure they are well shuffled.

Procedure
1 Divide your class into groups of four.
2 Give each group a set of cards, which they should place face down on the desk.
3 Tell each player to take four cards from the top of the pack.
4 Explain that the aim of the activity is for the players to get rid of all four of their cards as quickly as possible. They do this by taking it in turns to answer the questions on their cards. They must answer both parts of their question correctly (except in the case of the key word transformations, where their sentence must be perfectly correct). The other members in the group should decide whether or not the answer is correct.
5 If they are correct, they lay that card down on the desk. If they are wrong, they must place that card to the bottom of the main pile and take another card from the top.
6 As soon as one student has got rid of all his/her cards, he/she should check their answers with you. If they have *not* answered all their questions correctly, they should continue playing.

ANSWERS
1 forward/from
2 when/since
3 explanation/financially
4 (a) tell (b) performance
5 (a) annoyed (b) failed
6 far easier to pass
7 unfortunate/inexperienced
8 ~~the~~ home/~~a~~ hospital
9 (a) absolutely (b) fairly
10 little/any
11 I'll have been at
12 be/so
13 (a) telling (b) says
14 ~~been~~ upset/can't ~~have~~
15 been/were
16 whose/where
17 hadn't failed, he could
18 supportive/furious
19 was/If
20 (a) much (b) would
21 ~~was~~ used/~~to~~ spend
22 such/too
23 reminded me to bring
24 ~~such~~ like/~~to~~ avoid
25 (a) paced (b) stared
26 on condition that
27 (a) accused (b) denied
28 ought / have/miss

© Pearson Education Limited 2004 **PHOTOCOPIABLE**

First Certificate in English Quiz p190

ANSWERS

1 Only in Paper 4 (Listening) where you get five minutes at the end of the test.
2 Pencil.
3 This will be marked wrong, so you should rub one out.
4 Minor errors are tolerated if they don't impede communication.
5 No.
6 You cannot pass or fail any individual paper, but you need an average of about 60% to get a Grade C.
7 Results usually come out about six weeks after the exam Certificates are sent about a month after that.
8 Four.
9 To get a good idea of what the text is about.
10 You should look at the text first in Parts 2 and 3. You should look at the questions/headings first in Parts 1 and 4.
11 Two. The question in Part 1 is compulsory; in Part 2 you can choose one task from five.
12 No, you must write in pen.
13 Yes, but make sure the examiner can read your work.
14 No, because you won't have time. After you have made a plan you should write your composition neatly.
15 Yes. It makes it easier for the examiner to read and mark.
16 If your handwriting is difficult to read, the examiner may mark you down.
17 Grammar, spelling and punctuation.
18 You will be marked down. If your answer is too short, you may not have given all the necessary information and if it is too long, you may have included things that are irrelevant.
19 Both questions are worth equal marks, so you should spend approximately equal time on them.
20 Five.
21 Two. Part 1 is multiple-choice, and tests vocabulary. In Part 2 no options are provided because it tests structures.
22 You should try again as it is incorrect.
23 If both answers are correct then you will get a mark. If one of the words is wrong then you will not get any marks.
24 Twice.
25 Simple words should be correct. Other minor errors are not marked down.
26 Two.
27 Yes.
28 Yes.
29 Examiners are trained to deal with this, so it shouldn't be a problem.
30 Try to find another way to say it.

usually	ever	ever	for	when	already
for	yet	since	since	since	for
since	already	never	already	when	yet
never	ago	never	when	ago	ago
for	already	ever			

Game 1

1 I've known him well
   .... we were children.

2 This is the first time I've
   .... eaten Japanese food.

3 I've seen this film five
   times ....

4 The last time he called
   was six months ....

5 This is a good book, but I
   haven't finished it ....

6 I wanted to be an architect
   .... I was a boy.

7 I .... eat lots of salad with a
   meal. It's very good for you.

8 I've .... met such an
   unpleasant man before.

9 I can't remember ....
   I first started hating seafood.

Game 2

10 I last went swimming three
    years ....

11 Have you .... had lunch?

12 I've lived here .... as
    long as I can remember.

13 You can borrow this book if
    you like. I've .... read it.

14 I can hardly believe I've
    worked here .... five years.

15 This is the first time I've ....
    been abroad for my holidays.

16 I knew him well ....
    we were children.

17 I've wanted to be an architect
    .... I was a boy.

18 Today was the first day I've
    .... been on an aeroplane.

Game 3

19 It's been almost three years
    .... I had any real time
    off work.

20 I first began having breathing
    difficulties about two
    months ....

21 I've .... tasted anything
    as disgusting as this before.

22 I've hated seafood ....
    as long as I can remember.

23 I've .... seen this film
    five times. It's absolutely
    brilliant!

24 Have you done your
    homework .... ?

25 I almost .... eat salad.
    I avoid it because it's just
    so boring.

26 He's obviously not talking
    to me, because he hasn't
    called me .... six months.

27 I've lived in the same
    place .... I was born.

Team A

FINISH

12 I'm **determine** to succeed, whatever happens.

11 I can't give you any money at the moment. I'm afraid I'm suffering from a few **finance** difficulties.

10 I'm not really very keen on **compete** sports. I'd rather sit at home with a good book!

9 My brother's a **survive** expert. He's able to survive on just one credit card!

8 Could you give me a good **explain** why you've missed so many classes?

7 I don't think I'm **prepare** for the exam. I've worked hard, but can't seem to remember anything.

6 He had hoped to pass his exam, but **disappoint**, he failed one of the papers.

5 One of the most **enjoy** things in life is a picnic on the beach with some good friends.

4 There's an old English saying that **flatter** will get you nowhere. Rubbish! It will get you *everywhere*!

3 My father's a travelling salesman, and is **regular** away from home.

2 **Perform** in the school play was one of the highlights of his year.

1 There was so much **confuse** in the room.

START

Team B

FINISH

12 In order to be successful, you need lots of money, and even more **determine**.

11 I would love to be **finance** secure, but as soon as I get any money I have to spend it on shopping and bills.

10 We decided to take part in a **compete** to see who could eat the most hot dogs in twenty minutes.

9 Were there any **survive** from the plane crash?

8 Stop **explain** why you missed our appointment. I don't want to hear your excuses!

7 Have you done much **prepare** for the party, or are you just going to take things as they come?

6 We hoped the film would be good, but it was a major **disappoint**.

5 I don't want to spoil everyone's **enjoy** of the party, but we should really turn the music down.

4 I'm **flatter** that you think my English is so good. Personally, I think it's not up to much.

3 He missed his English lessons with alarming **regular**, and eventually was asked to leave the school.

2 He was an actor by profession, but became famous as a live comedy **perform**.

1 He was completely bald, but was **confuse** known as 'Curly'.

START

Team A's answers (this copy to be given to Team B)

1 confusion   2 Performing   3 regularly   4 flattery   5 enjoyable   6 disappointingly   7 prepared

8 explanation (*not* explaination)   9 survival   10 competitive   11 financial   12 determined

Team B's answers (this copy to be given to Team A)

1 confusingly   2 performer   3 regularity   4 flattered   5 enjoyment   6 disappointment   7 preparation

8 explaining   9 survivors   10 competition   11 financially   12 determination

Remember:

- Use between two and five words for each gap.
- Do not change the form of the **key** word.
- Write your answers on the answer sheet.
- Only write the missing words on the answer sheet. Do not write the whole sentence.
- Contractions (I've, He's, etc.) count as two words.

		Points risked			Total
1	I've never met such an interesting person. **the** He's .... person that I've ever met.	5	10	15	
2	James doesn't drive his car as dangerously as his father does. **his** James' father .... than James does.	5	10	15	
3	My new computer wasn't quite as expensive as my old one. **little** My new computer was .... expensive than my old one.	5	10	15	
4	Tom isn't nearly as intelligent as Zoë. **lot** Zoë .... than Tom.	5	10	15	
5	Driving a sports car is much more exciting than driving a 4x4 off-roader. **nearly** Driving a 4x4 off-roader isn't .... driving a sports car.	5	10	15	
6	In my opinion, westerns are the most boring films to watch. **as** In my opinion, no other films .... to watch as westerns.	5	10	15	
7	The film I saw last night wasn't quite as long as this one. **little** The film I saw last night was .... this one.	5	10	15	
8	I prefer watching television to reading books. **rather** I'd .... books.	5	10	15	
9	You aren't nearly as tall as your sister. **far** Your sister .... you.	5	10	15	
10	I thought the Maths exam was much more difficult than the English exam. **far** I thought the English exam was .... the Maths exam.	5	10	15	

--✂------------------------

Answers

1 the most interesting   2 drives his car more dangerously   3 a little less   4 is a lot more intelligent
5 nearly as exciting as   6 are as boring   7 a little shorter than / a little less long than
8 rather watch television than read   9 is far taller than   10 far easier than / far less difficult than

Dear Ms Harcourt. Thank you very much for your letter confirming my place on English course at St Luke's in Cambridge. I am very much looking forward to joining course. There are few details that I need to correct. First of all, I am attending course for six weeks, not four. Secondly, I am arriving on June 23, not July 23. Furthermore, I am staying in college accommodation while I am there, and not at hotel. As far as my classes are concerned, I would like to concentrate on speaking and listening in morning, as my job requires these skills. In afternoon, I would like to join FCE class, as I will be taking exam in December. I would be grateful if you could tell me whether there is canteen at the college. Could you also let me know how far the college accommodation is from college itself? I look forward to hearing from you. Yours sincerely,

Articles box:

1	on the English course
2	
3	
4	
5	
6	
7	
8	
9	
10	
11	

Paragraph breaks:

1	...Ms Harcourt	and	Thank you...
2		and	
3		and	
4		and	
5		and	
6		and	

1 Don't forget your scarf and gloves when you go out.
2 I was worried about telling my boss I wanted to leave the company.
3 There are several things to remember when you go climbing.
4 What a fantastic day today!
5 I saw the child run across the road in front of me, and I swerved my bike to avoid him.
6 He glared at us and shouted 'You stupid idiots' at the top of his voice.
7 She thought we would all be late.
8 He was very short – probably no more than 1.4 metres tall.
9 She was either Australian or British.
10 He said he didn't have his homework with him because the dog had eaten it.
11 Put the fan on, please. Let's get a breeze going.
12 She told us she was going to have dinner in the best restaurant in town.
13 I didn't think much of the bit in the film where the main character is arrested.

a) Perhaps the most important thing is to make sure you are s...................... fastened to your ropes and harness.
b) I'm afraid I'm not c...................... sure which.
c) However, he was p...................... built, and as strong as a horse.
d) She was t...................... wrong of course, as we were punctual as always.
e) The weather is a...................... marvellous.
f) The whole scene was much more v...................... described in the book.
g) However, we weren't convinced, since she was so p...................... dressed.
h) It was an e...................... narrow escape for both of us.
i) It's i...................... hot in here.
j) It was a f...................... unpleasant moment for everybody.
k) I'm afraid I found his excuse r...................... unconvincing.
l) In the event, I found it s...................... easy to hand in my resignation.
m) It's u...................... cold for the time of year.

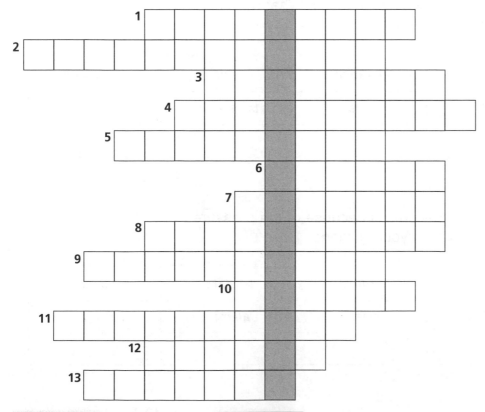

Team A (questions to ask Team B)

1 A friend of yours wants to get fit and healthy. What advice would you give him or her?

running/jogging	(balanced) diet	eat	swimming	smoking
give up	cut down on	exercise	drink	avoid

2 Do you think you eat a healthy diet? Why or why not?

fat	fibre	fruit	vegetables	meat
sugar	balanced	organic	fish	protein

- - - - - - - ✂ -

Team B (questions to ask Team A)

1 A friend of yours wants to change his eating habits. What advice would you give him or her?

give up	cut down on	increase	fruit	vegetables
cholesterol	diet	fibre	balanced	fat

2 Do you agree that many people become ill because of the pressures and stresses of modern life? Explain your opinion.

work	overtime	deadlines	targets	pollution
job	exercise	meals	allergy	lifestyle

A	*Direct*: 'I don't spend a lot of money.' *Reported*: This person **eedidn** spending a lot of money.
B	*Direct*: 'You spend a lot of money.' *Reported*: This person **cadcsue** somebody of spending a lot of money.
C	*Direct*: 'I do spend money on things I don't need.' *Reported*: This person **datmdite** spending money on things she didn't need.
D	*Direct*: 'I need to have the latest fashion accessories because I want to look cool.' *Reported*: This person **peladienx** why he needed to have the latest fashion accessories.
E	*Direct*: 'I really won't spend so much on fashion accessories from now on.' *Reported*: This person **rpiodsem** not to spend so much on fashion accessories.
F	*Direct*: 'You ought to save money whenever possible.' *Reported*: This person **sdviade** someone to save money whenever possible.
G	*Direct*: 'I'm sorry for spending your money.' *Reported*: This person **sopagdolie** for spending somebody's money.
H	*Direct*: 'I love it. It's therapy. You feel so good when you spend money.' *Reported*: This person **sddcibeer** the pleasure of spending money.
I	*Direct*: 'Don't waste so much money.' *Reported*: This person **dotl** someone not to waste so much money.
J	*Direct*: 'I need my money for important things.' *Reported*: This person **isda** he needs his money for important things.

The situations
Students A and B

1

Student A: John left the underground station and headed north. He went into the first building on his left, and said to the assistant:

Student B: *Have you got something for athlete's foot?*

2

Student A: He then went next door and asked an assistant:

Student B: *Which floor is it for electronic equipment?*

3

Student A: After that he went into the building opposite and said:

Student B: *I'd like this to go air mail please.*

4

Student A: He then walked north until he got to the T-junction. He turned right and went into the first building on his left. He said:

Student B: *I bought these last week and they're a bit tight around the toes. Can I exchange them?*

5

Student A: Next, he walked into the building to the south, on the other side of the road and said to the assistant:

Student B: *Have you got any last-minute deals for a weekend break somewhere warm and sunny?*

6

Student A: He turned right outside the building and took the second road on his left. He went into the last building on his right (just before the crossroads) and said:

Student B: *I'd like to return this. I really enjoyed it. Do you have anything else by the same author?*

7

Student A: After that he went west, and entered the first building on his left. He said:

Student B: *Two for this evening's performance, please.*

8

Student A: Then he went into the building diagonally opposite and to the west, next to the car park, where he said:

Student B: *I'd like to cash this please. Could you give me two tens and four fives?*

9

Student A: When he left the building, he headed east and took the second road on his right. At the end of the road, he went into the shop on his left, and said:

Student B: *I'm looking for a good dictionary. Preferably something for under £10.*

10

Student A: After that, he went along the footpath opposite, stopping at the building on the corner, where he said:

Student B: *A large iced coffee, please.*

11

Student A: He drank his coffee, and walked west to the end of the footpath. At the end of this path, he turned right, and at the crossroads he turned left. He walked into the first building on his right, and said:

Student B: *I'm looking for something that will grow quickly and give me lots of nice, colourful flowers.*

And then he went back to the station.

The map

Students C and D

bank   shoe shop   cinema   garden centre   library   department store
travel agent   café   post office   chemist   book shop

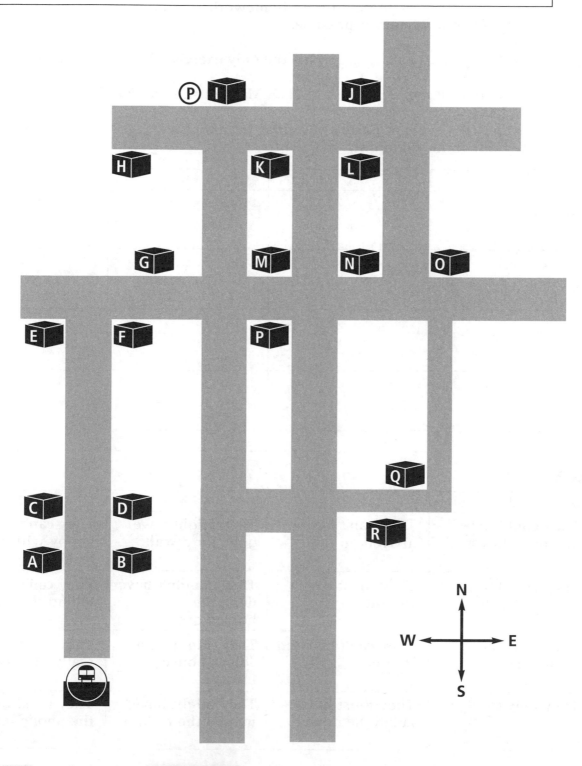

Group 1

1 They're shivering. .... Why don't they turn the heating on?

2 They're not here yet. .... They're usually so punctual.

3 They passed all their exams. .... Now they can go to university.

4 They say their students all hate doing their homework. .... They always seem to avoid it whenever possible.

5 They aren't at home. .... It's the only exercise they get these days.

6 They haven't written to me. .... Maybe I should give them a call.

7 They tell me that they were at Carol's yesterday evening. .... She was with me until about midnight.

	1	2	3	4
A				
B				
C				
D				

Group 2

	1	2	3	4
A	They could have lost my address	They can't have arrived on time	They might have gone for a walk	They can't be very happy with the results
B	They could have been cooking dinner	They must be freezing	They couldn't have done their homework	They can't be telling the truth
C	They must have been here	They can't be lying to me	They might be at John's house instead	They must be really pleased
D	They may be right	They must have failed the others	They might have missed the train	They must be on the phone instead

Part 1

Read this text carefully, and try to remember as much information as possible.

Jules Jordan was born in 1973. His parents died when he was only a baby, so his aunt and uncle, James and Janice Peabody, brought him up. They didn't treat him very well; they rarely gave him enough food to eat and never showed him any real affection. When he was only 7 years old, they sent him to boarding school. He was very unhappy there, and often got into trouble with the teachers. After only two terms, they expelled him, and his aunt and uncle sent him to live with his grandfather, Joseph Jordan. Joseph encouraged Jules to work hard. He became interested in information technology when he was 15 years old, and he set up his own website design company when he was only 18, a remarkable achievement considering that people were still developing the internet and were unsure in which direction it was heading. Since then, his company, Cranberry Technology, has designed thousands of websites around the world, and he has made in excess of £170 million. In 2001, the *Society for Excellence in Industry and Technology* presented him with a Golden Crown award for services to British industry. People all over the world know his name, and the author Max Jeffries is currently writing his biography.

- ✂ - - - - - - - - - -

Part 2

1	Jules Jordan was born in 1973. His parents died off when he was only a baby, so he
2	.... by his aunt and their uncle, James and Janice
3	Peabody. They didn't treat with him very well; he .... rarely .... enough
4	food which to eat and .... never .... any real affection by them. When he
5	was only before 7 years old, he .... to boarding school. He was very
6	unhappy there, and often got into a trouble with the teachers. After only two terms,
7	he .... , and .... to live with his grandfather, is
8	Joseph Jordan. He .... to work hard by his grandfather. He became
9	interested in information technology when he was 15, and he set up for his own
10	website design company when he was then only 18 years old, a remarkable
11	achievement considering that the Internet .... still .... and
12	people they were unsure in which direction it was heading. Since then,
13	thousands of websites around about the world .... by his
14	company, Cranberry Technology, and he has been made in excess of £170 million.
15	In 2001, he .... with a Golden Crown award for his services to
16	British industry. His name it .... to people all over the world, and
17	his biography .... currently .... by the author Max Jeffries.

Part 1

1   Going camping is more expensive than you think

2   A remarkable and adventurous couple

3   The luxury holiday you've always dreamed of

4   A return to the past is yours – for a price

5   Modern technology can drive you mad

6   Living and working with a bad-tempered boss

7   The pleasures of mountain climbing

8   Living with the threat of illness and disease

9   Home or away – which is *really* better for you?

10   Go back to basics – and save yourself some money at the same time

11   The perfect people for the job

12   Working together – and loving every minute of it!

Part 2

A

Every summer for two months, Kate Hedley and her daughter Anne do something .... most of us wouldn't even consider. They disconnect their electricity, gas, water and telephone, lock up their house and move to the back garden, ... they have set up a tent. 'It's something .... gets us back to nature,' explains Kate, 'and of course we don't have to pay any bills for two months. If our ancestors could live like this, so can we! The most remarkable thing is how much healthier we become during the summer.'

B

Think back to a time .... there was no electricity, no television, modern medicine didn't exist, and there were none of the luxuries .... make modern life so comfortable. Sounds terrible? Well, believe it or not, there is a holiday company .... specialises in recreating the good old days for adventurous people who are willing to part with lots of money just for this experience.

C

What's my boss like? Well, I've got two bosses, actually. Married to each other. They're a good-natured couple. They're people .... believe in treating their employees as equals. They listen and respond to any problems or questions .... their workers have. They like to save money whenever possible, of course, but they pay us well and we get generous holiday and sickness leave, ... we make the most of.

D

Think about the different things you did yesterday. .... mobile phone did you borrow? .... did you share a lift with? Did you drink out of a coffee cup .... someone had just washed up? Better get yourself checked out immediately; you've probably caught some of the millions of bacteria that are around us all the time.

E

She held the letter in her hand. .... should I send it to, sir?' she asked. 'How should I know their name?' Jenkins snapped at her, irritable as ever. 'Just write "To .... it may concern" at the top, and leave it on my desk.' Mary smiled patiently, despite the headache .... had been driving her mad all day. She decided it was time for a good, long holiday.

F

John and Sally Weatherthorn, ... have been married for almost sixty years, yesterday became the oldest people to reach the summit of Mount Everest. They both said it was an experience .... they never thought they would achieve. 'As holidays go, it was certainly different,' laughed Sally. Her husband, ... arthritis became less painful on the trip, agreed.

G

Remember that beautiful fishing village .... you spent the summer? Those carefree hours .... you spent walking along the beach or sitting in a poolside bar? That feeling of total relaxation .... you watched the sun setting over the sea? Well, believe it or not, the chances are you were probably doing yourself more harm than if you stayed at the office, being shouted at by the boss! Your first enemy is the sun – it might turn you a golden brown, but do you realise the damage it is doing to your skin?

Group A clues

A Travelling around India was a **wonderful** .... , and one that I'll never forget.

B I'm trying to save up enough money to rent an apartment, so I really can't afford **unnecessary** .... at the moment.

C We were able to measure the distance from the Earth to the Moon using a variety of **scientific** .... which we borrowed from the school.

D There have been some remarkable **technical** .... in recent years, especially in the field of information technology.

E There's going to be an eclipse of the sun later today. The .... for viewing it are **good**; a clear sky with a slight haze.

F You've made **good** .... with your English. Overall, your grammar, vocabulary and pronunciation have all improved.

G Here's a .... **key** so that you can let yourself in if I'm not at home.

H It's an excellent .... **book**, full of delicious recipes for any occasion.

I *To the Queen an Empire* is a fascinating .... **novel** set during the reign of Elizabeth I.

J Have you heard the .... **news**? The government is planning to raise taxes yet again!

K She's such a .... **runner**. Perhaps we should consider putting her in the school athletics team?

L There's a good article here about **recent** .... in computer technology.

Group B clues

A She decided that working on a summer camp for children would be a **valuable** .... , as she wanted to become a teacher.

B Computers and mobile phones, once considered **expensive** .... , are now everyday necessities.

C There's a shop on the High Street that sells an excellent variety of **musical** .... I bought my guitar there.

D Not all **scientific** .... have benefited humankind. The development of dangerous weapons is just one example.

E Our office has **excellent** working .... ; the offices are large, the furniture is comfortable and the air conditioning is at just the right temperature.

F I'm afraid your .... isn't very **satisfactory**. You've missed a lot of lessons, and haven't made any effort to catch up.

G It looks like we've got a puncture. We'd better get the .... **tyre** out.

H The chef at school is terrible. Maybe we should suggest sending him for .... **lessons**!

I Roberta Davenport's biography of Mary, Queen of Scots, involved a huge amount of .... **research**.

J Give me the .... **gossip**. Is it true that Marie is going out with Eduardo?

K I need a .... **reply** to this request. We need to make a decision as soon as possible.

L On the programme tonight, we will be telling you about the **latest** .... in the war against car crime.

A	B	C	D
Thanks for the invitation to your party. I really like …	… to tell …	… for the post of managing director, and was successful! What's next? Maybe I'll start my own multinational company.	
I know your suggestion is the most sensible one. However, please understand that I prefer …	… telling …		
	… to apply …		
	… applying …	… too many things at once. I believe in working at my own pace and taking regular breaks.	
Of course I remembered …	… to do …		
	… doing …	… me to shut up and give everyone else a chance to speak!	
I don't have many memories of the meeting last month. However, I do remember everyone …	… to worry …		Sensible
	… worrying …	… things my way to any other.	Talkative
	… to post …		Thoughtful
Of course I'd like …	… posting …	… about my job, my relationship problems and my financial difficulties. As far as I'm concerned, things can only get better from now on!	Ambitious
I don't want to tell everyone how successful and powerful I am in my job. I would prefer …	… to meet …		Generous
	… meeting …		Modest
			Stubborn
I've stopped …	… to have …	… your letter and buy you some milk when I went shopping.	Sociable
I was in a terrible hurry, but I could see that Anne was upset. So I stopped …	… having …		Optimistic
	… to make …	… a donation to your charity. Here's a cheque for £10,000.	Reliable
I don't try …	… making …		
I tried …		… them that I'm just an ordinary office worker.	
		… new people. Shall I bring something to eat, or a bottle of something?	
		… a chat with her and cheer her up.	

Student A

Picture 1

Student B

Picture 2

✂

Police are .... the disappearance of two children.	She started off as a family doctor, and .... become a successful surgeon.	We've done nothing all day. It's time we .... some serious studying.
Everybody said he should retire, but he .... working until he was 91.	I don't speak the language fluently, but I .... a few words when I was there on holiday.	Are you listening? Have you .... anything I've said to you?

My mother says she's .... meeting you next week.	I needed a hobby, so I .... photography.	Has anyone tried to .... how much the tickets will cost?
What do you want to be when you ....?	When I was young, children were .... to respect the law.	I'll just .... the word in my dictionary.

When I was young, children were .... to respect the law.	I'll just .... the word in my dictionary.	We need to .... how much food we'll need for the party.
The Ferrari team want to .... their new car on the racetrack.	How long have you been .... her?	Mrs Garcia .... anyone who hasn't had a college education. She thinks she's much better than they are.

How long have you been .... her?	Mrs Garcia .... anyone who hasn't had a college education. She thinks she's much better than they are.	Do you .... a lot, or do you do a lot of cooking at home?
I've always .... Bill for his courage and determination.	He's .... a nice apartment in the city centre.	She started off as a family doctor, and .... become a successful surgeon.

We've done nothing all day. It's time we .... some serious studying.	I've always .... Bill for his courage and determination.	I'm always very busy, but I can usually .... time to see my friends.
We must .... the simple fact that drugs are dangerous.	Has anyone tried to .... how much the tickets will cost?	Mrs Garcia .... anyone who hasn't had a college education. She thinks she's much better than they are.

Phrasal verb cards

look into	pick up	look forward to	bring up	go out with	look out for
go on to	take in	take up	look up	look down on	
get down to	get across	find out	work out	eat out	
go on	fit in	grow up	test out	look up to	

Finish

30 It was great to hear .... you again and to hear your news.

29 Problems: 1. Some younger students use their phones .... text each other during lessons.

28 Suddenly I .... up and I realised it was all a dream.

24 I refer to your advertisement .... the *Newbury Gazette* ...

25 Have you ever wondered what it's .... to be rich and famous?

26 I would like to complain .... the service I recently received in your hotel.

27 Give me a ring or email me .... you're free this Saturday.

23 I was waiting for her to arrive .... suddenly the phone rang.

22 In my opinion, *Reserved Hogs* would make .... ideal video for our film night.

21 People say that food in Britain is terrible. How wrong .... are!

20 On the one .... , computers help us in our everyday lives. On the other hand ...

16 In conclusion, I .... like to say that exams are unnecessary because ...

17 Hi! Thanks a lot .... your letter and birthday card.

18 In my opinion, young people .... too much freedom these days.

19 .... they were waiting for the train, they saw a man run across the track.

15 So what are you waiting ....? Get out, get running and get fit!

14 As soon as he opened the door, he realised he had .... a terrible mistake.

13 I would like to outline the problems caused by the use .... mobile phones in our school.

12 Your advertisement falsely claimed that your prices were .... best.

8 If you would .... any more information, please do not hesitate to contact me.

9 Why do people complain .... young people are lazy?

10 Some people claim that there is too .... violence on television.

11 I would like to present the argument .... and against corporal punishment.

7 The information and recommendations here are based on interviews .... our students and teachers.

6 If you want to know more .... keeping fit, read on!

5 Anyway, hope to see you on Saturday .... about 6.

4 We recommend .... students should leave their phones turned off during lessons.

Start

1 I'm really looking .... to seeing you again and catching up properly.

2 I .... be grateful if you could send me more information.

3 Emma couldn't believe .... she saw in front of her.

START	Special offer! If you decide buy a TZX phone card, …
… work hard and don't forget to grovel!	If prices continue to rise as fast as they are now, …
… you will never be able to enjoy by yourself!	Take an umbrella with you …
… only unless it rains.	If we spent more of time at home, …
… I would probably have stayed on.	If I had been like more ambitious when I was younger, …
… the bank was always being happy to lend me some.	I'm going to buy a new computer …
… on condition that I paid it back to within 6 months.	Providing as you are prepared to work overtime, …
… provided that you cook for me a meal tomorrow.	You're very welcome to use my trainers …
… I would have been in considerable trouble.	Don't eat those apples …
… sound the alarm and run to the nearest exit.	If you didn't do work so hard all the time, …
… I wouldn't give you any thing of my money.	**FINISH**

… you get another one absolutely free!	If you want to succeed in the life, …
… we won't have enough to live on for anymore.	If you spend all your money on necessities, …
… in case there it rains later on.	We can go for a walk later …
… we wouldn't spend so much of our money all the time.	If my boss she had paid me a bit more, …
… I wouldn't be stuck in this boring, dead-end job now.	If I ever needed extra money, …
… even if I have to steal the money away from someone!	The bank was always willing to lend me money …
… you can make a lot of money in this job.	I'll let you borrow my car …
… if you will clean them properly after you've used them.	If you hadn't warned with me about it first, …
… unless they've been quite washed first.	In case of the fire, …
… you wouldn't feel so tired every day.	Even if I was a millionaire, …

Agreeing with somebody
That's my *view exactly*.
I think you're …
That's …
I can't help …

Disagreeing with somebody
I'm afraid I …
I'm not entirely …
I'm not so …
I see things …

Asking somebody to say something again
I'm …
I'm afraid I didn't …
Could you …
Would you mind …

Giving yourself time to think
May I think about …
Let me …
I haven't really …
Hm, that's an …

Asking somebody what they think
What's your …
What are your …
What are …
How do you …

Saying things in another way
What I …
To put it …
In other …
What I'm …

Interrupting someone
Sorry to …
Could I just …
Could I just …

… sorry?

… sure about that.

… say that …

… right.

… absolutely right.

… don't agree.

… thought about it before.

… sure about that.

… repeat that please?

… interrupt, but …

… mean is ….

… see.

… feelings about it?

… come in here and say …

… differently myself.

… repeating that.

… that for a moment?

… thinking the same.

… interesting question.

… your views on …

… another way …

… feel about …

… ~~view exactly.~~

… words …

… opinion?

… trying to say is …

… catch that.

Part 1

believe chew creep gasp gaze glance gobble grip hug imagine knock
mutter peer punch scream shout sip slap smack stagger stammer stare
stroll suffocate wade weep whisper wonder

- ✂ - - - - - - - - - -

Part 2(A)

Across

1   Make sure you .... your food properly before swallowing it.
4   Stop .... to each other. if you have something to say, let us all hear.
7   We didn't want to wake anyone up, so we .... quietly up the stairs.
8   The old woman .... at me angrily, turned round and walked away.
9   We spent Saturday afternoon .... in the park and feeding the ducks.
12 Have you ever .... why British people drive on the left-hand side of the road?
13 He .... in sheer terror as the snake slid up his leg.

Down

2   Aunt Jessie .... me so tightly I thought she would crush me to death.
3   My boss was so furious, she .... my report on the table and told me to do it again.
5   It was so hot and stuffy in the room, I thought I would ....
6   The boy sat in the corner, ... quietly to himself.
8   She .... her cola, and watched me carefully to see what I would do next.
10 She .... at the paper, trying to read the tiny print.
11 Some parents don't believe in .... their children if they are naughty.

Part 2(B)

Across

1   She .... uncontrollably when she found out she had failed, and nobody could say anything to cheer her up.
2   'P-p-please can I c-c-come in?' she .... nervously.
3   She ran out of the burning building and fell on the ground, ... for air.
6   I heard someone .... on the door. 'Come in,' I said.
7   Nobody .... her when she said she was going to get married.
9   You don't need to .... I'm not deaf, you know.
10 She .... the gun tightly in her hand. 'Come any closer, and I'll shoot you!' she said.
11 As I walked into the room, they .... quickly at me, then went back to their discussion.

Down

1   At one point the river was only about half a metre deep, and we were able to .... across it from one side to the other.
2   The injured man .... into the hospital and collapsed on the floor.
4   From the top of the hill, we .... out over the countryside below us.
5   When the bell rang the boxer ran into the ring and .... his opponent.
8   I can't .... being penniless and living on the street. Can you?
11 You shouldn't .... your food like that - you'll get indigestion.

PHOTOCOPIABLE

Remember:
- Use between two and five words for each gap.
- Do not change the form of the **key** word.
- Write your answers on the answer sheet.
- Only write the missing words on the answer sheet. Do not write the whole sentence.
- Contractions (I've, He's, etc.) count as two words.

		Points risked			Total
1	At any one time, I'm usually doing several jobs. **go** I have several jobs .... any one time.	5	10	15	
2	I usually like historical novels more than modern stories. **prefer** I tend .... modern stories.	5	10	15	
3	I'd like to work in Japan. **appeals** The idea of .... me.	5	10	15	
4	Jennifer hasn't appeared in class recently. **made** Jennifer .... in class recently.	5	10	15	
5	There's someone walking around downstairs. I think it's a burglar. **sounds** There's someone walking around downstairs. It .... a burglar.	5	10	15	
6	I really wanted to speak to Marlene. **word** I wanted to .... Marlene.	5	10	15	
7	I met Steve at the Jericho Tavern and talked to him over coffee. **chat** I met Steve at the Jericho Tavern and .... over coffee.	5	10	15	
8	It's pointless to do endless grammar exercises. **worth** It's .... endless grammar exercises.	5	10	15	
9	We should cancel the barbecue because I think it's going to rain. **looks** We should cancel the barbecue because .... going to rain.	5	10	15	
10	'Don't speak to me like that again,' the teacher said to us. **warned** The teacher .... to her like that again.	5	10	15	

---✂--------------

Answers

1 on the go at   2 to prefer historical novels to   3 working in Japan appeals to   4 hasn't made an appearance
5 sounds like   6 have a word with   7 had a chat with him   8 not worth doing   9 it looks like it's
10 warned us not to speak

Scoring system:
so = 2 points   very = 4 points
too = 3 points   such a = 5 points
such = 4 points   enough = 6 points

1 <u>Unfortunately</u> in there friends were few of class his the .

Complete sentence	Points

2 <u>The</u> boring film cinema was that we the left .

3 <u>Everyone</u> him likes nice he's guy because .

4 <u>Have</u> leaves a before we got time to have coffee our train ?

5 <u>It</u> was went beach the hot to work, so we to .

6 <u>Unfortunately</u> I round think go there's pizza to don't .

7 <u>I'm</u> be job trusted afraid you're this to with unreliable .

8 <u>Luckily</u> during damaged were storm houses few the .

9 <u>We're</u> moment hot having weather at the .

10 <u>I</u> being company him he's with good love because .

11 <u>He</u> boss horrible a resigned was that his employees half .

12 <u>The</u> decided do was difficult I not to it that homework .

Set A

1   Do you realise that it's been over 50 years since Hilary and Tensing climbed the Mount Everest.
2   I know that public transport is much safer than private transport, but to tell you the truth I would rather to travel by car than by train.
3   Nowadays it's considered very fashionable to be wear something made by a designer from the past.
4   I don't mind lending you my car tonight as long as you would promise to take good care of it and pay for any petrol you use.
5   Students are being allowed to use the computers in the library as often as they want, provided they look after them.
6   I've got a lot of lovely things at home, but the thing which I value it the most is my grandmother's necklace.
7   The man by the door talking to Jenny seems like very familiar – I wonder if we've met before.
8   I don't know if Julie has any plans for tonight; she may have want to come to the film – why don't you ask her?
9   I didn't go out yesterday because it was a terrible weather, so I stayed at home and watched television all day.
10 People such like David Beckham and Julia Roberts have to spend their whole lives being followed by the press – it must be a real nightmare!

Set B

A   I'm not sure who broke my computer, but I would always suspected that my younger brother had something to do with it.
B   As you can imagine, I was absolutely furious when my suitcase got lost at the airport, but fortunately my luggage was being insured against loss or damage.
C   You look like really angry; I do hope I haven't done something to upset you.
D   If you come late again, please don't have make up any more stupid excuses like the one you gave me yesterday.
E   It was a such terrifying experience and I never want to repeat it, even if I live to be a hundred years old.
F   I try to eat well and sensibly, avoiding food that is high in fat and always eating lots of vegetables, corn and a brown rice.
G   Be careful what you say to him; he's a bit of a gossip and really can't to be trusted to keep a secret.
H   It all seems a bit strange at the moment, but I'm sure I'll find my feet and be get used to living here.
I   He doesn't really know what to do with his uncle's inheritance, so the money it will probably be given to charity.
J   I know I give the impression of being very confident and sociable, but I'm actually quite shy and would really hate to give a talk in the public.

✂

1   **Fill in the gaps with an appropriate word.**

I look .... to hearing .... you soon.

2   **Fill in the gaps with an appropriate word.**

I moved to Glasgow .... I was a child, and I've lived there .... then.

---

3   **Put the words in bold into their correct form.**

She gave us a long **explain** about how to become **finance** independent.

4   **Choose the best alternative from (a) and (b) to complete the sentence.**
Could you (a) .... me what time tonight's
(b) .... of *Romeo and Juliet* begin?
(a) explain   say   describe   tell
(b) perfomance   acting   play   display

---

5   **Choose the best alternative from (a) and (b) to complete the sentence.**
I was really (a) .... with myself when I
(b) .... my driving test.
(a) thrilled   amazed   annoyed   flattered
(b) lost   failed   succeeded   won

6   **Complete the second sentence so that it has the same meaning as the first sentence.**
I think passing the FCE is a lot easier than some people think.
far
I think it's .... the FCE than some people think.

---

7   **Put the words in bold into their correct form.**

It was **fortune** he lost the game, but he was such an **experience** player.

8   **Identify two words that should not be in this sentence.**

She usually lives at the home with her parents, but at the moment is in a hospital for an operation.

---

9   **Choose the best alternative from (a) and (b) to complete the sentence.**
Your English is (a) .... fantastic. You must have worked (b) .... hard to get it to that level.
(a) absolutely   fairly   very   a bit
(b) utterly   just   fairly   totally

10   **Fill in the gaps with an appropriate word.**

Coffee makes me feel dizzy, so I drink very .... of it. In fact, I haven't had .... today at all.

---

11   **Complete the second sentence so that it has the same meaning as the first sentence.**
I came to this school exactly a year ago tomorrow.
at
Tomorrow .... this school for exactly one year.

12   **Fill in the gaps with an appropriate word.**

This time tomorrow we'll .... arriving in New York. I'm .... excited I can't stop shaking!

---

13   **Choose the best alternative from (a) and (b) to complete the sentence.**

I'm really bad at (a) .... jokes, but everyone
(b) .... I would make a good comedian.
(a) saying   talking   telling   speaking
(b) tells   says   talks   speaks

14   **Identify two words that should not be in this sentence.**

You must have been upset him somehow – he can't have be angry for no reason.

© Pearson Education Limited 2004   **PHOTOCOPIABLE**

15 **Fill in the gaps with an appropriate word.**

Your essay should have .... finished by Thursday last week. All the others .... handed in then.

16 **Fill in the gaps with an appropriate word.**

That's Brian, ... father works in London. He has a small shop .... he sells souvenirs.

17 **Complete the second sentence so that it has the same meaning as the first sentence.**
He failed, so he couldn't move up to the next level.
he
If he .... have moved up to the next level.

18 **Put the words in bold into their correct form.**

She's very **support** of everything I do, but gets **fury** if I do things without asking her first.

19 **Fill in the gaps with an appropriate word.**

I'm too tired to get up. I wish it .... Saturday today. .... only I hadn't stayed up so late yesterday!

20 **Choose the best alternative from (a) and (b) to complete the sentence.**
We didn't have (a) .... money when I was a child, so (b) .... go camping for our holidays.
(a) many   much   lots   some
(b) will   used   would   must

21 **Identify two words that should not be in this sentence.**

History was used to be my favourite subject at school, and I would to spend hours reading history books.

22 **Fill in the gaps with an appropriate word.**

It's .... a hot day today. It's far .... hot to do any work.

23 **Complete the second sentence so that it has the same meaning as the first sentence.**
'Don't forget to bring a sleeping bag,' she said to me.
reminded
She .... a sleeping bag.

24 **Identify two words that should not be in this sentence.**

I don't like people such like her. I would rather to avoid her if possible.

25 **Choose the best alternative from (a) and (b) to complete the sentence.**
He (a) .... rapidly up and down the corridor a few times, then (b) .... angrily at me for a minute or so before leaving.
(a) strolled   crept   paced   tiptoed
(b) gazed   peered   glanced   stared

26 **Complete the second sentence so that it has the same meaning as the first sentence.**
I'll lend you the money providing you pay it back by Monday.
on
I'll lend you the money .... you pay it back by Monday.

27 **Choose the best alternative from (a) and (b) to complete the sentence.**
He (a) .... me of stealing his wallet, but I strongly (b) .... it.
(a) blamed   refused   accused   admitted
(b) admitted   denied   agreed   refused

28 **Fill in the gaps with an appropriate word.**

You really .... to visit the cathedral while you're there, and you mustn't .... the fantastic light show at night.

First Certificate in English Quiz

Try this quiz to see how much you know about the exam.

1   Is there any extra time for transferring answers to the mark sheet? ....
2   Do I have to write in pen or pencil on the mark sheets? ....
3   What happens if I shade in two lozenges on the mark sheets? ....
4   Does spelling have to be correct? ....
5   Is there any negative marking in multiple-choice questions? ....
6   What general pass mark do I need in each paper? ....
7   How soon do get my results? ....

Reading

8   How many parts are there in the paper? ....
9   Why is it important to read the title and subtitle of a reading text? ....
10 In which part(s) should I look at the text first, and in which part(s) should I look at the questions first? ....

Writing

11 How many questions do I have to answer? ....
12 Can I write answers in pencil? ....
13 Can I use correction fluid? ....
14 Is it a good idea to rewrite my composition neatly? ....
15 Is it a good idea to write on alternate lines? ....
16 Does handwriting count? ....
17 What kind of mistakes should I check for? ....
18 What happens if my answers on the writing paper are too short or too long? ....
19 Should I spend equal time on each answer? ....

Use of English

20 How many parts are there in the paper? ....
21 How many cloze passages are there? What is the difference between them? ....
22 What happens if I write more than five words in key word transformations? ....
23 What happens if I write two words for one gap in the cloze passage? ....

Listening

23 How many parts are there in the paper? ....
24 How many times do I hear each part? ....
25 Does spelling matter? ....

Speaking

26 How many people will be involved in examining? ....
27 Is it all right to ask the interlocutor to repeat their instructions? ....
28 Will I lose marks if I don't talk for a minute in Part 2? ....
29 What happens if my partner is too quiet or too talkative? ....
30 What happens if I don't know a word? ....

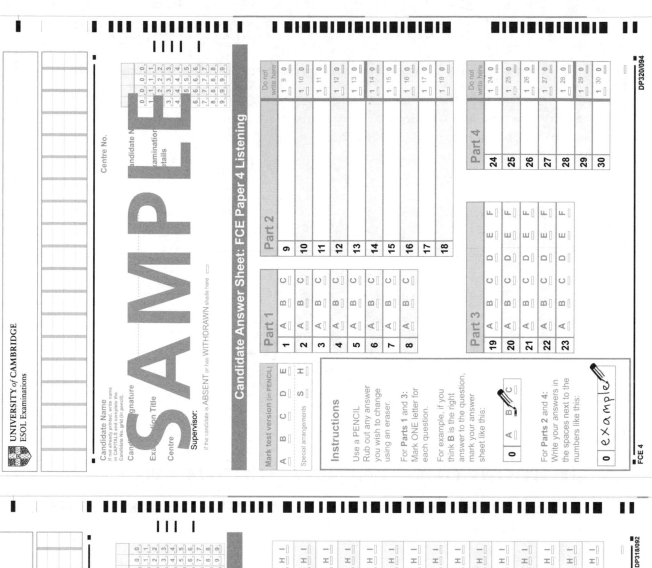

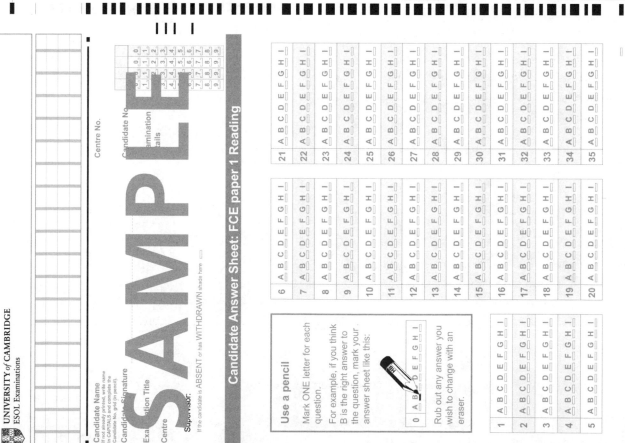

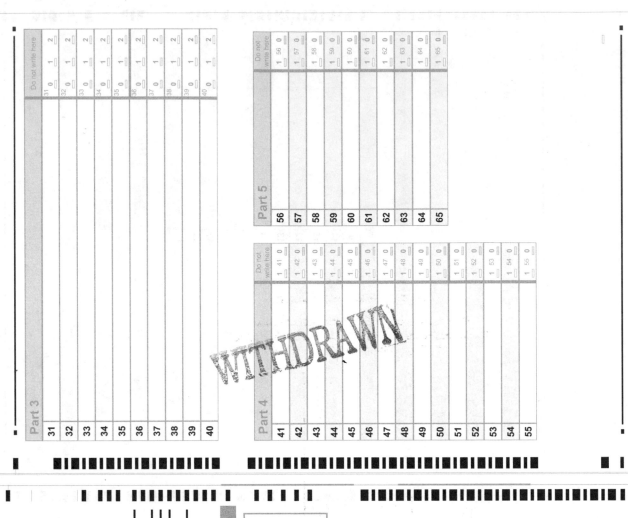

UNIVERSITY *of* CAMBRIDGE
ESOL Examinations

Candidate Name
If not already printed, write name
in CAPITALS and complete the
Candidate No. grid (in pencil).

Candidate Signature

Examination Title

Centre

Supervisor:

If the candidate is ABSENT or has WITHDRAWN shade here ☐

Centre No.

Candidate No.

Candidate Answer Sheet: FCE Paper 3 Use of English

Use a **PENCIL** (B or HB). Rub out any answer you wish to change with an eraser.

For **Part 1**: Mark ONE letter for each question.
For example, if you think **C** is the right answer to
the question, mark your answer sheet like this:

For **Parts 2, 3, 4** and **5**: Write your answers in
the spaces next to the numbers like this:

0 | A | B | C | D

0 | *example*

Part 1

	A	B	C	D
1				
2				
3				
4				
5				
6				
7				
8				
9				
10				
11				
12				
13				
14				
15				

Part 2

		Do not write here
16		1 16 0
17		1 17 0
18		1 18 0
19		1 19 0
20		1 20 0
21		1 21 0
22		1 22 0
23		1 23 0
24		1 24 0
25		1 25 0
26		1 26 0
27		1 27 0
28		1 28 0
29		1 29 0
30		1 30 0

Turn over for Parts 3 - 5 →

DP319/093

FCE 3

Part 3

		Do not write here
31		31 0 1 2
32		32 0 1 2
33		33 0 1 2
34		34 0 1 2
35		35 0 1 2
36		36 0 1 2
37		37 0 1 2
38		38 0 1 2
39		39 0 1 2
40		40 0 1 2

Part 4

		Do not write here
41		1 41 0
42		1 42 0
43		1 43 0
44		1 44 0
45		1 45 0
46		1 46 0
47		1 47 0
48		1 48 0
49		1 49 0
50		1 50 0
51		1 51 0
52		1 52 0
53		1 53 0
54		1 54 0
55		1 55 0

Part 5

		Do not write here
56		1 56 0
57		1 57 0
58		1 58 0
59		1 59 0
60		1 60 0
61		1 61 0
62		1 62 0
63		1 63 0
64		1 64 0
65		1 65 0